EUROTRASH

EUROTRASH

*Why America Must Reject the Failed Ideas
of a Dying Continent*

DAVID HARSANYI

BROADSIDE BOOKS

HarperCollins books may be purchased for educational, business, or sales promotional use. For information, please email the Special Markets Department at SPsales@ harpercollins.com.

Broadside Books™ and the Broadside logo are trademarks of HarperCollins Publishers.

FIRST EDITION

Library of Congress Cataloging-in-Publication Data has been applied for.

ISBN 978-0-06-306601-4

21 22 23 24 25 LSC 10 9 8 7 6 5 4 3 2 1

To Oren and Boaz

There are two kinds of Europeans: The smart ones, and those who stayed behind.

—*H. L. Mencken*

CONTENTS

Europeanization

After the events of the 20th century, God, quite reasonably, left Europe.

—*P. J. O'Rourke*

About three times as many Europeans leave their homelands and immigrate to the United States every year as the other way around.[1] This fact shouldn't surprise anyone. Europe, still one of the wealthiest places on the planet, has begun collapsing under the weight of its top-heavy institutions, economic fatigue, moral anemia, and cultural capitulation. The modern legacy of Europe is one of unregulated and destructive mass migration, overregulated and constrictive economic life, high unemployment, a lack of entrepreneurship, eroding civic society, low replacement rates, creeping authoritarianism, and most devastatingly, a loss of faith in their best ideas.

Yet, even as Europe's faith and traditions continue to decay, a growing number of American elites—politicians, academics, pundits, journalists, among others—argue, with increasing popularity, that we should look across the Atlantic for solutions to our most pressing problems. These Europhiles prefer modern European institutions, ethics, and policies to the ones found here. They sneer at the jejune and vulgar nature of American life.

They see America as a place teeming with uneducated, obese, gun-toting, television-obsessed, box-store-shopping, slack-jawed yokels who are in desperate need of paternalistic guidance. For them, a Europeanized population is an enlightened, educated, and selfless one, willing to sacrifice for their conception of the "common good." They are antagonistic toward the societal characteristics embedded in the American psyche that work against the success of contemporary European ideas: our embrace of risk taking, individual liberty, and traditional Judeo-Christian ideas.

Indeed, the most vociferous champions of the European systems of governance in the United States are invariably the most passionate critics of the dynamism and glorious messiness of American life. The factors that propel our economic superiority— the unplanned and unregulated, individualistic, and seemingly disordered free markets—chafe against their technocratic sensibilities. Europhiles detest individualism and self-sufficiency and definitely the unfettered self-assuredness of their average fellow countrymen. For them, American exceptionalism, the idea that the United States occupies a unique position in world history, is ugly and plainly wrong.

It's not just American leftists who look to Europe for answers. While a large part of the European temptation emanates from the political left, which values centralized control over individual choice, American nationalists and theocratic intellectuals are also increasingly looking toward places like Hungary, Russia, and other Eastern European nations for answers on how to stem the diminishing birth rates, dramatically dropping church attendance, and what they see as our moral decline. This book, however, is predominately concerned with the destructive love affair left-wing Americans have with Western Europe and member states of the European Union. When Europhiles admiringly gaze across the Atlantic, they are not jealous of the political structures of Turkey, Bulgaria, or Albania—even though many of those nations have adopted socialistic systems that Europhiles favor. Europhiles are predominately gushing about France, Germany, and Scandinavia. And that's bad enough.

There are three fundamentally dishonest facets to the Europhiles' arguments for European policy.

First, declarations about Europe's superiority are often wildly overstated. The temptation to portray Europe as a utopia is given traction by a stream of deceptive activism from journalists and intellectuals, who not only overstate European triumphs but denigrate American ones. Europhilic arguments for adopting European norms and policies are most often predicated on the idea that our own country is in steep economic and moral decline, even though, by every quantifiable measure, Americans are living healthier, wealthier, and freer lives today than they were forty or twenty years ago—and easily outpacing Europe on nearly all fronts.

Not that you'd know that from the mainstream reporting on Europe. In a recent *New York Times* piece headlined "How Europeans See America," readers learn that "European governments prioritize citizen welfare, offering national assurances like universal health care and affordable education. Americans have grown accustomed to the exorbitant costs of basic human services, the absence of parental leave protection and the unregulated presence of chemicals in food—things that would 'cause riots' in Europe."[2] This oft-repeated mythology—from the notion that greedy Americans allow chemicals to kill off their countrymen to the idea that they pay "exorbitant costs" for "basic human services" to the lie that we live with subpar medical care—is debunked when the data is analyzed with honesty.

Though we must concede that the *Times* is right about riots. Europeans riot over nearly everything.

Second, while Europeans *are* quite good at numerous ventures that are highly valued by American elites—ensuring "free" health care for everyone or limiting "inequality"—Europhiles refuse to acknowledge the trade-offs that accompany these successes. They either ignore or dismiss the tremendous economic downsides that European societies take on when implementing social welfare programs. They either ignore or dismiss the numerous core freedoms, both individual and communal, that are lost when living under the bureaucratic thumb of a monolithic enterprise like the European Union. They either ignore or dismiss the negative externalities that accompany mass immigration without assimilation, one-size-fits-all energy policy, or socialized medicine. This book will explore those trade-offs, and many other instances in which we often don't hear the full story.

Finally, Europhiles refuse to acknowledge that many of the European continent's most notable genuine successes are achieved by embracing what we can now call American ideas. Europeans have long attempted to emulate the United States—from adopting "federalism" to deregulating certain industries and trade—to fix their problems. Most good ideas head from west to east, not the other way around.

DISDAIN FOR EUROPEANS HAS BEEN something of an American rite. The very creation of the United States, after all, was a rejection of Europe. Nearly every American is acquainted with the inspirational lines from Emma Lazarus's grandiose "The New Colossus." They should be. *"Give me your tired, your poor . . ."* is a beautiful rhetorical affirmation of our promise to immigrants who, like my own parents, came to the United States to escape, variously, the strictures, ethnic violence, monarchism, religious oppression, wars, feudalism, ancient hatreds, fascism, class-driven injustices, communism, or economic immobility of the Old World. Written by Lazarus in 1883 to help raise funds for the pedestal below the Statue of Liberty—a sculpture of Libertas, the Roman goddess of liberty, gifted to America by the French in 1886—the poem was finally cast onto a bronze plaque and mounted in 1903.

Almost invariably, those quoting "The New Colossus" skip the line that immediately precedes it, which instructs those who enter, "'Keep, ancient lands, your storied pomp!' cries she / With silent lips." In other words: The United States wants you, but please leave the stifling customs and ideas of your old home at the door. From the beginning, the egalitarian American citizen carried with him a deep-seated and well-founded skepticism about European dogmas and norms.

This aversion was entrenched deeper in the national consciousness with every subsequent generation that fled the inequalities, indignities, and indigence of the European continent. The Monroe Doctrine, the principle laid out by President James Monroe to Congress in December 1823, is today largely remembered as an assertion of American hegemony over the Western Hemisphere, but also a stern warning to Europeans—the English and Russians, in particular, but it didn't really matter who—to stay out of the neighborhood. The American instinct to tenaciously resist post-Enlightenment European ideological fads—many of which would evolve into homicidal movements—has served us well. Such an effort isn't as easy as it sounds when we consider that the vast majority of newcomers for our first two centuries of existence had been Europeans.

There is good reason for our suspicion. Europeans might have come up with the foundational liberal ideals of the American project, but they've rarely been able to live by them themselves. Since 1776—nay, since perhaps the fall of Rome—the inhabitants of Europe have lived under the threat of poverty, monarchy, dictatorships, or war. Sometimes all three. It is only in the past seventy years or so, and only under the watchful eye of American power, that there has been anything resembling a lasting peace.

Only a year after Lazarus's poem was written—two decades after the American Civil War began to correct our most egregious immorality—the major European powers were meeting in Berlin to figure out how to carve up the entire western half of

the African continent. Europe itself had been violent and unstable for centuries. The conference was a couple of generations
removed from 1848, the "Year of Revolutions," where uprisings
had once again swept through Europe—including a *third* French
Revolution. The continent would spend a century revving up for
two of the worst bloodletting orgies of the twentieth century.
The ideologies of fascism and communism would dominate the
mid-twentieth century. They not only would engulf their continent but would export deadly consequences across the globe. No
wonder the huddled masses fled.

It's also fair to say that contemporary American antagonism
toward Europe had become something perfunctory, and quite
often evolved into apathy. These days Americans don't really
know much about Europeans, which is why Europhiles often get
away with misleading the public. Though Europeans might ob-
sess over politics in the United States, we often forget Europe's
existence altogether—except perhaps when curtly reminded by
another spasm of violence. More than 100,000 American casu-
alties of war are buried in Europe, yet most Americans couldn't
tell you the difference between Brussels and Bucharest. When
the European Union was formed as a direct competitor to U.S.
economic supremacy, Gallup found that 77 percent of Americans admitted to knowing nothing about the organization.[3]

On the other hand, what Europeans *think* they understand
about the United States—a cartoonish dystopian landscape in
which relentless competition, destructive selfishness, repressed
sexual mores, and unfettered violence rule the day—is absurd.
Western Europeans have always enjoyed denigrating and grousing about American culture and power. Such irritation became
most obviously trendy in the 1970s. The high art of poet Harold
Pinter, who earned his fame belittling Americans, and the low
art of punk rockers like the Clash—famously lamenting, "Yan-
kee detectives are always on the TV, 'cause killers in America
work seven days a week"—come to mind. Of course, like most

pop artists of the past century, the Clash nicked, as they say, their music from the United States.

This attitude about Americans isn't limited to the intellectuals or artists. When the Associated Press recently asked some random Europeans what they thought of when someone mentioned the United States, this is what some of them came up with:[4]

Capitalism. Money rules everything. Overweight people, Donald Trump, elections, shootings.

—*Ingerlise Kristensen, sixty-eight, retired bank employee, Copenhagen, Denmark*

America is food . . . fast food and (Coca) Cola. It's cars. It's the many electronics we have . . . the bridge in San Francisco.

—*Ksenia Smertova, twenty one, student, Moscow*

Americans are American because they feel (they are) better than the rest of the world but in reality we are as good as they are. They simply don't see us as their equal . . . but we are. Sometimes we are even better than them . . . but don't tell them (laughing).

—*Kenni Friis, twenty-eight, computer technology student, Copenhagen, Denmark*

A black-and-white look at the world. They miss nuances.

—*Knut Braaten, forty-three, handyman, Oslo, Norway*

What Europeans don't see is how America's world domination in devising and manufacturing technological advances makes modernity possible. They don't see the world-class university system and open markets that propel that dominance, or the widespread tolerance that allows hundreds, if not thousands, of people of all ethnicities to coexist in relative peace and enjoy the wealth.

Negative conceptions of America are not new. It is often said that World War II turned America into a global power. The truth is that the United States had been a world economic power for a century. The Europeans have been aping our technology, manufacturing, and economic ideas since the early 1800s, and yet disparage our culture. Indeed, by the mid-nineteenth century, "from Europe's perspective," writes Richard Pells in *Not Like Us*, "Americans appeared irredeemably materialistic, avaricious, frantic, violent, crude, without spirit or soul—in vivid contrast to the mature, tolerant, sophisticated, socially conscious, and responsible European civilization that was adept at preserving the amenities of human life. . . ."[5] By the early twentieth century European cultural critics and thinkers were accusing us of being "monolithic," "culturally imperialistic," and engaging in "indoctrination" and "cultural genocide." As William Thomas Stead, the Victorian-age journalist, famously predicted in his book *The Americanization of the World*, the twentieth century would be dominated by the young nation. Europeans would look on in a strange mix of jealousy and contempt.

Europhiles often dismiss American mass culture. There's probably good reason, however, why chains like McDonald's, KFC, and Starbucks have proliferated across all of Europe, but you've never eaten at a Kochlöffel. Or why American movies dominate the European box office every year—in the past, nations had tried to put quotas on American films to temper their popularity—but the vast majority of you do not watch European films.

None of this is to contend that the Impressionists were garbage. Or that the works of Dante and Dostoevsky and Dickens are not worth our time. Nor is it to say that the Notre-Dame Cathedral in Paris, the parliament building in Budapest, or the Florence Cathedral aren't awe inspiring. Europe is filled with wondrous cultural and societal accomplishments of an ancient society. Nor is it to contend that the European people themselves are nefarious or our enemies. It is, after all, the second-best place on earth.

It is to say that there is an American identity, a set of values that bind us. Yet, this is not a place that demands cultural conformity, but rather one that has room for the progressive Brooklyn vegan, the evangelical conservative farmer, and the suburban moderate. And in the aggregate, human flourishing does better under the American traditional principles—born of European culture, indeed, but improved upon for two centuries—than anywhere else. Americans and Europeans, their morality, perceptions, habits, and culture, have evolved in fundamentally different ways.

We, in many ways, are the true inheritors of Europe's liberal philosophical and cultural legacy—one that they have often abandoned. We have mined the best aspects of European thought—ideals of the Enlightenment, the moral codes of Judeo-Christianity, the economic dynamism of capitalism—and improved on them. This is as true today as it was in 1883. Which is why Europe should be looking to us for solutions, and not the other way around.

2

The Nordic "Utopias"

"In Scandinavia, we have no poverty," a Swedish economist once told American Nobel laureate Milton Friedman.

"That's interesting, because among Scandinavians in America we have no poverty, either," Friedman responded.[1]

There are no countries in the world more extravagantly praised and celebrated by American Europhiles than the Nordic nations. A closer look at these success stories, however, shows that not only are the Nordic Europeans far from socialist paradises, many of their successes are a result of their becoming more like the United States, not less.

This does not deter Europhiles from enthusing about Nordic utopias. "In strong and vibrant democracies, a generous social-welfare state is not a road to serfdom but rather to fairness, economic equality and international competitiveness," the writer and academic Jeffrey Sachs noted, in an article praising Nordic welfare states.[2] An exasperated *New York Times* columnist Paul Krugman once groused that every time he hears "someone talking about the 'collapsing welfare states of Europe,' I have this urge to take that person on a forced walking tour of Stockholm."[3]

Daydreaming about forcing the average Americans to see things his way is very European of Krugman. He's far from alone. The dream of a Scandinavian America has slowly been mainstreamed by the political left. Ezra Klein, former editor of the popular liberal "explainer" news site Vox, once noted that contemporary Democrats "want to make America look a lot more like Denmark" and "pass generous parental leave policies, let the government bargain down drug prices, and strengthen the social safety net."

Socialist Bernie Sanders has maintained that America "should look to countries like Denmark, like Sweden and Norway, and learn from what they have accomplished for their working people."[4] But it's not only "democratic socialists" who praise the Nordic Model as an exemplar of righteous governance. During the Democratic Party primaries of 2020, moderates like Pete Buttigieg declared that the "last time I checked, the list of countries to live out the American Dream—in other words, to be born at the bottom and come out at the top—we're not even in the top 10. The number one place to live out the American Dream right now is Denmark."[5]

As we'll see, this is all hokum. Scandinavians are undeniably a successful people, but it has nothing to do with embracing the top-down constrictive economic ideas that are peddled by Europhiles. The opposite, in fact, is true. Nations like Denmark, Sweden, and Norway (and for our purposes we'll include Finland and Iceland, who share the same social mores and ideas about governance, though they technically aren't part of Scandinavia) rely on strong American-style capitalistic policies to prop up high standards of living and generous social welfare programs. Furthermore, digging into the facts reveals that many of the benefits of the Nordic nations are down to national habits, which immigrants export and maintain. Their much-vaunted claims to be the world's happiest countries are suspect, to say the least. And finally, to Europhiles' greatest distress, the Nordic Model wouldn't work in America even if it worked in Europe.

Which it doesn't.

Scandinavia Is Capitalist

The nation of Denmark ranks as the eighth most economically free country, judged not by the liberal *New York Times* or *Washington Post* but by the conservative Heritage Foundation in its 2020 Index of Economic Freedom.[6] Nordic countries rank quite high on nearly every index of economic freedom. The World Bank grades Nordic nations as some of the easiest countries to do business with globally—with Denmark coming in third worldwide, behind the other small, highly capitalistic sanctuaries Singapore and New Zealand.[7]

As *The Economist* once put it, Scandinavians are "stout free-traders who resist the temptation to intervene even to protect iconic companies."[8] Or in other words, they do not rely on many meddlesome policies and higher regulatory burdens most often advocated by Europhiles, but rather ones Americans have depended on for their own high levels of economic attainment.

The American misconception about Nordic nations being acutely regulated socialistic paradises had grown into such a popular myth that in 2015 Danish prime minister Lars Løkke Rasmussen was forced to try to set the record straight when visiting Harvard's Kennedy School of Government: "I know that some people in the U.S. associate the Nordic model with some sort of socialism. Therefore, I would like to make one thing clear, Denmark is far from a socialist planned economy," he said. "Denmark is a market economy. The Nordic model is an expanded welfare state which provides a high level of security for its citizens, but it is also a successful market economy with much freedom to pursue your dreams and live your life as you wish."[9]

Though it still remains one of the best places to reside in the world, the ability to pursue your dreams has been somewhat fading, not growing, in Scandinavia. As the historical record shows, it was only after a great run of laissez-faire economics that Nordic nations like Sweden, the region's most populous country, began adopting socialistic policies in the 1970s and '80s—which were the cause of, not the answer to, an array of societal problems.

In 1870, Sweden was one of the poorest nations in Europe, plagued with destitution and mass emigration. By 1970, before most of the intrusions and mandates that are favored by American Europhiles had been implemented, Sweden had transformed itself into the fourth-richest country in the world.[10] While the Scandinavian society embraced free-market liberalism, they also relied—and still do—on strong social cohesion, a robust Protestant work ethic, linguistic and cultural homogeny, and widespread civic involvement.

During its welfare state expansion from 1970 to 1991, on the other hand, Sweden's economic growth rate was slower than in Italy, France, Germany, or the United Kingdom. After copious interventions and a slew of labor regulations in the 1970s, Sweden dropped from its perch as the fourth-richest nation in per capita gross domestic product (GDP) ranking in the world to sixteenth by 1995. In the early 1970s, taxes and corporate rates were so high that people like Ingvar Kamprad, the founder of IKEA—one of Sweden's most famous exports—were forced to move, in his case first to Denmark and then to Switzerland. In many ways, the country never recovered its former economic glory. High taxation dampened entrepreneurship and job creation.

From 1870 to 1936, Sweden was home to the highest growth rate in the industrialized world. However, from 1936 to 2008, its growth rate was only thirteenth out of twenty-eight nations. Large swaths of the workforce began relying on the largesse of the state rather than private-sector innovation. For every 100 Swedes whose income was derived from private enterprise in 1960, there were 38 Swedes whose main source of income was derived from the public sector—either through working for the government or through welfare payments. By 1990, that number had risen to 51—in other words, there was a significantly growing faction of the population that was not creating wealth.[11] From 1965 to 1975, Sweden nearly doubled its civil servant force. From 1970 to 1984, the public sector was the largest creator of new jobs in the country.[12]

In the 1990s, Sweden slowly began adopting American-style economic reforms, cutting and simplifying its taxes, rolling back some of its welfare system, adopting voucher systems for schools, privatizing a number of state-controlled monopolies, and injecting more competition into the economy. By the 1970s Sweden's inheritance tax—an idea that American Europhiles are quite fond of—had hit a high of 65 percent. By the 1990s the country began trimming it, until 2004, when Sweden's parliament unanimously abolished it. Sweden ended its "wealth tax" as well. And though labor unions, as in most European nations, still hold considerable sway, there is little state interference in negotiations or outcomes. Neither Sweden, Denmark, Iceland, nor Norway has a statutory minimum wage. Yet salaries are high compared with those in the rest of the European continent.

Yet, as the economist Milton Friedman pithily noted, Europhiles ignore the most vital component of Scandinavian success. It isn't the existence of a welfare state, or the "democratic socialism," or the generous social safety net, or the discovery of oil, but rather Scandinavians themselves.

We know this because the descendants of Scandinavians find similar success around the world. There is a question fans of the Nordic system need to answer: Why do Scandinavians thrive more in the boisterous capitalism of the United States than they do under the Nordic Model? There are somewhere around twelve million descendants of Nordic nations in the United States, where the median household income hit an all-time high in 2019 of over $68,000. Among those who identify as Danish, Swedish, or Norwegian American, that rate is nearly $10,000 higher than average, and far higher than the median income in any Nordic nation.[13]

"The poverty rate among immigrants in the US today is half the average poverty rate of Americans—this has been a consistent finding for decades," the Swedish author Nima Sanandaji points out. "In fact, Scandinavian Americans have lower poverty rates than Scandinavian citizens who have not emigrated. This suggests that pre-existing cultural norms are responsible for the low levels of poverty among Scandinavians rather than Nordic welfare states."[14]

Many immigrants from Norway and Sweden—some of whom left for reasons of poverty, but also due to religious and political persecution[15]—initially faced just as much deprivation in the United States as they did in their home countries. They certainly faced more destitution than new immigrants do in Europe or the United States today. Between the years 1820 and 1920, nearly a million Norwegians immigrated to the United States—more than a quarter of Norway's entire population.[16] Their economic rise far outpaced that of their relatives at home. Even among those Norwegian immigrants who ultimately returned to their native land, the majority held higher-paid occupations relative to those who never left, despite initially coming from poorer backgrounds.[17] Many of those immigrants accumulated wealth in the United States and brought it back to their homeland.

Contra Pete Buttigieg—the Harvard-educated former presidential candidate of Norwegian descent—not only is the American Dream alive and thriving in the United States, but the Scandinavian dream is found here as well.

Scandinavian Culture Makes the Difference

If the Scandinavian systems, as Europhiles claim, are more moral and decent than our own, why do immigrants, including Nordic ones, achieve more in the United States?

Scandinavian nations offer an array of immigration policies, some more open and some more restrictive, but all of those nations have struggled to assimilate newcomers. Sweden, the largest Scandinavian country, has generally been the most liberal, taking in more refugees during the recent migrant crisis from the Middle East than any other European country.[18] Denmark has been the most restrictive, sometimes aggressively so, going as far as placing ads in Arabic newspapers dissuading more refugees from attempting to immigrate to their nation,[19] and halting trains coming from Germany in an attempt to stem the tide of refugees.[20]

In 2015, Sweden had more new refugees than new births.[21] The massive flow of immigrants—not only from Syria but from many other Islamic-majority nations including Turkey—fused with Sweden's inability to assimilate newcomers and a welfare state that incentivizes immigrants to rely on the government, has been disastrous. After only seven months, the Social Democrat prime minister Stefan Löfven went from lamenting the notion of a closed border to grousing that "Sweden is no longer capable of receiving asylum seekers at the high level we do today. We simply cannot do any more."[22]

Löfven's position was driven by a harsh political reality. Almost instantaneously, a very specific type of crime began skyrocketing in Sweden, which had historically benefited from some of the lowest crime rates in Europe. Reported rapes in Sweden would spike 10 percent by 2017, jumping nearly 25 percent over the decade.[23] In one two-week period in 2018, five explosions took place in the once-peaceful country, all of them perpetrated by new immigrants.[24] In 2016, Malmö, the country's third-biggest city, had a higher murder rate than New York State for the same year.[25] Gang murders had jumped from four per year in the early 1990s to around forty in 2018, most of them perpetrated by groups of immigrants.

Immigrants make up 26 percent of Sweden's prison population and about 50 percent of those in prison for serious violent offenses.[26]

It is likely, and commonly thought by the people, that most gang members in Sweden are first- and second-generation immigrants. We aren't sure because there's been a concerted effort in Sweden to hide immigrants' connection to the rise in crime. As of this writing, there hasn't been a single recent study in Sweden attempting to estimate the connection between immigration and sexual assault or homicide rates. Further, there is no data on crimes committed by immigrants. Sweden has either not kept those numbers or hasn't made them public since 2005.[27]

That said, the statistics from 2005—before the recent spike in newcomers—revealed that immigrants were significantly overrepresented as offenders of crime. In fact, the numbers showed that immigrants were 2.5 times more likely to be registered as a suspect for a crime than a native Swede.[28] Since the 2005 report, Swedish politicians have ensured no more statistics are released. In 2017 Parliament even rejected a motion to produce updated crime statistics based on national origin.[29]

It is indisputable that many nationalist and far-right-wingers exploit the rise of crime for political purposes. It is also indisputable that Sweden went from being a nation with one of the lowest homicide rates in Western Europe to above average within a few years. For the first time in its history, "law and order" was among the most vital issues cited by voters.[30]

In many ways, the immigrant crisis exposed just how brittle the Nordic Model really is when it isn't relying on near-complete homogeneity of a small population. Sweden accepted around 600,000 immigrants from 2015 to 2020. The labor force grew by over 7 percent since early 2015. It grew only 4.7 percent in Denmark and only 4.9 percent in Norway.[31] And while the unemployment rate among native Swedes remained at around 4 percent, foreign-born unemployment rose to around 15 percent (and we should take into consideration that some newcomers are Finns, who share social and cultural ideas of Swedes). The rate among immigrants' children was even higher. Unemployment of immigrants with high educational attainment remains around eight percentage points higher than of native-born Finns and Swedes.

As noted above, the progeny of Swedes tended to find more success in the United States than those who remained in Sweden. An even more instructive example is to compare immigrant groups that land in both Sweden and the United States at around the same time. Among these, the most useful example are Somalis.

Around one-third of all Somalis who have immigrated to the United States settle in Minnesota, a state where around a fifth of the 5.5 million population still claim Scandinavian descent.[32] Most polling puts the number of Somalis in the state somewhere around 70,000. Sweden, a nation of 10 million, has somewhere around 60,000 Somalia-born residents.

According to Swedish economist Benny Carlson, who's studied and contrasted the successes and failures of this African-born community, Somali employment in Minnesota is more than twice as high as in Sweden, and self-employment is around eight times higher. Nordic nations like Norway and Denmark do not fare much better.

In the United States, Somalis have found great success in health care and education, but they also include conspicuously high numbers of small business owners. This entrepreneurship among Somalis lays the foundation for generational success that simply isn't found in Sweden. Carlson credits a number of reasons

for this trend—most would dismay Europhiles. For one, the inability of newcomers to rely on welfare programs and safety nets
for extended periods of time tends to incentivize them to make
their own way. Add to that the ingrained entrepreneurial spirit
of the United States and a system that encourages small business
owners with a low bar for entry and comparably few labor regulations, and you have a recipe for success.

All of this also leads to more cultural assimilation. Somalis
in Minnesota are generally better educated—with most of their
education being attained in the United States. Somali Americans are more likely to speak English, more quickly, than Somali
Swedes are to learn Swedish.[33] Then again, unemployment rates
among immigrants with low educational attainment in Sweden
aren't just high compared to the United States, they're high compared to any English-speaking nation. America's dominance in
assimilation is not new and merely a case of Sweden struggling
with the high influx of recent immigrants. In 2006, nearly ten
years before Europe's migration crisis, there were thirty-eight
Somali-run businesses in Sweden. There are eight hundred in
the city of Minneapolis.[34]

Myths of Scandinavian Happiness Should Be Treated with Skepticism

The *real* gauge of a Nordic society's success, Europhiles will re-
tort, isn't economic indicators but the levels of social satisfaction. Studies, as Europhiles incessantly point out, illustrate that
Scandinavians are—or claim to be—"happier" than most people
in the world. According to the 2020 World Happiness Report,
for instance, Finland was the happiest country in the world, followed by Denmark, Switzerland, Iceland, and Norway.[35] The
United States had fallen to 18, down from its peak of 11 in 2012.

"Happiness," despite all the bromides we hear about money

not buying you love, is indeed wealth. Social satisfaction is tied to wealth. That is why one of the key measurements the report takes into consideration is per capita GDP. Richer people generally consider themselves happier than poorer people no matter where experts poll. That is the case in the world polls. Wealth offers the security and freedoms that poor people strive to achieve. And Scandinavians, like all the others in the top echelon of the happiness index, are comparatively wealthy to most people of the world.

Europhiles like to blame capitalistic "inequality" as a leading reason for societal unease. There is little evidence to suggest much correlation. Nor, in fact, is there much evidence that Nordic nations offer any better outcomes for workers in this regard. In a study conducted by James J. Heckman, a Nobel Prize–winning economist at the University of Chicago, Denmark, the nation most often pointed to as an exemplar of social equality, creates little mobility. If a Dane's parents did not have a college education, chances are high that their kids will end up at the same level because of "disincentives to acquire education arising from the redistributional policies."[36] Danes are "happy" because they are wealthy.

Of course, the notion that researchers can actually detect, compare, codify, and rank levels of authentic happiness between wealthy nations with specificity is ludicrous. Every group—nay, every person—has a unique and self-defining conception of contentment. There is no effective method to properly contrast one person's version of contentment to another's, much less entire societies'. Most often it is an opaque value judgment. Psychiatrists and experts still conduct vigorous debates about how they can even define "happiness." Certainly, the authors of these studies, the people who craft the questions and come to the determinations, have, like all of us, subjective views of contentment. Some are never happy no matter how well the state works around them.

Nordic people, despite their violent early history, are quite agreeable. In the small country of Finland, for example, 91 percent of all respondents say they are satisfied with their president.[37] In the United States, a pluralistic nation, which must make room for a wide array of ideological, geographical, religious, and ethnic diversity, this kind of political "unity" would be—and should be—considered destructive. As one Finnish expert explained, his nation's comity during the coronavirus pandemic was predicated on people being "willing to follow instructions and trust that everyone will do their part. Every time the president or the prime minister holds a public speech about the issue, the overwhelming response is one of trust and commitment."[38] To an American, the Finns might sound like a pathetically compliant society—we are not, to the endless consternation of Europhiles, willing to follow directions.

While the Finns can avoid the difficult debates and critical thinking necessary to preserve a healthy heterogeneity, Americans cannot. The Finnish kind of compliance may work in a small homogeneous society that has the luxury of agreeing on virtually all things because the vast majority of people share the same background and cultural ideas. Like the Scandinavian economic system, the conception of happiness does not comport or scale in the United States.

But, more than all that, do we really know that Finns are happy? As one local joke goes, "An introverted Finn looks at his shoes when talking to you; an extroverted Finn looks at your shoes." What Scandinavia really excelled at, one journalist noted, was minimizing unhappiness.[39] And as the Danish newspaper editor Anne Knudsen once put it, it is "shameful to be unhappy" in her Scandinavian nation.[40] "Over the years I have asked many Danes about these happiness surveys—whether they really believe that they are the global happiness champions—and I have yet to meet a single one of them who seriously believes it's true," noted the author Michael Booth, who lived in Scandinavia, on and off, for more than a decade. "They tend to approach the subject of their much-vaunted happiness like the victims of a practical joke waiting to discover who the perpetrator is."[41]

Now, some of us would be left without careers if grousing about politics and culture fell into disfavor in the United States. This aspect of the Nordic mentality, most common in Denmark, is called "Law of Jante." This set of informal social norms says things like, "You're not to think you are anything special" or "You're not to think you are as good as we are." Basically, every one of them is a call to stop complaining.

Thus, what Nordic people tell pollsters does not always match reality. There is a stigma around admitting unhappiness. A recent report by the Nordic Council of Ministers and the Happiness Research Institute in Copenhagen—Scandinavians seem exceptionally interested in measuring happiness—suggests that the wealth and relatively docile dispositions mask a significant rise in mental health and social problems. "More and more young people are getting lonely and stressed and having mental disorders," one of the report's authors, Michael Birkjaer, told the *Guardian* newspaper. "We are seeing that this epidemic of mental illness and loneliness is reaching the shores of the Nordic countries."[42]

Finns are the European leaders in alcoholism, suicide, and antidepressant use. One-third of all deaths among fifteen- to twenty-four-year-olds in Finland are caused by suicide. According to the Nordic Council of Ministers and the Happiness Research Institute in Copenhagen, some 16 percent of Finnish women aged eighteen to twenty-three and 11 percent of young men define themselves as "struggling" or "suffering" in life.

A 2019 European Union study found that hopelessness, feelings of marginalization, and lack of education and unemployment are increasingly pushing young Europeans toward a "mental health crisis." Around 14 percent of all young people aged fifteen to twenty-four were was at risk, but the nation most susceptible was Sweden, with 41 percent of youngsters "at-risk of depression" based on World Health Organization guidelines.[43]

All of this seems to line up with most Western nations. Even the supposedly unhappy ones.

More important than any statistic, however, is that Europhiles offer no evidence that alleged high levels of Nordic satisfaction are connected to the political system Scandinavians live under rather than existing societal and cultural norms and the natural disposition of the people. One strongly suspects, if Americans with Scandinavian backgrounds would answer the same queries about social satisfaction, they would likely score similar levels of contentment.

The Nordic Model Wouldn't Work Here

Ultimately, whether or not a generous welfare state would make Americans happier is largely irrelevant because it would be unsustainable both economically and constitutionally.

Europhiles are enamored with the Swedish political concept of *folkhemmet*—the literal translation meaning "the people's home"—which is basically the idea that society should be tasked with perpetually taking care of its citizens' every need. At one time, the majority of Americans would mock this kind of governance as a "cradle to grave" welfare state. (Though, as the humorist P. J. O'Rourke once noted, "Between elaborate sex education and the constitutional status of the Lutheran Church, Sweden provides for its citizens from, as the Swedes put it, 'erection to resurrection.'")[44]

Such an all-encompassing system that is reliant on the generosity of transfer programs is no doubt enticing to some, but it poses moral hazards for society as a whole. As the money and benefits of transfer programs become more generous, increasing numbers of citizens are incentivized to set aside their tradition-ally strong work ethic and rely on the state.

Or cheat. In the 1980s, somewhere around 80 percent of Swedes agreed with the statement that "claiming government benefits to which you are not entitled is never justifiable." By the mid-2010s, only 55 percent did.[45] Beginning in the 1990s, somewhere around a fifth of Sweden's working-age population was relying on unemployment, sick leave, or early retirement benefits. Scandinavians, who pride themselves on good health, are somehow also the sickest people in the world. The number of people on government-paid sick leave in Sweden continues to ex-plode, exceeding the military and education budgets combined. The country finally had to try to reform the system recently—just as American Europhiles were arguing we should import it.

Young Nordic workers have become less competitive than their parents, and as the population ages, this will manifest into a long-term economic erosion. The spike in welfare services costs coincides with an aging population. Yet, Sweden's young are far less inclined to compete than the generations that came before them, and the country is losing ground to Central European and Asian cities in important engineering and technology skills.

Europhiles, moreover, often overstate the underlying eco-nomic health of Scandinavian economies. In Norway, the Ekofisk oil field, first discovered in 1969, allowed the nation to create the Government Pension Fund Global. From this over–$1 trillion reserve, checks are sent to the nation's small population of 5.5 million. Denmark, Western Europe's largest oil and gas producer, also relies heavily on fossil fuels to bolster its economy. The International Monetary Fund is constantly warning these countries that their reliance on one commodity, in this case oil, threatens their economic health.

Mostly, though, Nordic nations rely on high taxes to fund their wide social safety nets and welfare programs. Even reformed tax rates in most Nordic countries would likely spark a violent revolution in the United States. Though American voters have their own grievances about the federal tax system—namely that voters are convinced the wealthy don't pay their fair share (in reality, the rich pay the vast majority of income taxes)—they are likely the most tax-averse people in the Western world. Around 40 percent of Americans say they pay *more* than their fair share, while 53 percent say they pay about the right amount. Only 4 percent of Americans believe they pay less than their fair share.[46]

It still isn't politically feasible in the United States for a politician to propose that the state take the majority of earnings as it does in Nordic nations, so the Europhiles work incrementally. Fans of the welfare state like Senators Elizabeth Warren and Bernie Sanders argue that they can create an American version of social welfare without raising taxes on the middle class.

The rich do not pay most taxes in Nordic nations. Everyone pays. In 1960, Sweden's tax rates were approximately at the same level as the United States right now. Today, more than half of Sweden's economic output is taken by the government.

Sweden's top statutory personal income tax rate is 57.1 percent.[47] Denmark's is 55.9 percent.[48] In 2018, Denmark's tax-to-GDP ratio—which gauges a nation's tax revenue relative to the size of its economy—was 44.9 percent. Norway's is at 39.0 percent. Sweden's is at 43.9 percent.[49] Add to that a national sales tax of 25 percent in Denmark, Sweden, and Norway on most goods.

In Bernie's beloved Denmark, 24.5 percent of tax revenue as a percent of GDP came from personal income taxes and social security contributions, compared with only 16 percent in the United States. Denmark's top statutory personal income tax rate, which kicks in at 1.3 times the average income, is 55.9 percent. In the United States, that would translate into taxing everyone who makes more than $65,000 at 55.9 percent. On the other side, Denmark's corporate tax rate is 22 percent, compared with a combined state and federal American corporate tax that stands at 25.9 percent.

If the United States wanted to duplicate Scandinavia's munificent social welfare on a massive scale, we would need to significantly raise income taxes on the middle class to broaden the tax base and adopt a value-added tax—a consumption tax put on all goods whenever value is added during the supply chain—which will be paid for by the middle class.

In comparison, the ratio of government taking in the United States is 24.3 percent. Put it this way: In American terms, a person earning $60,000 a year would be subjected to a 60 percent tax rate in Sweden.[30] What do you get? You get what the government decides you get, in the way government decides to give it to you. That is why Sweden has been slowly trying to cut more taxes, scale back the welfare programs, and create a more vibrant private sector. The norms and bonds of a strong Scandinavian society are being corroded by the Nordic Model, not strengthened.

Were Scandinavian institutions as successful as their champions claim, there is still no way such a state would successfully scale to the size of the United States, nor would it comport with its ideals, its geographical and cultural diversity, or its traditions. It would require exceptionally un-American ideas.

Even President Barack Obama, quite the Europhile, understood the problem of scale and tradition when pushing back against the notion of the United States acting like Sweden during a fiscal crisis. "They took over the banks, nationalized them, got rid of the bad assets, resold the banks, and, a couple years later, they were going again. So you'd think, looking at it, Sweden looks like a good model. Here's the problem; Sweden had like five banks. We've got thousands of banks. You know, the scale of the U.S. economy and the capital markets are so vast and the problems in terms of managing and overseeing anything of that scale, I think, would—our assessment was that it wouldn't make sense. And we also have different traditions in this country."[51]

There are fewer than 6 million people in the nation of Denmark, as opposed to about 330 million people in the United States. The idea of transferring that kind of massive wealth to fund programs of that scale to be efficiently run by our federal government is implausible. And why would we do any such thing? There are good reasons that for decades successive governments in Scandinavian nations chose to adopt capitalistic free markets over more state interventions. The question should not be "Why isn't the United States adopting the Nordic Model?" but rather: "Can you imagine how successful and happy Scandinavian nations would be if they adopted the American model more quickly?"

3

Europe's Health Care Disasters

America's health care system is second only to Japan, Canada, Sweden, Great Britain, well . . . all of Europe. But you can thank your lucky stars we don't live in Paraguay!

—Homer Simpson

Perhaps the most damaging myth perpetuated by Europhiles on the American populace is the claim that health care in the United States is inferior. This falsehood has been internalized by the nation's political class, by the media, and by its popular culture. Americans are subjected to a torrent of punditry and news stories that either obsequiously praise the European health care system as morally superior or frame our lack of socialized medicine as the great inequity of American life.

"Europeans," explains the *New York Times* columnist Roger Cohen, "don't get why Americans don't agree that universal health coverage is a fundamental contract to which the citizens of any developed society have a right."[1] "The Best Health Care System in the World: Which One Would You Pick?" a *New York Times* interactive piece asks.[2] (It's not the United States, if you're wondering.) "Is Germany's health care system a model for the U.S.?" asks NBC News. (Yes!)[3] "The fix for American health care can be found in Europe," *The Economist* asserts.[4] "France's health-care system was ranked as the world's best—here's how it compares with the US," says CNBC, leaving little to the imagination.[5]

Few Americans, of course, would contend that our health care system *isn't* in need of improvement. Most of the popular arguments calling to abolish the private health care insurance system, however, are highly misleading. The Europhiles' case usually boils down to three facile assertions of alleged American failure: life expectancy, infant mortality, and costs. As a recent Reuters piece put it, the United States "spends about twice what other high-income nations do on health care but has the lowest life expectancy and the highest infant mortality rates."[6] When the congressional Democrats sponsored a European-style Medicare-for-all bill in 2020, the accompanying letter maintained "that life expectancy in the U.S. is lower than other nations, while our infant mortality is much higher."[7]

There are significant problems with each of these claims.

Shorter life expectancy rates in the United States have very little to do with how we deliver health care, and more to do with culture.

Stripped of context, European longevity is indisputably better—Americans live on average 78.7 years while, according to the World Health Organization, citizens of top-performing nations like Italy and Spain live to over 83.[8] Yet, this is a false comparison on a number of fronts. With its eclectic range of behaviors, its high levels of ethnic diversity, its array of environmental factors, and its perpetual flow of immigration (of people who often spend their formative years in non-Western subpar health care systems), American health care outcomes have as much to do with choices, habits, and socioeconomic situations as they do with the delivery of services.

A far better comparison is to place European rates alongside American states with similar cultural compositions. When comparing the life expectancy and health outcomes of Minnesotans, who predominately rely on private health insurance, with the outcomes of Swedes, who live in an area that is more or less of the same size and ethnic makeup—*and* has government-run health insurance—the populations of the two have basically the same longevity. As researchers have pointed out, the health outcomes in Minnesota have a lot more in common with those of Denmark than they do with Mississippi.[9]

Another good way to compare European-style government-provided health insurance plans with private-sector insurance would be to see how each of them functions within the United States. When researchers looked at the outcomes of nearly 900,000 major operations, ranging from coronary artery bypass grafts to organ removal, they found that patients on state Medicaid were more likely to die in the hospital and more likely to have complications and infections than those who were on private insurance plans.[10] Those on Medicaid remain in the hospital longer and they cost more. By nearly every metric available, private insurance outperformed state-provided Medicaid.[11] Some studies show that people with *no insurance* experienced better outcomes than those who relied on Medicaid.[12]

When the National Bureau of Economic Research examined Americans who had gotten state-provided health insurance through Medicare, it found patients were 45 percent more likely to die than those with private insurance.[13] This, alone, doesn't mean European models underperform private health insurance, but it does show that they underperform in the United States.

Societal forces and local practices have a large part to play in how long we live, as well. "It's great that the Japanese eat more sushi than we do, and that they settle their arguments more peaceably," Avik Roy, president of the Foundation for Research on Equal Opportunity, once quipped, "but these things don't have anything to do with socialized medicine."[14] Researchers at the *Journal of the American Medical Association* found that nearly two-thirds of variation in life expectancy could be attributed to "behavioral and metabolic risk factors" rather than any difference in the health care system.[15]

If you believe that Americans should lead more salubrious and less risky lives so they can match the marginally better life expectancy rates of Belgium or Portugal, that's an argument for more calisthenics and broccoli and an attitude change, not for socialized European health care.

One of the most obvious factors between Americans and Europeans affecting longevity is how we use cars. We drive them. A lot. A larger number of Americans get in an automobile every day so they can go back and forth from their sprawling suburbs and mansion-size homes to work. This has been a generational choice. The sheer size of the areas that suburban Americans traverse in a single year would likely equal a lifetime of driving for some urbanites in European cities. Americans drive around 13,500 miles per year on average.[16] The British, the busiest drivers in Europe, drive around 6,500 miles per year, or nearly 50 percent less than the average American.[17]

Though vehicular deaths have fallen everywhere over the years because of improved safety and medical technology, the fact is that more driving leads to more accidents. The United States, which has far less density than any Western European nation, experiences nearly 13 deaths per 100,000 while that number is below 5 in most European nations (other than similarly sprawling nations like Russia—sans the mansions—where it is nearly 16 per 100,000).

Now, many Europhiles find reliance on cars and life in the suburbs to be a vulgar lifestyle choice, but the deaths that drive down life expectancy have nothing to do with access to medical care.

Less positively, Americans also experience more violent crime—which is one of the few areas we lag behind Europe. When researchers at Texas A&M and the University of Iowa began removing all fatal injury deaths from the life expectancy tables of developed nations, the United States rose from the bottom end of the list of industrialized nations to first.[18] Again, socializing medicine would not change any of these factors—other than, perhaps, making families poorer.

It would still be misleading to say that personal health choices are entirely at fault for the discrepancy in life expectancy. In the United States parents are also far more likely not to abort children with genetic and chromosomal conditions like Down syndrome, who often have shorter life spans.

The United States has a higher infant mortality because we value every life and try to save "hopeless" cases that European numbers don't even count as live births.

Another popular indictment of the United States health care system is that it has a comparatively high rate of infant mortality—which is usually defined as death within the first year after birth. Recent studies have found that the United States has nearly 6 deaths per one thousand live births, and is 32nd among 35 of the most developed countries, according to the Organisation for Economic Co-operation and Development (OECD).

Big hay is made of this fact. "US kids shouldn't be 55% more likely to die by age 19 than European kids," contends *New York Times* columnist Nicholas Kristof.[19] "American kids are 70 percent more likely to die before adulthood than kids in other rich countries," says Vox.[20] Headlines like "Preterm Birth Rates Have Increased in the U.S." or "U.S. Top of List for First-Day Deaths in Rich Nations" are used to juxtapose the allegedly sorry state of American medicine with Europe's high rates of survival for babies. The reasons for this disparity have a lot more to do with our moral outlook on life than with the health care system.

Comparing infant mortality rates on both continents is already difficult because the factors aren't consistent. In nations like Germany and Austria, for example, a premature baby weighing less than 500 grams isn't considered a living child.[21] In France, only babies born after twenty-two weeks of gestation are considered alive and in Poland a baby has to weigh more than one pound, two ounces to count as a live birth.[22] In many other European nations underweight premature babies are listed as "unsalvageable" and are never considered living in the first place.

Furthermore, numerous peer-reviewed studies find that neonatal deaths have been underreported in Western European nations by anywhere from 10 to 30 percent.[23] Buried in the world health literature you will find that it's been a "common practice in several countries (e.g., Belgium, France, Spain) to register as live births only those infants who survived for a specified period beyond birth" and those who do not are "completely ignored for registration purposes."[24] That kind of reporting will obviously skew numbers to make it seem that the United States is home to third-world-level health care.

More relevantly, Americans count every life they save. Thus, for example, Harper Rose Schultz, a 312-gram baby born in Saginaw, Michigan, in 2020, would not have been considered a "life" in most European nations.[25] While many preemie babies are not as lucky as Harper Rose, in the United States we calculate all births that display "any evidence of life" in our infant-mortality statistics—spending millions of dollars trying to save them. Naturally, America is going to experience higher neonatal-mortality rates than countries that do not. When we adjust for low birth weights alone, the United States jumps to fifth among all countries.[26]

That survival rate continues to improve as hospitals spare little expense in their efforts. Today, babies twenty-six weeks and above are quite likely to live—and the number keeps getting better.

Given this philosophy of valuing and counting every life, it should be obvious that:

Hell yes, Americans pay more for medical care!
There is no question we spend *a lot* on health care in the

United States. This is mostly a function of us spending a lot more on everything. American consumption levels easily out-pace every nation in the world on almost all fronts. Why should medicine—perhaps the most vital purchase a person makes in their lifetime—be any different? Britain, the country that comes closest to our per capita spending, sits at around 85 percent of the level of American consumption. The next best, the Germans and French, are at around 70 percent.[27]

It is unsurprising that one of the biggest complaints consum-ers level against the American system is the cost. There are, without any question, plenty of wasteful and inefficient costs embedded in the American health care system—many of them due to government intrusions and regulations—but lots of our spending goes toward advanced medical technology, new drug therapies, and high-end care.

A system built to save every life incentivizes technological advances. The United States leads in technologies with high numbers of surgical and cardiovascular procedures and imaging studies. None of it is cheap. At least, not yet. It is the United States, not Europe, that is home to the world's best lifesaving medical innovation. There are more clinical trials conducted in the United States than in any other country—or continent.[28] The United States is home to more new medical patents and medicine than every other country combined.[29] It's estimated that new medical or improved medical technologies contribute anywhere from 30 to 50 percent of increases in annual spending.[30]

The best way to measure a nation's health care spending isn't by relying on crude life expectancy numbers—which are quite high across the industrialized world—but rather by looking at what happens after medical intervention. One of the reasons we outperform other nations in this regard is the aggressive treatment of ailments, most noticeably when it comes to cancer. American doctors catch more cancers, and they catch cancer earlier.

One study found that Americans averted 265,000 more

deaths of colorectal cancer compared to Western Europe between 1982 and 2010 because of aggressive treatment.[31] The United States' all-cause mortality rates relative to those of other developed countries improve dramatically after the age of seventy-five years.

For decades now, studies have found that most cancer patients in the United States live considerably longer than Europeans after diagnosis. The death rate from cancer in the United States declined by nearly 30 percent from 1991 to 2017, but the past years have seen some of the largest single-year drops ever recorded, according to the American Cancer Society.[32] More than 90 percent of American breast cancer patients lived at least five years after treatment, compared to a survival rate of only 85 percent in the rest of the advanced world.[33] The same goes for survival for rare cancers.[34] And the trend is accelerating.

Another reason European nations often do a better job containing medical costs is that they have embraced government-rationed care. And one of the ways they keep costs down is by fixing prescription drug prices. In the United States we spend nearly double on pharmaceutical drugs—$1,443—compared to the average of other countries, $749—per person.[35]

Shouldn't we put caps on drug prices? One reason not to is that allowing companies to profit from their patents incentivizes research and consistent improvement. The United States is home to strong intellectual property laws and open markets for pricing that prompt pharmaceutical giants to research and bring more drugs to the marketplace. Without the possibility of recouping the enormous investment of capital that is plowed into the development of new drugs—on average somewhere around ten years and nearly $3 billion[36]—the world would have far fewer lifesaving drugs on the market. American companies are given a twenty-year monopoly over a drug, which typically brings them a healthy profit. This kind of agreement is often derided as profit mongering. But without a market relationship, not only would Americans be without many advances, but the world would as well.

The disconnect in Europe between the marketplace and the cost of pharmaceuticals undermines innovation and disincentivizes technological advances. Europe pays for its restrictive policies in many ways. One is by denying its citizens expensive cancer treatments such as the new immunotherapies for cancer. Of all the cancer drugs that were brought to market between 2011 and 2018, 95 percent were available in the United States, while only 74 percent were available in the United Kingdom, Europe's top-performing nation, and only 8 percent in Greece.[37] While 90 percent of new antiviral drugs are available in the United States, only 60 percent of these new drugs are available in Britain. While 91 percent of new cardiovascular drugs are available in the United States, only 73 percent of these therapies are available in Britain.[38]

Americans get better drugs and they get them faster. From 2011 to 2015, the Food and Drug Administration (FDA) approved 170 new drugs while the European Medicines Agency approved 144. Furthermore, the FDA had a median review time of 306 days, 80 days fewer.[39] And despite being faster, the oversight is more rigorous.[40] The American philosophy of valuing every life also means the United States leads the world in orphan drugs—those developed to treat rare medical diseases that aren't profitable. Around 40 percent of all approved drugs in the United States every year are orphan drugs. In Europe, it is only 25 percent.[41]

Another factor boosting health care prices is the high salaries of doctors. Physicians in the United States earn the highest annual salaries in the world at $313,000—with Germans coming in at a distant second place, at around $163,000.[42] Due to high remuneration—as well as an array of other quality-of-life factors—American doctors are more satisfied with their jobs (91 percent) than those in the highest-performing nations like France (71) or Spain (73). More than one in four doctors in the United States were born in another country, but the entice-ment of working in America extends to the entire health care profession. Researchers who analyzed U.S. census data of over 164,000 health care professionals in the Unites States found that 17 percent weren't born in America and almost 5 percent were not even citizens.[43]

Now, some may argue that doctors don't deserve such high salaries. But pushing down the organic market-driven level of salaries is a dangerous game. From 2005 to 2015, more than 10,000 doctors left Italy to go find "meritocracy, better career prospects, and higher salaries," according to one study.[44]

Britain's National Health Service (NHS) has a major problem with staffing shortages. The United Kingdom has a significant doctor shortage and an even bigger nursing shortage. The United Kingdom has a shortfall of 11,500 doctors and 42,000 nurses.[45] In contrast, by 2030 almost every state in the United States will have a surplus of nurses.[46] At the end of June 2018 the NHS had 107,743 unfilled positions.[47]

One doctor wrote in the *Guardian*'s "Blood, Sweat and Tears" series that the NHS is training him to lose his humanity. He de-scribed being so overworked that he is forced to forgo normal interactions with his patients like laughing at a joke, smiling at them, or listening to them talk as they lay dying. For him, the choice is between being kind and polite or getting vital work done that will keep his patients safe. In the end he chose to blame the system rather than himself for forcing him to choose between his humanity and saving another human's life.[48]

In contrast, the United States attracts medical professionals from around the world. Part of the draw for doctors all around the world is the fact that the United States pays its doctors $100,000 more on average than British doctors make. Further, starting pay for nurses in the United Kingdom is one-third that of nurses' in the United States.[49] No wonder so many British nurses are quitting to work as grocery store clerks, where the pay and the hours are better.[50] Talk about an upside-down world.

This European brain drain became a serious problem during the COVID-19 pandemic. After the coronavirus first hit Europe, many of the nations that had the best systems, according to the WHO, struggled to keep up because of lack of beds, protective equipment, and doctors are just some of the issues faced in Europe, as the coronavirus crisis exposed the weaknesses of the region's national health systems. The president of the Portuguese Medical Association was left to appeal to retired doctors to return to the national health service and help during the emergency. This has also been the case in Spain and Italy, where the lack of medical staff has been a key issue during the pandemic.[51]

"For years, we have heard Spain's leaders say that we had the best health care in the world," wrote David Jiménez after the coronavirus pandemic hit Spain. "This political fantasy has now met with a rude awakening. We have learned the hard way that being deemed the healthiest nation in the world by the World Economic Forum is not the same as having the best health care system." The problem, he pointed out, wasn't that hospitals had reached their limit because of COVID-19, but rather that they had reached their limit before the cases had ever arrived. It was not, he notes, uncommon for a single doctor in a Spanish hospital to treat up to sixty patients a day before the coronavirus epidemic.[52]

What About the NHS?

Europe features many iterations of socialized medicine, some more effective than others. The United Kingdom's system is by far the most centralized, in the worst shape, and also the most popular among American Europhiles. *New York Times* columnist

Paul Krugman, one of the nation's most prolific Europhilic writers, recently contended, "In Britain, the government itself runs the hospitals and employs the doctors. We've all heard scare stories about how that works in practice; these stories are false."[53]

Are they?

The United Kingdom has a single-payer model where the government is the primary provider of health insurance.[54] The National Health Service (NHS), founded in 1942, has been the national pride of Britain, treated with patriotic reverence. Not only is the NHS a single-payer system, but it is truly socialized in that the government owns the medical facilities and medical personnel work directly for the NHS.[55] The system is financed through high taxes. Health care is only "free" in the sense that there is no charge at the point of care. There are also no deductibles or copays.[56] However, as the system becomes increasingly stressed, patients are increasingly asked to pay for more things themselves.

As with other European systems, the only way the NHS can control spending is by regulating fees and drug prices and enforcing a centralized method of policing care that often disregards local needs and the unique care that diverse populations need. The notion that Americans would abide with treatment allocated by government bureaucrats is probably wish-casting, no matter how much headway Europhiles have made.

One of the truisms I've learned covering politics over the past couple of decades is that the more acronyms a reporter is forced to use to describe something, the more authoritarian that thing is. This section is *loaded* with them.

The NHS agency in charge of aggressively restricting the procedures, treatments, and drugs patients receive is the National Institute for Health and Care Excellence (NICE). In other words, the ironically named NICE oversees rationing. Rationing isn't a dirty word in the British system; it is the system.

NICE, in fact, quite transparently lets citizens know how it decides who will be allotted lifesaving treatment and who will suffer in pain or die. NICE's metric for determining whether a treatment is worth paying for is called the quality-adjusted life year (QALY). NICE boards calculate the amount of years a procedure, drug, or treatment might add to a person's life, and they multiply that by that person's expected quality of life. To NICE each QALY is worth £20,000. If the treatment is £20,000 per QALY or less it will likely be approved.[57]

If not, patients can choose to pay for the procedure themselves. Every new drug, procedure, and treatment in the United Kingdom has to go through NICE as well. A new, more expensive treatment must exceed the old one by enough QALYs to be approved by the NHS. This has greatly restricted access to the newest, most innovative medical advances in the United Kingdom.

Since the NHS is in perpetual financial crisis, it has been cutting surgeries that used to be considered routine but have been labeled as being of "limited clinical value." Among these procedures are hernia repair, cataract removal, continuous glucose monitoring, as well as hip and knee replacements.[58] This does not mean that these surgeries are never covered under the NHS, but it does give clinical commissioning groups (CCG), the local organizations that run hospitals, discretion about whether to allow them or not. For instance, 104 out of the 195 CCGs in England are restricting cataract surgery.[59]

Many CCGs require a significant deterioration in vision prior to allowing the surgery. However, as some have pointed out, if the elderly aren't able to see they will be less independent and thus need more care. Similarly, bad vision increases the risks of falls and accidents for the elderly.[60] How would Americans react to such inhibitions of service?

In a similar situation the NHS initially told elderly patients with wet age-related macular degeneration that they would need to go blind first in one eye before they would be prescribed

Lucentis, a two-year treatment that is known to stabilize the condition and even sometimes reverse blindness. After a public outcry the decision was reversed.[61] What happens next time?

When the British can't get care, incidentally, they often come to the United States. The United States regularly has a trade surplus of over a billion dollars when it comes to medical travel. Annually 100,000 to two million travelers flying into the United States are what is known as medical tourists (we just call it "going to a doctor"). These are people who come to the United States for a medical purpose. Around 25 percent come from Europe.[62]

The NHS's top-down decision making doesn't translate to a system that only prioritizes the most serious ailments. In fact, the NHS's priorities are often strangely warped. There is now a clinic to treat those thirteen to twenty-five who are addicted to playing video games.[63] Thousands of children might have to forgo continuous glucose monitoring for their diabetes and some elderly might have to go blind, but we can all rest assured that today's youth will no longer be addicted to *Candy Crush* and, God forbid, *Minecraft* or *Fortnite*.

In 2017 alone, the NHS spent £220,000 on prescriptions for Neutrogena shampoo and £1.6 million on Aveeno bodywash, yet they deemed hernia operations of "limited clinical value."[64] When a fifty-one-year-old man named Ross Clark developed a hernia just like his father, he was told by his doctor that new NHS guidelines dictate that if his condition was not causing him pain, and his job did not involve heavy lifting, he did not qualify for an operation. Though he hadn't been to the doctor in five years, during that time he paid an estimated £30,000 in taxes specifically to the NHS and now they wouldn't pay to repair his intestinal wall.[65] That same year the NHS spent £22 million on transgender surgery and £730 million on methadone for drug addicts.[66]

Long wait times are a chronic problem across government-run

health care systems. The United Kingdom has a particular problem with meeting their own wait time standards. A report from April 2019 stated that more than 220,000 people had been waiting more than six months to receive medical treatment in the United Kingdom and more than 36,000 had been in line for treatment for nine months or more.[67]

Prior to the pandemic, the total number of people waiting to get surgeries like hernia repair, cataract removal, or hip or knee replacement stood at 4.4 million.[68] Further, an NHS report from February 2020 states that the number of patients waiting more than eighteen weeks for a treatment referral rose from 556,000 to 722,000. Additionally, there were 1,467 patients who were waiting more than fifty-two weeks.[69]

Journalist Susannah Thraves claimed in 2019 that waiting for her kidney surgery caused her more pain than her actual condition. Thraves starts her article off by describing her weekend, hanging out with friends watching stand-up comedians. Then she describes being curled up in her theater seat with heating pads on her skin to keep the excruciating pain away. Thraves says it felt like her organs were being squeezed inside of her. Her pain is due to a pelvic ureteric junction obstruction in her kidney. Because one of her kidneys does not filter properly, it balloons up. Thraves writes that it took months of tests and appointments to get to the point of being referred for a kidney surgery. She says she struggles with the anxiety brought by being on "what seems like a never-ending wait list."[70]

In contrast to the United Kingdom, more than 60 percent of patients in America can schedule a surgery within a month of being advised they need it.[71]

Wait times can also be deadly, especially for cancer patients. According to the NHS's data, almost 25 percent of cancer patients did not start their treatment on time despite an urgent referral from their general practitioner. Don't forget that "on time" for the NHS is sixty-two days after referral.

This is possibly one reason why only 81 percent of breast cancer patients and 83 percent of prostate cancer patients in the
United Kingdom live at least five years after diagnosis compared
to 89 percent of breast cancer patients and 97 percent of prostate cancer patients in the United States.[72] Faster care, especially
where cancer is concerned, yields better results.

The United Kingdom's emergency rooms, known as Accident
and Emergency (A&E) centers, are notorious for being over-
crowded and understaffed. Ultimately this means long wait
times, if you get seen at all. After becoming known for infamously
long wait times the NHS imposed four-hour treatment targets
on A&E centers. Ninety-five percent of patients are supposed to
be seen within four hours of arriving at an emergency room. The
target is rarely met.

Getting admitted isn't the end of the story. There is often a
delay between the admittance agreement and the hospital actually being able to find an open bed for a patient. These are
called trolley waits because they often involve putting people in
temporary holding areas like corridors on uncomfortable trolley
beds. In December 2019, 98,452 patients spent more than four
hours waiting on a trolley from decision to admission. Of those,
2,347 had a twelve-hour trolley wait.

One report notes that nearly 5,500 patients died while waiting on a trolley between 2016 and 2019, meaning many likely
died in a corridor.[73] At one UK hospital, two patients died in one
week while on trolleys. One of these patients died from cardiac
arrest after waiting on a trolley for thirty-five hours.[74] The hospital said it was unusually busy.

Waiting doesn't just happen in hospitals. Ambulances in the
United Kingdom have become habitually unreliable. Between
2017 and 2018, ambulances from four different services took
twenty-four hours to respond to patients. After falling and breaking her hip, a seventy-nine-year-old woman was left on the
ground for three and a half hours. Apparently, Sylvia was lucky.

Three other patients waited fifty hours, and another waited sixty-two hours for an ambulance to show up.

Handoffs from an ambulance to an A&E are supposed to take no more than fifteen minutes, but they are regularly taking over an hour. In 2008, there were almost 15,000 occasions where an ambulance took at least an hour to hand over a patient in London's thirty-five hospitals.

Negligence is also rampant in the NHS. In 2018, the NHS made 336 payouts of more than £1 million and 869 payments that were in seven figures. The NHS litigation authority says it expects to spend £7.8 billion in clinical negligence litigation and payouts in the next three years.

SO MANY OF THE NHS'S problems could be solved with a freer, more competitive, less centralized health care system. The U.S. health care system has its issues, but nothing to this extent. Consistently the United States has better health outcomes than the United Kingdom. Patients in NHS hospitals were four times more likely to die than in a U.S. hospital. Among severely ill patients the disparity was even worse. Sicker patients were seven times more likely to die in a British hospital than in a U.S. hospital.[75] The medical professionals in the United Kingdom are not blind to the problems. Eighty percent of medical personnel that responded to one survey said that they believed patient safety and quality of care were at risk due to staffing shortages.[76]

The United Kingdom's seventy-two-year experiment with socialized medicine is a gift to the United States in that it teaches us what not to do.

4

"The United States of Europe"

The men who founded our Republic did not aspire to emulate Europeans at all—to the contrary, the project of drafting the American Constitution was largely about ensuring that the American people would never languish under the yoke of a European-style government.

—*Antonin Scalia*[1]

A European superstate is a long-running utopian project of the continent's elite. It was once championed by figures as diverse as Dante, Kant, Voltaire, Bentham, Saint-Simon, and Garibaldi, to name just a few. It was a hope, in widely divergent ideological forms, of Charlemagne, Napoleon, Hitler, and the scores of postwar liberal Western European leaders—including British icon Winston Churchill, who, only a year and a half after the cataclysmic violence of World War II had ended, informed a crowd in Zurich that the continent "must now build a kind of United States of Europe."

Indeed, the intellectual and historical roots of the modern European Union go back to at least the 1920s. And by the time Clarence K. Streit, an American living in Geneva, wrote the bestselling *Union Now*, which called for an American-style federation of the "North Atlantic democracies" with a constitution, a common defense, and a single currency, the idea was well known to a Europe that was barreling toward another world war.

A transnational European state was the dream of the continent's leaders and intellectuals and, allegedly, its people. In his 1983 book, *The Europeans*, the noted Italian journalist Luigi Barzini claimed that at the "bottom of the heart of every European [is] this ancient desire to see Europe pacified and merged into one political unit; to admit openly once and for all what we knew all along and what foreign visitors perceive immediately; that in spite of the infinite diversities, the many separate histories, religions and cuisines, the innumerable languages and patois, we are all basically the same kind of people, comfortable with each other's countries, and in each other's homes."

These were lofty words, indeed, expressing an aspiration held by many European intellectuals. Yet, even Barzini, despite arguing that the people's latent desire for comity had them clamoring for a superstate, remained skeptical that the diverse personalities of Europe could be placated and coexist under a single political body. As long as Europe found itself sandwiched between the belligerent Soviet Union and the powerful United States, he reasoned, the arrangement would be a necessity.

Well, within a few years the Soviet Union would be no more, due in large part to the long-term global efforts of the United States. The European project was reimagined as predominately an economic organization powerful enough to compete with the United States. Whatever romantic notions the union might have once represented, it was born of weakness and self-doubt in the face of American power and prestige. "Post-national, welfare-state, cooperative, pacific Europe was not born of the optimistic, ambitious, forward-looking project imagined in fond retrospect by today's Euro-idealists," notes the historian Tony Judt. "It was the insecure child of anxiety."

IN MANY WAYS, EUROPHILES' PROMOTION of the EU as a progressive alternative to unruly American democracy is ironic since EU

founders liberally plundered American civic ideals to rhetorically pitch their new community. The hundreds of delegates
who gathered at the European Parliament in Brussels in 2002 to
finally draft the European Union's constitution envisioned their
conference as something akin to the ratification of the United
States Constitution in 1787. Such an optimistic framing of their
project had long been the conceit of the EU builders. When the
Belgian socialist Paul-Henri Spaak, one of the philosophical
founders of the European Union, presented plans for a proto-
constitution in 1957, he repeated George Washington's letter in
support of ratification of the American Constitution verbatim.[2]
"It is obviously impracticable in the federal government of these
states, to secure all rights of independent sovereignty to each,
and yet provide for the interest and safety of all," Spaak optimis-
tically said, mimicking the first American president.

Spaak's choice of source was not a strange one. The United
States was not only the first truly modern democratic republic,
but also the most stable and enduring one in the world. This
fact is sometimes forgotten because of her relatively young and
dominant culture.

The first challenge with seeing a united Europe as the equivalent of the United States, however, was that Europeans, unlike
Americans, had not grown into their country. Not only had most
Europeans failed to see themselves as a single continental tradition, but many still struggled to see themselves as a single national
identity. One might be Prussian but not German; Basque but
not Spanish; Parisian but not anyone else. "If there is an analogy
to the US in Europe," the scholar Ted Bromund once noted, "it
is the Federal Republic of Germany, or the United Kingdom of
Great Britain and Northern Ireland—not the European Union."[3]

The United States, by contrast, is wedded by common beliefs. It is true that America has benefited, as many Europeans
like to point out, from the great luck of history and geography,
giving it the space and time for its ideas to incubate and bloom.

Some Europeans, however, fool themselves into believing the American experiment owes *everything* to its geographical windfall and abundance of natural resources. If American success was predicated on its coal mines, wheat fields, and forests, rather than a set of superior ideals and habits, they would not be alone in their success. Russia is big, and largely isolated. Brazil is big, and rich in natural resources. China is big.

What elevating set of principles, after all, did the European Union offer citizens that might replace their own centuries-old histories and customs? The EU is a colossal, yet wholly insipid, bureaucratic arrangement. Such an institution might excite the technocratic Europhile, but it's unlikely any Estonian or Scot would voluntarily grab a rifle and risk his life to defend the "Council of Europe" (not to be confused with "European Council").

Why should they? The citizens of the EU had never banded together to win their independence or banish the old guard or abolish ancient injustices. No Polish pioneers had gotten into covered wagons and taken a perilous trek across the continent into the vast empty spaces to build a new world. Europeans shared no common experiences that might cultivate continental solidity or solidarity, much less cultural continuity or devotion. Americans might have engaged in a bloody civil war to form a more perfect union, but Europeans had largely slaughtered each other in efforts of conquest and revenge. Their new union was a concocted one, their laws collated by men sitting around boardroom tables in Belgium.

The contrast between the founding documents of the United States and the European Union illustrates just how different, both functionally and philosophically, the projects have been.

The U.S. Constitution's fifty-two-word preamble is a sharp declaratory statement of shared beliefs, which offers no political predetermined outcomes, no special accommodations, no promise to soothe majoritarian impulses. It simply aspires to "form a more perfect Union, establish Justice, insure domestic Tranquility, provide for the common defense, promote the general Welfare, and secure the Blessings of Liberty to ourselves and our Posterity, [and] do ordain and establish this Constitution for the United States of America."

Whether an American citizen can recall every clause and amendment of the Constitution or not, they've almost surely internalized its straightforward protections and intent. In more than two hundred years of existence, Americans have amended their founding document only twenty-seven times—and only twice in the past fifty years—most vitally, to rectify the injustice of failing to bestow on all its citizens its central promise.

On the other hand, the treaty establishing a constitution for Europe that was adopted by the twenty-five European nations in Brussels in June 2004 was birthed with 448 Articles, 36 Protocols, 30 Declarations, 20 Declarations on the Protocols, and 2 Annexes, and was 70,000 words of fashionable policy concerns (now 250,000). The European Constitution did not read like an organization of a national consciousness, but rather like the minutes of a corporate merger.

Jack Straw, then Britain's foreign secretary, noted at the time that intentions were nice, but "size tells another, more important story—that of coherence." Straw might well have been echoing James Madison, who had presciently warned that a long-winded constitution might "be of little avail to the people" if laws were so "voluminous that they cannot be read, or so incoherent that they cannot be understood."

How can a people rally around a set of ideals if they have to cross-reference an index to find out what's in it? Few even understood it when it was created. As one poll commissioned by the Elcano Royal Institute, a Madrid think tank, found at the time, only 1 percent of Spaniards could even explain what the convention had been formed to achieve.[4]

Conversely, the shared ideal and heritage of Americans—the thing that unifies them—*is* the liberty, bolstered by a robust civic society and the promise of economic opportunity. It is codified by a constitution that is an elegant declaration of organizing principles, with both a rigid defense of enduring ideals of the Enlightenment and a malleability that accommodates progress and change in a massive, culturally, geographically disparate multiethnic state.

The American Bill of Rights, the first ten amendments to the document, largely restricts the state from interference in the rights of individuals. Some of the Founders believed these rights were so self-evident that writing them down would be superfluous at best and destructive at worst, as it would give license to authoritarians to chip away at their meaning. On the other hand, the Charter of Fundamental Rights, the second part of the European Union's constitution, offers a laundry list of rights to citizens, including things like paid maternity leave, free placement services, housing assistance, and environmental protection. Equating such often-fleeting concerns with essential liberties destroys the indissoluble character of natural rights that precede it in the document.

Essential liberal rights are given perfunctory mention in the EU's constitution, and they always seem to be up for debate while progressive policy concerns that lard up the document are zealously protected.[5] As the late justice Antonin Scalia once noted, every "banana republic in the world has a bill of rights." Soviet republics, after all, had constitutions with long lists of protections including free speech and due process. Upholding those rights, keeping unitary power under control, is the essential difference.

America excels in its system for checking power. While the three branches of the U.S. federal government are intended, ideally, to obstruct the abuse of power through a series of checks and balances, the European executive (Commission), legislature (Parliament and Council of Ministers), and court (Court of Justice) perpetually reinforce, expand, and centralize the power of the European superstate. Add to this a terminal case of mission creep, and you get a recipe for endless intrusions on both the nation-state and individual level.

Both the European and American federal governments are tasked with enumerated powers that limit the national power. The hitch is that the mechanisms of the EU constitution allow authorities to continue to appropriate powers by implicitly and explicitly directing national governments, which rather than assert their own autonomy usually fold.

All of this, no doubt, sounds like a fantastic deal for American Europhiles, who also harbor relativistic ideas regarding liberty and morality. They are prone to dismiss the Constitution as antiquated, crude, and an impediment to progress. They abhor federalist institutions and immutable natural rights—speech, self-defense, economic freedom, you name it. Headlines like "America's Constitution Is Terrible. Let's Throw It Out and Start Over," "The Constitution Is Outdated; Let's Change It," "The U.S. Constitution Is Hopelessly Outdated. It's Time to Re-envision It," and "The Constitution Needs a Reboot" pollute major American periodicals. The Constitution has fallen out of favor with most intellectuals, journalists, and social justice warriors (often the same people).

The American conception of governance is seen as an obstruction by the Europhile, as it places the individual's sovereignty above that of the state, and the individual state's sovereignty above that of the federal government. When the late justice Ruth Bader Ginsburg, a leading proponent of malleable rights and adopting international law in American jurisprudence,[6] was asked about the pitfalls of writing a new constitution, she relayed that she "would not look to the United States Constitution if I were drafting a constitution in the year 2012," recommending, instead, among other documents, the more pliable European Convention on Human Rights.[7]

Federalism? Not So Much

Many of the intellectual founders of the European Union—Paul-Henri Spaak, Aristide Briand, Jean Monnet, Altiero Spinelli, and others—stressed the importance of American-style federalism to surmount the realities on the ground. The European Union's architects and champions, however, would come to see federalism as a mechanism that would coax nations to adopt their edicts under the fabricated notion of "unity"—which, of course, has the American idea upside down. Instead of bonding its citizens with common culture and beliefs, the EU chooses to tightly bind them with copious amounts of red tape. Such an arrangement could never fly in America's union of independent states.

Britain's testy relationship with the EU is a good example of this tension. For obvious historical reasons, the British remain among Europeans, both temperamentally and culturally, most similar to Americans. This book, no doubt, betrays a soft spot for our Anglosphere cousins—once, and still, the best hope of the continent. As Barzini noted, it was the British who imposed on their subjects "such unwonted virtues as earnestness, parsimony, prudence, diligence, discipline, perseverance, honesty as the best policy, correct accounting, punctuality, selfless patriotism, courage, the acceptance of death in battle, tenacity, self-control, fair play but, at the same time, the survival of the fittest, loyalty, the pursuit of profit," among others.[8] Many of these traits are likely to sound familiar to us because Americans have, more than any other people, internalized them. As Alexander Hamilton may or may not have said, we "think in English."

One hopes there will be a renaissance of British ideals *in* Britain. And surely Brexit, the 2016 referendum for a "British exit" from the European Union and the European Atomic Energy Community, finally formalized in December 2020, was an excellent start. The United Kingdom's withdrawal (it had joined the European Communities in 1973) shouldn't have been all that unexpected. Not even Churchill had foreseen the British participating in a common state, arguing instead that the union "must be a partnership between France and Germany" and not the United Kingdom, which had built a special bond with the United States during the war.[9]

National sovereignty was the crux of the matter. The primary reason Brexiters gave for leaving the European Union was a modest and patriotic belief that "decisions about the UK should be taken in the UK."[10] Few predicted they would prevail. But Brexit began with calls to reinstate "regulatory sovereignty," and ended with the chancellor of the Exchequer, Sajid Javid, declaring, to the consternation of Remainers and other Europeans, that Britain would no longer be a "rule taker."[11]

The Europeans had long groused about the United Kingdom's reluctance to "integrate," as British proles continued to cling to ideas of queen and country. The British had never surrendered their currency nor joined the Schengen agreement, which functionally eliminated borders within Europe. Since the Thatcher years, a consequential number of Britons had cultivated something of an aversion—at least, by European standards—to central economic planning. However, the country had seen marked economic growth. Perhaps Brexiters had noticed that the United Kingdom's forty years of deregulation, anti-trade-union laws, and privatization had more to do with that economic growth than any diktat from Brussels.

An average American, one hopes, would find an insistence on self-governance an uncontroversial position. For Europhiles, who tend to believe being coddled by a welfare state is the highest form of liberty, such sentiments as those expressed during Brexit were radical. As one *New Yorker* writer noted, "Outside of London and, perhaps, Birmingham and the university towns, support for *liberalism* appeared to have evaporated almost altogether."[12] The italics are mine, as they highlight how Europhiles often confuse decentralized governance with illiberalism. They, of course, have it backward. While the British, alas, have adopted many of the invasive bureaucratic and multicultural ideas of continental Europe, the notion that they were less liberal than the French or Spanish or Italians—or the EU itself—for aspiring to self-governance was highly risible.

What kind of regulatory regime impelled Britons to leave? The European Union's single market system sounds on paper like a free marketer's dream. It's ostensibly a place where all participating nations face negligible regulatory obstacles to the movement of goods and services across borders. The EU's single market system, which now encompasses somewhere around 500 million consumers and 22.5 million small and medium-size businesses,[13] had promised to stimulate competition and trade, improve efficiency, raise quality, and help cut prices. But whereas this trade arrangement may have once benefited European economies, the superstate that emerged has constricted the movement of goods and capital, and dictated the national fiscal policies and everyday behavior of denizens of the continent. As the scholar Theodore Bromund once pointed out, the EU isn't free trade as much as a "managed market."[14] And managed markets are the highest ambition of American Europhiles.

This was an inevitable development. The organic trajectory of any huge bureaucratic machine is to consolidate its power. The EU is no different. Without any hard constitutional limitations on its reach, and any army of empowered administrators, the European Union is no longer "federalist" by any conception, but rather an institution that demands economic and regulatory conformity, just as the 1957 Treaty of Rome promised. And with every crisis, from the 2008 financial collapse to the mass migration of 2015 to 2016, the EU mandarins have worked to further consolidate EU governance.[15] Even in 2020, as the coronavirus ravaged Western Europe, the European Commission president, Ursula von der Leyen, used the €750 billion EU recovery program to push forward the European Green Deal and exert greater control over member states.[16]

This was tradition. In the early 1980s, the number of EU laws reached 14,000.[17] The EU passed 25 directives and 600 regulations per annum in the 1970s, but those numbers rose to 80 directives and 1,500 regulations by the early 1990s.[18] By 2005 the EU had passed 170,000 pages of active legislation and 666,879 since its inception in 1957.[19] As of June 2019, 80 percent of the United Kingdom's environmental laws had been tethered to EU policy. According to the House of Commons Library, only an estimated 6.8 percent of British primary legislation and 14.1 percent of British secondary legislation from 1997 to the end of 2009 was connected to EU law in one way or another.[20] One British government study estimated that approximately 50 percent of legislation in the United Kingdom with a significant economic impact had originated from EU legislation.[21] As such, the true impact of EU regulations is often impossible to calculate. Much of its influence comes through the administrative state and "soft laws," laid down through thousands of "communications, declarations, recommendations, resolutions, statements, guidelines and special reports from EU institutions" that influence member states.[22]

European standardization policy, championed by the likes of Elizabeth Warren—who gives it a collectivist spin, calling it "economic patriotism"[23]—is meant, according to the EU, to "ensure the interoperability of complementary products and services" as well as protect "health, safety, security, and the environment." Or, in other words, *everything*, from printing paper to envelope sizes to airbags to surgical masks to data technologies to how a person must brew coffee. Yes, every brewing device sold to tens of millions of people across the EU is required to have a "standby mode." Not because of safety reasons, but because some head of an Orwellian department in Brussels decided that it would save people on electricity bills.[24]

How many people does it take to change a lightbulb? the British had asked during the Brexit referendum. The entire supranational European state, that's how many. So went the joke when a priest in Suffolk, England, who had hired a man to climb a ladder to change lightbulbs around his church, was forced, because of "the European Union's Working at Heights Directive," to stop engaging in this kind of dangerous activity. The priest, obliged to follow Caesar's laws, was compelled to build a scaffold that cost him $2,000 every time he needed light.[25] This was just one of the thousands of nannyistic intrusions conceived by administrators, both physically and philosophically thousands of miles removed from the average men and women who live under their rule.

Sure, plenty of "Euromyths" exist—exaggerations about the reach and power of the EU. It is, however, still a nightmare of micromanagement and bureaucratic overreach. The EU, unable to help southern-tier nations break free from a decade of double-digit unemployment, has no problem vigorously enforcing gender quotas on corporate boards or regulating the aesthetic quality of bananas. The EU's tortuous agricultural regulations have become one of the major causes in the rise of food prices across EU member states. While Americans spent an average of 9.5 percent of their income on food, Europeans spent 13.5 percent on average.[26]

The EU also whittles away at sovereignty by pressuring nations to amend or withdraw domestic laws that do not comply with EU desires. Since its inception the Court of Justice has declared scores of staid, completely innocuous laws and deregulations in nations like Belgium, Germany, Greece, Spain, France, Ireland, Italy, Luxembourg, and the United Kingdom as infringements on EU laws.

American federalism, it's not.

IT WAS LIKELY AFTER THE financial Eurozone crisis of 2009 that increasing numbers of British citizens became wary of the assimilated economic fortunes of Europe. The interconnected nature of the continent's monetary policy meant one country's welfare could threaten all of them. Greece, a small nation, had almost brought down the continent in the late 2000s. What happens when the inevitable comes for France and Italy?

Many EU elites blamed the 2008 financial crises on "light-touch Anglo-Saxon regulation."[27] Yet, prior to the crash, the Eurozone, the monetary union of nineteen member states, had forty acronym-rich supervisory authorities already, often with conflicting charges and weak interagency coordination. Here is a list of just a few of the governing bodies: "the Committee of European Banking Supervisors (CEBS) for the banking function and the Banking Supervision Committee of European System of Central Banks (ESCB). For securities, there is the Committee of European Securities Regulators (CESR) and for insurance and pension the Committee of European Insurance and Occupational Pensions Supervisors (CEIOPS)."[28]

How did the EU plan to fix the problem? They decided to establish yet another coordinating committee of regulators to develop common supervisory approaches for all financial firms and create a single set of harmonized rules.[29]

The EU's excessive standard guidelines create layers of bureaucracy unseen in the United States. Companies must use conformity assessment bodies to demonstrate that their product or service complies with the relevant EU legislation to get the okay for their product.[30] Products must meet all applicable EU requirements before they can be placed on the EU market.[31] The cost of testing, inspections, and certification to businesses is tremendous, but people are no safer than they are in the United States, despite the constant grousing of Europhiles.

One major difference between the EU's regulatory tyranny and the United States is that the latter has a stronger self-regulatory system. American industries police themselves through bodies such as the Financial Industry Regulatory Authority, the

Investment Company Institute, the American Insurance Association, the Financial Planning Association, the American Bar Association, the American Bankers Association, and many more.[32] The United Kingdom also has a stronger self-regulatory system than the EU, which is one reason there has been so much clash between the two. For instance, the United Kingdom has a Fairtrade Foundation and a Marine Stewardship Council. Germany has pressured these independent bodies to be consumed by the EU's government system of quality labeling prior to Brexit.

The reality, of course, is that Britain will not be able to fully separate itself from the EU—its top trading partner. Huge consumer markets often dictate the rules of trade. For example, states like California ordain car emissions standards for the entire nation since it is a massive market. Still, states like Texas and Florida can continue competing for corporations, jobs, and people by lowering their regulatory burden and taxes. There are few mechanisms for competition among European Union member states who are under the thumb of a convoluted managed economy.

Many Europhiles peer over the ocean at the fifty byzantine bureaucracies of the EU in jealousy. Yet, such controls are antithetical to American economic life, not only because strict unitary regulatory bodies would undercut the tenets of federalist governance and open markets, but because they demand a caustic conformity. And I don't mean this merely in spirit. The men and women who serve the EU in Brussels—or in Strasbourg or Frankfurt, where its other institutions are housed—are literally bound by a pledge to uphold the interests of the EU above their own nations.[33] This kind of vow would, quite rightly, be considered distasteful and nearly treasonous by Americans, though perhaps not by Europhiles, who often believe international law has a moral legitimacy that supersedes our own.

"Fully embracing the European Union and supporting European integration efforts that bolster the strength and resilience of Europe's union should be core to a new American approach," says the Center for American Progress,[34] a powerful liberal think tank that has produced numerous Democratic administration officials over the years, including Joe Biden's failed nominee as Office of Management and Budget manager, Neera Tanden. Virtually all of the group's positions align with the technocratic supremacy of a unitary government.

The cost of erecting that welfare state, one that American Europhiles believe is broadly preferable to our own system, has taken a serious social toll on Europe. Despite being micromanaged and taking on a massive tax burden, Europeans do not experience less poverty or less suffering than the average Americans. Moreover, they often have less economic mobility and fewer genuine opportunities to succeed. While the European welfare state hurts the lives of individuals—stripping men and women of their agency—it does not offer any more "fairness." Those who have done the heavy lifting are bearing a larger and larger burden, carrying both immigrants and the young who seem to be perpetually unemployed and have never paid into the system. The European welfare state compounded the continent's problems every generation. Youth unemployment rates are nearly 50 percent in Greece, 39 percent in Italy, and 25 percent in France. Worse, ambitious and educated young people are emigrating from Europe in record numbers to meritocracies like the United States.

Margaret Thatcher once argued, "The welfare state will end when they run out of your money." This, sadly, has not come to pass yet. And any reform of the welfare state has been all but impossible. Even the most moderate political attempt to alter policy has sparked widespread, and sometimes violent, protests. Why would we want to put ourselves in a similar position?

You're Welcome, Europe

Forget economics for a moment. The EU's greatest achievement, its champions will assure you, is the creation of a stable, interdependent continent that's avoided any major military conflicts for nearly seventy years—easily a record.

Doubtlessly, trade encourages peace and harmony among peoples. Yet, as many historians have also pointed out, Europe had bucked this trend before, notably preceding the First World War, when the continent was experiencing unprecedented intracontinental trade—both of goods and capital—and still got itself entangled in one of the most destructive conflicts in world history.

Let's not forget that it was Europe that dragged the United States into two colossal wars over the past century in which tens of millions perished. It was the sophisticated Europeans, and not America, that had perpetrated two of the worst genocides in mankind's history (and numerous smaller ones that are either ignored or forgotten). The two most nefarious and destructive ideologies of the age, fascism and communism, were among the tragic quackeries of the European intellectual.

If anyone deserves credit for taming the Western European bellicosity, it was the Americans, who, in addition to the heavy lifting liberating Western Europe from the Nazis, an effort that came at a high cost in both lives and treasure, also guaranteed a peaceful and prosperous postwar Western Europe. America accomplished this feat not only through charity and trade, but by nearly single-handedly ensuring the peace through military might.

"In this Pearl Harbor day, we should remember that the US refused to side with France and the UK to confront the fascist powers in the 30s," Gérard Araud, ambassador of France to the United States, said in 2017.[35] But without the United States,

Araud might well have been celebrating the seventy-fifth year of Vichy rule. These counterhistorical hypotheticals are nothing but guesses. The question is: Would liberalism have thrived in postwar Europe without the United States? It's hardly outrageous to suggest that without us, Europe was likely to be swallowed up by more economic and political turmoil.

Indeed, it was the American taxpayer who funded the Economic Cooperation Act—the Marshall Plan—to the tune of $17 billion—over $200 billion in 2020 dollars (not counting billions in aid that preceded the 1948 bill). All of it was to be used in the effort to rebuild Western Europe (it had been offered to, and rejected by, Eastern European nations). To put this $17 billion in context, the United States' entire federal budget in 1948 was $35 billion.[36] Its entire GDP was $258 billion. Americans saw a rapid economic recovery as the best way to stem the tide of communism in Western Europe, especially in France and Italy, where communist parties were growing in popularity and gaining traction.

Still, as well as being practical, it was, as many American projects are, steeped in idealistic intentions. The stated purpose of the legislation was to "promote world peace and the general welfare, national interest, and foreign policy of the United States through economic, financial, and other measures necessary to the maintenance of conditions abroad in which free institutions may survive and consistent with the maintenance of the strength and stability of the United States."[37]

The Marshall Plan was just the beginning, and perhaps not even the most vital aspect of the United States' efforts to repair war-torn Europe. The fiscal effects of the Marshall Plan have long been debated by economists and historians. Though Americans believed it had primed the pump and given Europe the boost it needed, the Europeans often dismiss it as marginally important, accounting for approximately 3 percent of the spending. The Marshall Plan never exceeded 5 percent of the gross national product of the recipient nations. Whatever the case, it was at that point an unprecedented act of international generosity.

Not since the French bailed out the American revolutionaries, incidentally, has there been any need for European dollars or troops to flow in the other direction.

More important was the reality that the Americans had finally been forced to assume responsibility for the maintenance of Europe. It would be the United States' armed forces that defended the nations of Western Europe from any expanding communist intrusions of the second half of the twentieth century. It was the United States that allowed Germany, France, and even England to foster strong economies and stable governments, saving them the potential military confrontation with Soviets, and also the massive cost of building a military large enough to do the job.

In the film *A Fish Called Wanda*, the brutish American, Otto, rhetorically asks a snooty British woman if she would like to know what the fate of England would have been without "the good ol' U.S. of A." to protect it. "The smallest fucking province in the Russian Empire, that's what!" he says. Undoubtedly, in the absence of an American force, Western Europe would have been compelled to spend lives and treasure resisting the Soviet Union.

The reality is that the United States picked up the tab for the free world. Of course, the United States also benefited from the salubrious liberal institutions that emerged in postwar Western Europe. Per capita GNP grew 33.5 percent in Western Europe from 1948 through 1951. It must be stressed that most of the economies improved before any of the European Union's precursor agreements had been signed. It was reforms of people like Walter Eucken, Wilhelm Röpke, and Franz Böhm, advocates of Angle-Saxon-style market liberalization in West Germany, that brought about the *Wirtschaftswunder*, "the Miracle on the

Rhine," the reconstruction of the decimated economies of West Germany and Austria.

There were others. France's *Trente Glorieuses*, the "Glorious Thirty" years, from 1945 to 1975, saw nearly uninterrupted economic growth, as did booms in Belgium, Greece, Italy, Sweden, and elsewhere. (Britain, which had not been defeated by the Nazis, struggled most in these years.) These periods of economic growth are generally referred to as "miracles" by Europeans. In the United States, we just call them "decades."

It was only when Europe turned from American-style governance in the 1970s that the economic growth stalled in many of these places.

A Kinder, Gentler Reich

As the Cold War came to an end, the famed American diplomat Jeane Kirkpatrick argued that the time had come for "drawing down American forces and commitments overseas."[38] The United States, she contended, had an "unnatural focus" on Europe and the world and the time had come to become "a normal country in a normal time."

The North Atlantic Treaty Organization (NATO) had been conceived as an intergovernmental military alliance meant to thwart Soviet ambitions. It now has thirty member countries, all of them reliant on the United States and few of them in any genuine danger of invasion or attack. Instead, Europeans used the American military to subdue another potential bloodbath in the Balkans in the 1990s. When Arab Spring rebellions broke out across the Middle East, France and Britain pressured the United States to intervene in Libya. Mostly, it is the presence of the United States, Europeans contend, that impedes Russian renewed ambitions that could easily threaten a dozen small nations.

Germany, incidentally, boasts a nearly $4 trillion national

GDP while Russia has a GDP of under $2 trillion. Yet Germany perpetually fails to keep its alliance pledge to put a meager 2 percent of GDP toward defense spending. In fact, only nine of NATO's thirty nations have hit the threshold as of 2019, and the United States continues to bankroll the protection of Europe.[39] Germany has already notified other nations it will miss defense spending, with it estimated to fall to 1.25 percent of GDP in 2024.

Germany now promises to meet the 2 percent level, perhaps by 2031.[40] As the Heritage Foundation's Ted Bromund once put it, "Germany's characteristic posture since World War II has been to shuffle around on its knees while hitting everyone else over the head with its own moral superiority."[41]

When the Trump administration—as the Obama administration had before it—griped about the lack of payments, Johann Wadephul, a ranking member of Chancellor Angela Merkel's Christian Democratic Union, said "that the Trump administration is neglecting an elementary task of leadership, to bind coalition partners into decision-making processes."[42]

Germany simply ignores its commitments while lecturing the rest of the world about its behavior, arguing that they pick up financial slack in other ways, as in accepting Syrian refugees. Creating a refugee crisis in Europe was a German choice, indeed, but the cost was dictated and borne by the continent as a whole. The reality is that Germany, under the protection of the United States, has taken control of the continent without firing a shot. "German power in Brussels," *The Economist* recently noted, "is the political equivalent of dark matter: invisible, difficult to measure and yet everywhere. Now the Germans are stars, shining so bright as to be impossible to ignore."[43]

Luigi Barzini, author of *The Europeans*, understood that "the future of Europe appears largely to depend today once again, for good or evil, whether we like it or not, as did for many centuries, on the future of Germany." The view that Germans would find themselves on equal footing to the Romanians, Greeks, Portuguese, and Slovakians was always a pipe dream.

Not that Germans embrace such power openly. Not with the guilt over the past. As a European matter, this is positive and negative. The Germans will demand that their frail client states embrace austerity and open trade, but they do not have the power to imbue them with a Prussian work ethic and social cohesion. It's Berlin that decides who is bailed out, who has an oversized public sector, and who carries too much debt. It's Berlin that dictates immigration policy. It's Berlin that demands client states fight climate change while dismantling their own nuclear energy infrastructure. It's Berlin that demands client states stand up to Russian intrusions, while building massive natural gas pipelines that enrich Vladimir Putin. Berlin is the maker of rules, and also the breaker. Germany leads the continent with seventy-four infringement proceedings by the European Commission for failing to implement EU regulations properly in German law.[44] Berlin makes up the rules as it goes along.

Henry Kissinger had once supposedly asked, "Who do you call when you want to speak to Europe?" You certainly don't call any diffused federalist institution that is charged with protecting the rights of minority populations and individuals.

The correct answer is Angela Merkel.

5

America Is Far More Tolerant Than Europe

UNITED IN DIVERSITY

—*motto of the European Union*

In my suburban Washington, D.C., neighborhood there resides a dizzying array of racial, ethnic, religious, and national identities. Not only do all these groups coexist peacefully, they send their kids to the same schools and overpriced universities; they shop in the same big-box stores and stream the same silly television shows. In my high schooler's senior yearbook, I can discern no fewer than twenty-five distinct nationalities—and I know there are probably more. Historical enemies have become friends and engage in communal projects rarely displaying a residual ethnic, racial, or religious animus.

My kid's graduating class has descendants of both the Chinese and their onetime Japanese oppressors, of Jews and their onetime would-be German annihilators, of Bangladeshis and their onetime Pakistani tormentors, and of Nigerians and their onetime Anglo colonizers—and an array of other backgrounds and faiths that would, anywhere else, be weighed down by a thorny and violent history of cultural animosity. These children collaborate, date, compete in sports and academics, argue, and study together. They are largely oblivious to any of the racial or ethnic divisions that would have torn them apart only a few decades ago.

In most cases, the parents of these kids are solidly in the middle or upper middle class. This too is unsurprising. Name *any* ethnic group in the United States, and they will have higher living standards, have higher educational attainment, and experience freer existences than those who live in the place they came from. Ethnic Japanese Americans have a higher standard of living here than people in Japan. Ethnic Russians have a higher standard of living in America than people in Russia. Same goes for Somalis. Palestinians. Vietnamese. Italians. Lithuanians. Jews. Mexicans.

Nigerians, one of the more recent immigrant groups in the United States, have escaped a nation that has the largest raw number of people living in extreme poverty on earth. Half the nation's population, somewhere around 87 million Nigerians, live on less than $1.90 a day.[1] In the United States, around 60 percent of Nigerian Americans over the age of twenty-five hold a graduate degree—compared to 32 percent of the population in general.[2] That is now a higher number of degrees than the second-highest-achieving minority population, Asian Americans. A high number of Nigerians work in public education systems and in universities, increasingly becoming doctors, entrepreneurs, or workers in other highly skilled and high-paying professions. Like most other successful immigrant groups, Nigerians not only invest in the business and charities here, but they tend to invest in their ancestral homes, sharing both their knowledge and newly attained wealth.[3]

As a recent study by the National Academies of Sciences, Engineering, and Medicine noted, more immigrants buy into the American Dream than native-born Americans: 70 percent believe their children will be better off than themselves, up from 60 percent twenty years ago. Among American-born parents, only 50 percent believe that.[4] "Current immigrants and their descendants are integrating into U.S. society," the report concluded. "Integration increases over time, with immigrants becoming more like the native-born with more time in the country, and with the second and third generations becoming more like other native-born Americans than their parents were."

The above story is often perfunctorily retold by Americans all the time. Still, it's worth reiterating. With all our imperfections and infighting, with all the partisanship and grievances, the United States represents one of the great miracles of mankind. It's an easy thing to forget when you live in it. But by any genuine measurement America is the most tolerant place on earth. The level of cooperation between people of truly diverse backgrounds—or anything even approaching it—is wholly unprecedented in human history. It exists nowhere else. Especially not Europe.

In fact, in Europe, minorities are worse off than in the United States. Anti-Semitism is on the rise, and European cultural habits make it nearly impossible for immigrants to assimilate successfully and smoothly.

None of this is to contend that prejudice doesn't exist in America. That would be preposterous. We have a lot of work to do. In June 2020, mass protests broke out across American cities sparked by the murder of a Minneapolis black man named George Floyd. Suspected of buying cigarettes with a counterfeit twenty-dollar bill, Floyd had been thrown to the concrete by a white police office named Derek Chauvin, who then kept his knee on Floyd's neck for nearly nine minutes, asphyxiating him. The incident—along with other deadly attacks on black men by police over the years—sparked large-scale protests that deteriorated into large-scale riots and looting across the country. The fact that most Americans had been cooped up in their homes due to the coronavirus quarantine surely made the environment even more combustible.

However, virtually every major politician in the country condemned the death of Floyd. Then-president Donald Trump, often accused of bigotry, ordered the Department of Justice to investigate the incident. Soon Chauvin was arrested and charged with second-degree murder. The three officers who watched Chauvin kill Floyd were also charged with abetting murder. There was plenty of legitimate anger over racial injustice in America. Some of it, however, is predicated on the false notion that the United States is—by its nature, its founding, its destiny—an inherently racist and xenophobic enterprise. This is manifestly untrue.

Certainly, a large number of Europeans seem to function under this illusion. So they too got in on the act, directing ire at their own societal inequities, but predominately focusing on the sins of the United States. Police fired tear gas at violent protesters at an anti-racism rally in Paris and in London leftists and right-wingers clashed with each other and police. In most European capitals, thousands took to the streets to peacefully protest policies in the United States that they almost certainly didn't understand.

According to polls, at least seven in ten adults living in France, Germany, Italy, Spain, and the United Kingdom believe racism is "a major problem" in the United States. That might be understandable if more than a tiny percentage of Europeans believed the same of their own nations.[5]

Perhaps these folks have been misled by European writers living in the United States (why they deign to reside in such a xenophobic place is a great mystery) or Europhiles, who continue to describe America as the least welcoming place in the world, a haven for human intolerance that was in perpetual war against minorities and immigrants. "To the World, We're Now America the Racist and Pitiful," read the headline by Robin Wright in *The New Yorker*. These days, the essayist, apparently unacquainted with the ethnic and racial animus of India, China, Brazil, the Islamic world, or the *banlieues* of France, noted, "the United States is destroying the moral authority it once had."[6]

"'I'm leaving, and I'm just not coming back': Fed up with

racism, Black Americans head overseas," read another headline in *USA Today* as the Black Lives Matter protests were unfolding.[7] "It wasn't until I had left the USA to experience Spain that I really got a sense of what freedom looks like. I was able to be 100% myself without having to worry about safety and without needing to have too much of a complex identity," said a Brooklyn native named Sienna Brown, who now resides in Valencia, on the Mediterranean coast. One must concede, surely, that a cloistered life in Valencia might be preferable to living in a borough of New York. As is the case with many Americans who visit areas teeming with luxury resorts, Brown confuses a prosperous area curated for tourists with the continent proper.

Barrett Holmes Pitner once explained to a BBC audience: "I've travelled a fair amount around the world, but America's racist status quo remains unique and alarmingly oppressive. American racism is entirely complexion-based and monolithic. One's nationality is immaterial."[8] To hit home this point, Pitner recalled that years earlier when visiting France, a woman at La Poste had refused to sell him stamps because she presumably thought he was French African. Once the writer explained that he was American, the woman smiled and acted as if everything was okay. Why targeted ethnic intolerance is preferable to other intolerance remains a mystery to me. Aside from that, there is plenty of evidence to illustrate that Europeans are far more intolerant of other ethnicities, races, and religions.

THESE JOURNALISTS' IMPRESSIONS BEAR LITTLE resemblance to the reality. In the real world, American universities like New York University have had to implement special programs to prepare students abroad for the rank racism they will surely encounter in places like Italy, France, and Spain. "Whenever I go back to my childhood home in Orange County, Florida," an exchange student who visited the NYU campus in Florence once wrote, "I am not surprised when I see the Confederate flag flying on high poles, plastered on car bumpers and worn proudly on T-shirts. But it surprises me that even the Dixie flag—and all it represents—doesn't get to me as much as the outright and physical disrespect I experienced very far from home."[9]

The stories of students reporting back from England are also replete with incidents of crass intolerance. "In Europe, sometimes it can feel as if segregation hasn't ended," wrote one African American woman who went to a London program of the Center for Global and Intercultural Study at the University of Michigan. "During my first week I was denied service at a restaurant because I'm black, and one of my friends on the trip was denied entry into a club for the same reason. In the States, I've never been denied service or told that I can't participate in something."[10]

These accounts are anecdotal, of course, but they are bolstered by social research and historical evidence. When researchers looked at all existing literature on international students in the south of England, of the 153 international postgraduate students, 49 had experienced some form of abuse. Most of the abuse was only verbal, but racism manifested physically for a number of students. "Strong emotional reactions were reported, including sadness, disappointment, homesickness and anger. There was a consequent reluctance to return to the UK as a tourist, or to offer positive word-of-mouth recommendations to future students," the authors noted.[11]

When the European Union conducted a study of black Europeans in 2018, it found that 30 percent of respondents said that they have been racially harassed in the past five years—with 5 percent having been physically attacked.[12] In places like Finland, 63 percent of minorities felt harassed. The highest rates of racist violence were also recorded in Finland (14 percent), Ireland, and Austria (both 13 percent). A sizeable majority of black Europeans felt that the police had racially profiled them within the last five years. A quarter of black Europeans claim to have experienced racial discrimination at work or in a job search.

Research from Northwestern University comparing conditions in nine countries—Canada, the United States, and seven European nations—found that racism in hiring practices in Europe was far worse than in America. The most discriminatory nations were France and Sweden. When Swedish economists attempted to gauge a country's level of racial tolerance, they turned to something called the World Values Survey, which has been measuring global attitudes and opinions for decades. Among the eighty questions that World Values asks, the Swedish economists found one that they believed best measured tolerance: Who would you *not* want as neighbors? The United States and other Anglo nations—the United Kingdom, Canada, Australia, and New Zealand—were least racist while a number of European nations—among them, yes, France—were among the worst.[13]

The French seem to be perhaps the least tolerant people on the continent, with 22.7 percent saying they didn't want a neighbor of another race. Then again, not a single European nation had a majority that believed increasing diversity was a net positive for their country, with the lowest numbers found in Sweden (36 percent) and Spain (31 percent). In places like Greece (63) and Italy (53), people believed that growing diversity makes their country a *worse* place to live. Roughly four in ten Hungarians (41) and Poles (40) agree.[14]

These numbers are strongly contrasted by Americans' positive view of diversity. About 60 percent of Americans say increasing diversity makes the country a better place to live, compared with just 7 percent who say it makes it a worse place.[15] A majority of Americans say the fact that the U.S. population is made up of people of many different races and ethnicities is a very good thing for the country—in a recent poll only 1 percent said it was "bad."[16] Now, we can't bore into the souls of poll participants and determine that they truly believe the answer they offer. We can, however, note that Americans understand that there is a national expectation to embrace all people, and answer appropriately.

Minorities Are Better Off in the United States Than in Europe

"Europe has long been suspicious—even jealous—of the way America has been able to pursue national wealth and power despite its deep social inequities," Robin Niblett, the director of the Royal Institute of International Affairs, explained to *The New Yorker*. "When you take the Acela and pass through the poorest areas of Baltimore, you can't believe you're looking at part of the United States. There's always been this sense of an underlying flaw in the U.S. system that it was getting away with—that somehow America was keeping just one step ahead of the Grim Reaper."[17]

Clearly, in this vision, America's sin of inequity is crippling. But if the United States is only one step ahead of the Grim Reaper, where does that leave Europe? One of the most common cases Europhiles make for implementing a welfare state is that it would heal the inequities of economic life. Surely, then, minorities who live under Europe's socialist economic policies— bolstered by the alleged tolerance of its denizens—are thriving in places like France and Britain. Not really.

Let's put it this way: If people of color in the United States formed a nation unto themselves, they would have a higher living standard and more wealth per capita than nearly any other country in the world—including most of Europe. Only 15 percent of black Europeans own property, as opposed to 70 percent of the EU's general population.[18] In the United States, African American homeownership has consistently stood at over 40 percent.[19]

Before the COVID pandemic broke out, black unemployment rates had reached near-historic lows in America. Over the past twenty years, American black entrepreneurship, already exceeding any European nation, jumped nearly 37 percent. Thirty-six percent of all black-owned businesses were headed by women, the highest share of businesses within any racial or ethnic group.[20] In Europe, black men under thirty regularly experience sky-high levels of unemployment—far exceeding the general population. According to the British Sociological Association, black Britons are more likely to be unemployed than African Americans, especially during recessions.

A long-term study found that during the past three downturns prior to COVID, unemployment among black British men was up to 19 percentage points higher than among black Americans.[21] Black women in Britain were far worse off than those in the United States, where, by 2019, they had added 1.6 percentage points to the employment rate since 2007's Great Recession, which was the second most of any prime-age working group after Hispanic women.[22]

The Europhile habit of portraying Europeans as tolerant cosmopolitans—think American jazz musicians wandering the streets of Montmartre in the 1950s—does not comport with history. Sandrine Le Maire, an expert on French colonialism, recently noted after the killing of a black man named Adama Traoré by the Paris police that her nation was "importing ideas from the US," because while the deaths happened in similar circumstances to George Floyd, "our historical baggage is not the same. There was no lynching here, or racial laws."[23]

There is, of course, no excuse for America's ugly history on race, but it should be noted that France is not only a trying place for contemporary black communities—which only really began immigrating in the mid-twentieth century—but it once subdued what are now the entire nations of Mauritania, Senegal, Mali,

Guinea, Côte d'Ivoire, Burkina Faso, and Niger, among others. It was a leading force in the slave trade, buying and selling millions in its African colonies.[24]

In the years leading up to World War II, only two thousand black men under French rule were afforded citizenship, while the vast majority lived under summary justice and forced labor.[25]

When researching this book, I ran across a 1973 piece in the *New York Times* headlined "The Immigrés Do What the French Won't." The reporter Edward Sheehan noted that *the* poorest French "are the Arabs, the Portuguese, the black Africans—that wretched subproletariat that performs the dirty and dangerous drudgery the French will no longer deign to do themselves." The piece might well have been written in 2020. It is unconstitutional for the French government to collect data on ethnicity or race, but it estimated that three to five million people, or somewhere above 7 percent of the population, are black.

In France's suburbs, third and fourth generations of immigrants from North Africa are still among the poorest in Western Europe. More than a third of households of immigrants from Africa live in poverty, compared to 13 percent of the general population.[26]

Americans are in a strong position to debate anyone in the contemporary world on tolerance. The true outrage in the United States isn't that minorities are worse off in Chicago than they are in Paris, but rather that they haven't reached the economic levels of others in the United States. There is no evidence that any European nation has concocted a better policy formula for equity. One can just look at the European Union's political institutions themselves.

Not long ago, after the Black Lives Matter protests broke out, an EU commissioner named Margaritis Schinas, whose self-proclaimed chare is "promoting the European way of life," argued that there "is no doubt that Europe as a whole has been doing better than the United States in issues of race, also because we have better systems for social inclusion, protection, universal health care."[27]

There is, in fact, great doubt that Europe is doing better than America on race. Just take a look at the European Union's modern governing body. After the George Floyd protests, the EU jumped into action, putting together a commission to study and debate racial tensions on the continent. Every person on the commission was white.[28] That is hardly shocking, considering that at the time, every one of the twenty-seven European commissioners was white. If you can't find a single minority to represent the people of an entire continent, perhaps your problems with race are more deep-seated than you contend.

There are somewhere around 15 million black citizens living in the European Union nations, and the number of ethnic minorities living within European states is somewhere in the vicinity of 50 million, or around 10 percent of the population. How many ethnic minority Europeans are employed by EU institutions? Around 1 percent.[29] In the 2014–2019 European Parliament session, only 17 of the 751 representatives were people of color, though that number went up to 30 MEPs in the next election. Once Britain left the Union after Brexit, that number fell back to 24, or 3 percent of all MEPs. Every single representative of South Asian descent, for example, was from Britain.[30]

By far, the most diverse international institution housed in the European capital of Brussels is NATO—and for that you can thank the United States.[31]

In Germany, there are over 500,000 black citizens but only one is a member of Germany's Bundestag: Karamba Diaby, who is the constant target of blatant racist sentiment.[32] His colleague Walter Lübcke, a pro-refugee politician, was murdered in 2019 by a neo-Nazi. When Italians finally elected their first black minister, Cécile Kyenge, in 2013, she was immediately subjected to hideous open racism. In one of her first appearances after the election, a man popped up out of the crowd and threw two bananas at the podium as she was delivering a speech. (This is not an isolated incident in Europe, as black soccer players often have to deal with bananas being thrown at them. Soccer is a sport rife with nationalist imagery and racism.[33]) "I love animals—bears and wolves, as everyone knows—but when I see the pictures of Kyenge, I cannot but think of, even if I'm not saying she is one, the features of an orangutan," a well-known populist senator named Roberto Calderoli said at a political rally, to the laughter of the crowd.[34] Calderoli, who never apologized, is still a major player in Italian politics.

The existence of this kind of racism in the halls of power would never be tolerated in the contemporary United States. There is no politician's career that would, thankfully, survive such remarks. Not because we have laws barring speech, but because the norms make such attacks a career killer. In the United States we are left to ferret out racist dog whistles.

The Oldest Hate

It must be stressed that the most reliable portent of illiberalism in Europe has been the rise of anti-Semitism. For centuries, Jews, other than Roma, were the only sizeable minority living in European communities. In times of trouble, no matter where on the continent they were, no matter the vagaries of the ideology or policies being adopted, it was almost inevitably Jews who ended up being scapegoated. And today, anti-Semitic sentiment is likely more prevalent in Europe than it has been at any time since the Nazis attempted to exterminate the Jews.

In modern Eastern Europe, where few Jews remain, right-wing nationalist parties have once again gained political clout, rewriting Holocaust history and blaming the minority for their domestic problems. In Western Europe, a place with its own rich tradition of Jew hatred, a new iteration has begun to thrive due in part to the influx of Muslim immigrants and the radicalization of leftist progressive parties.

Europhiles, aligned ideologically with the European left, like to blame right-wing nationalists for Europe's rise in anti-Semitism. It is hardly that simple. It was British Labour leader Jeremy Corbyn, running a major party in one of the wealthiest and most liberal European societies, who was perhaps the most prominent political figure excusing, and sometimes fostering, implicit and explicit anti-Semitism. Left-wing protests regularly feature anti-Semitic imagery and rhetoric. As one EU study found, of the most serious incidents of anti-Semitic harassment in the European Union, 31 percent include someone the victim did not know, but 30 percent were perpetrated by someone with extremist Muslim views; 21 percent with someone who held left-wing political views; 16 percent by a colleague from work or school, 15 percent by an acquaintance or friend; and only 13 percent by someone with known right-wing views. The normalization of anti-Semitism, as the study noted, was evidenced in the wide range of perpetrators, "which spans the entire social and political spectrum."[35] Granted, figuring out who is behind these incidents is difficult as leftist and Muslim anti-Semites have begun appropriating the rhetoric of the far-right radicals, and vice versa.

The state of Israel has provided a new focal point for alleged Jewish disloyalty. It's worth remembering that "anti-Zionist" terrorism over the past sixty years—whether perpetrated by Palestinians with homemade explosives, the Iranian government, or the leftist terrorists of the German Baader-Meinhof Group—has always targeted Jews as a whole, and not merely Israelis. It began long before a conservative like Benjamin Netanyahu was prime minister, and even before there were ever "occupied territories."

Today, the dual loyalty smear—questioning the patriotism of Jews because of Israel's existence—is rampant in Europe. In *The Protocols of the Elders of Zion*, a fabricated conspiratorial text first published in Russia in 1903, the rabbinic cabal meets secretly in Europe to plot world domination. Today, increasing numbers of Europeans believe that Jews have moved those meetings to the Knesset. The number of those who believe European Jews are more loyal to Israel than to their own countries is highest in Poland at 63 percent, but Spain is next at 62 percent, followed by Hungary, Belgium, Germany, Austria, and Italy—all of which are above 49 percent.[36] Not an inconsequential number.

The European Union helps fuel this animosity by singling out the Jewish state for endless and nearly exclusive reprimand, while at the same time ignoring the atrocities around the world. The Court of Justice of the European Union, for example, demands that foods and wines produced by Israelis in contested territories be sold with a special marking to European consumers—even though those Israeli companies in the West Bank hire thousands of Arab employees, who make more money working there than they would elsewhere. Eugene Kontorovich, director of the Center for International Law in the Middle East at George Mason University's Antonin Scalia Law School, refers to this as "a new kind of Yellow Star on Jewish-made products."[37] Simply put, the European Union doesn't demand similar labels for the people of any other occupations. Not for the ethnic Hungarians who live under Romanian rule in Transylvania, nor for the Kurds or Armenians who live under Turkish rule, nor the Tibetans who live under Chinese communist rule, and not for the thousands of situations where one group feels occupied by another. Only the Jewish state.

Such hatreds are often vindicated by the state. In 2017, a German regional court ruled that a 2014 firebombing of Bergisch Synagogue in Wuppertal, though an act of criminal arson, was not a hate crime. What made this case especially enlightening was that it illustrated both the mounting danger for Jews and the counterproductive nature of European "hate crime" laws, which allows the state to decide which intolerance is acceptable.

In this case, the German judge had upheld a lower court ruling deeming that the three Palestinian immigrants who had thrown Molotov cocktails at a Jewish place of worship were not anti-Semitic, but merely calling "attention to the Gaza conflict," which had recently flared up again.[38] The three men, who had admitted they were motivated by hatred of Israel, were ultimately given suspended sentences, since "no anti-Semitic motivation could be identified."[39]

Now, it's doubtful that many, or any, of the congregants at the Bergisch Synagogue were Israelis (not that it would make a terror attack okay). Certainly, none of the congregants had been polled by the attackers regarding their opinions of Israel's policies toward Gaza. The fact that German officials were justifying political violence against Jews in a city that was home to one of the first concentration camps is just an added reminder of its nefarious nature.

Germany isn't alone. Nearly a quarter of the French now believe in conspiracy theories involving Jewish world domination—and it remains especially high among the growing populist Yellow Vest movement and Muslim immigrants.[40] Nearly half of the French say that Zionism is some sort of world Jewish plot.[41] In France, home to the largest Muslim community (around five million) as well as the largest Jewish community (around 500,000) in Europe, conspiracies become harassment and violence. Jews are regularly accosted in the streets of Paris.[42] In France, 70 percent of Jews have personally experienced anti-Semitism. There is always, of course, the vandalism—ninety graves in a Jewish cemetery in eastern France were desecrated with swastikas in 2019, for instance.[43] But every year there is some act of gruesome violence, as well.

In 2012, a man named Mohammed Mera drove his scooter up to a Jewish school in Toulouse, France, and executed three Jewish children—aged three, six, and eight—and a rabbi.[44] In 2014, a French gunman named Mehdi Nemmouche strolled into the lobby of the Jewish Museum in Brussels and murdered four people. He was later arrested in Marseille, in the south of France, getting off a bus with a Kalashnikov rifle on his way to do who knows what.[45] In 2015, Amedy Coulibaly entered a kosher supermarket in Paris and killed eight Jewish shoppers.[46] In 2017, a sixty-five-year-old Orthodox Jewish woman, Sarah Halimi, was thrown from the third-floor balcony of her housing project in Paris. Kobili Traoré, a Franco-Malian Muslim, had crushed Attal's skull before throwing her over the railing. He had reportedly done it because she was Jewish; he called out "Allahu akbar" and, finally, "I have killed the shaitan" (devil).[47] The man was acquitted in 2021. In the same year a group of Muslim men stabbed Mireille Knoll, eighty-five, a Jewish woman who suffered from Parkinson's disease, before setting her body on fire, also yelling "Allahu akbar" and justifying the attack by saying: "Jews have money."[48]

These are the actions of individuals. But the fact that French soldiers are forced to regularly patrol streets in places like Sarcelles, where Jews and Arab immigrants live in proximity to each other, tells us something is deeply wrong. In 2015, France was compelled to send ten thousand troops across the country, to protect hundreds of Jewish sites.[49] Such an arrangement would be unthinkable in the United States.

A poll conducted by the Jerusalem Center for Public Affairs found that nearly 90 percent of European Jews have suffered some form of anti-Semitic threat, insult, or assault. Attacks against Jews have become a regular occurrence in places like Germany.[50] "Many Jews do not feel safe, do not feel respected in our country. This is one part of today's reality and it is one that causes me grave concern," Chancellor Angela Merkel recently noted.[51] In one infamous attack in April 2018, a man wearing a kippah—a Jewish skullcap—was assaulted by an attacker who whipped him with a belt in the middle of the day in a busy Berlin bar and restaurant area, yelling "Yahudi!"—which is Arabic for Jew.[52] "My opinion on the matter has changed following the ongoing brutalization in German society," the German government's anti-Semitism representative Felix Klein told a newspaper in 2019. "I can no longer recommend Jews wear a kippah at every time and place in Germany." Can one imagine such a capitulation by a government official to hatred in the United States?

It matters not whether there are many Jews or a few in a nation. This animosity manifests in ways both large and small. In one two-week span in 2020, for instance, a person could read about neo-Nazi protesters burning Israeli flags in Finland (1,800 Jews), someone leaving a bag with soap and anti-Semitic literature tagged with the Star of David outside a Holocaust exhibit in Sweden (20,000), and the words "Juden Hier" being graffitied on the front door of a Holocaust survivor's residence in Italy (45,000).[53]

Not long after the Bergisch incident, in Norway the state attorney dismissed a case against a rapper named Kaveh Kholardi, who had been hired by the city of Oslo to perform at a family festival to celebrate "diversity and inclusion." During his performance, Kholardi asked if there were any Jews in the audience, before going on a rant about the "f***ing Jews." A few days earlier, the rapper had tweeted that the "f***ing Jews are so corrupt."[54]

At the time of his outburst there were only 789 Jews left in Norway.[55] The court found that Kholardi's "remarks were demeaning, untruthful and offensive, but they are not breaching the law." This is a fine outcome if you, like me, believe that hate speech laws undermine an inherent and neutral right to free expression. But in Norway people do not. It is still illegal to "deliberately or grossly negligently publicly present a discriminatory or hateful expression," and it "shall be punished by fines or imprisonment for up to 3 years."[56]

When this fact was brought up to Tor-Aksel Busch, Norway's director of public prosecutions, he explained that while the comments by the Muslim rapper "seem to be targeting Jews" they can also be looked at as a way to "express dissatisfaction with the policies of the State of Israel."[57] I suppose Norwegian Jews should be relieved that no one was firebombed.

In 2018, eleven Americans were slaughtered in a Pittsburgh synagogue by a deranged white supremacist. In urban areas like Brooklyn, where many religious and Hasidic Jews reside, acts of violent anti-Semitism are not unheard of. We should never diminish the gravity and ugliness of these attacks. The American Jew is not only the most successful Jew in the world, he is still likely the safest Jew in the world. The American Jew is perhaps the safest Jew in history. Anti-Semitism is a serious, albeit relatively small, problem in the United States, where there are far more Jews than in all of Europe combined.

An American Jew is far more likely to encounter casual anti-Jewish sentiment from a Europhile leftist on a college campus than by white supremacists or Islamic terrorists in his own neighborhood. Then again, attacks perpetrated in ethnic, racial, and religious hatred are far rarer than most people imagine in the United States. Far rarer than in Europe. The United States, nearly always portrayed as a bigoted place by Europhiles, is home to few ethnic or hate crimes. And of all hate crimes, usually around 20 percent or less are due to religious bias. Among that group, most are anti-Semitic, with anti-Muslim and Christian acts coming in far behind. To put it in perspective, in a nation of 330 million people there are usually a total of 300 criminal hate incidents, most of them nonviolent, in which the perpetrators are openly motivated by anti-Muslim sentiment. Often, it's difficult to track these kinds of crimes, as we can't bore into the soul of criminals. Considering the plurality in the United States, crimes against one group are rare, since there are so many.

The reason violence on an ethnic or racial basis is treated as a grievous social sin is that it is so rare and intolerable.

Europe Is No Melting Pot

"Europe is a kaleidoscope of cultural diversity," wrote Jeremy Rifkin, in his poorly aged 2004 book, *The European Dream: How Europe's Vision of the Future Is Quietly Eclipsing the American Dream.* "The union's inhabitants break down into hundreds of different nationalities who speak eighty-seven different languages and dialects, making the region one of the most culturally diverse in the world."[58]

Indeed, when we speak about Europe as a whole, it is quite diverse. The problem is that this diversity is highly compartmentalized, not merely among individual nations, but often within those nations themselves.

From top to bottom, from the past to contemporary history, European society has been rife with intolerance and bigotry of all kinds—open and implicit. It is unsurprising, as Europeans have deeply ingrained disdain for one another, be it culturally, religiously, ethnically, or racially. For centuries the French and Germans, Italians and Austrians, English and French, Russians and Germans could hardly live next to one another without conflict, much less assimilate even a single minority group into their society without bloodshed. It is only in recent history, and under the protection of the American military, that war between European nations has abated. Before we came to the scene, these ethnic and ideological resentments, large and small, often manifested in tragedies.

That's one of the reasons we are successful at assimilation, whereas Europe is not. Europeans attempt to artificially replicate our arrangements by adopting vacuous and relativistic slogans—the European Union motto, for example—but miss the most vital ingredient. American cultural and political life offers space to honor the past, while making demands in the present. Despite much sloganeering, "diversity" does not make us stronger—though it is the flavor that enhances our personal and cultural lives. It is the ability to convince disparate people and cultures to adopt American norms and surrender many of their own. It could not happen without a unifying ideology, a shared understanding of civic life, a hierarchy of societal values, respect for law and order, a basic foundation of liberalism, an acceptance of a meritocratic society and social contracts and other cultures. The United States, notwithstanding all its inequities and sins, is built for it.

The European Union was conceived to compete with the United States. But Europe has never come close to replicating the comity of American life. No single country *in* Europe has come close to replicating it. The prospects of it happening in the future aren't looking great, either. Certainly not in the past, and definitely not today. In nearly every Western European nation, as well as many in Eastern and Central Europe, immigration and assimilation is one of the biggest political problems. There is no reason to turn to Europe for advice on tolerance, on racism, or on assimilation.

In the past, Americans might well have been guilty of exceedingly idealizing and romanticizing their history. Which nation did not? It was certainly preferable to the guilt-ridden self-flagellation that's been adopted by our many Europhiles who want us to look across the Atlantic for guidance on the matter of tolerance. If you happen to come from European stock—and around a third of Americans still do—rest assured the place your ancestors emigrated from was not as welcoming or pleasant as the United States, or you probably wouldn't be here. Even though the world has experienced tremendous change over the past two centuries, there has never been a wave of immigration out of the United States to Europe—or anywhere else for that matter.

None of this is to say that my neighbors in Washington do not harbor *any* residual grudges from the Old Country—all heritages come with the wounds of history, after all. Some may still prefer the company of their own ethnic group. All of that typically evaporates in a generation. And, of course, prejudice exists in America. Sometimes it is deadly. And, of course, not everyone can succeed here. And, of course, there is injustice. There is no utopia—not even in Germany or France. Humans are often terrible. The important question is, where can humans flourish best in spite of the ugliest actions of their worst people? Perhaps for the staff writer of *The New Yorker* the answer is Paris, but for millions of human beings searching for a better life it is, hands down, the United States.

6

Imagine, No Countries

Europe belongs to the Europeans.

—*Dalai Lama*

In 2016, European Commission president Jean-Claude Juncker informed an audience of European elites gathered in Austria that "borders are the worst invention ever made by politicians."[1] For Juncker, a native of the wealthy city-state of Luxembourg, the proposition of a nation-state with common culture, language, values, and history was not only obsolete, but entirely concocted. The only impediment to peaceful human coexistence, Juncker insinuated, was the arbitrary man-made lines that had been drawn across maps. Geography, it seems, was the barrier separating German culture and Somalian culture. It was as if centuries of history, war, reformations, revolutions, and awakenings had never happened.

The "community of nations" now meant *every* nation. When a slew of violent upheavals broke out across the Islamic world in the mid-2010s, a crush of Muslim refugees began migrating, by land, sea, and air, toward the European mainland. Without any genuine debate about the long-term societal or economic consequences for host or newcomer, or even a coherent continent-wide plan to deal with the cultural shock, the European Union—led by the Germans—opened their borders to somewhere around two million in 2015 alone.[2]

The consequences of the EU's reckless border policies had changed the continent forever. Even if Europe immediately froze all migration moving forward, Muslims, overall younger and more likely to have children, would continue to dramatically increase as a share of the population.[3] Though precise statistics regarding minorities are difficult to pin down in Europe, by 2016, Muslims already likely made up nearly 5 percent of Europe's population—most settling in Western Europe. Pew estimates that the number of Muslims in Europe has grown by 2.1 percent in the last twenty years, and they will reach a projected 8 percent of the continent's total population, or 58 million people, by 2050.[4]

The impact is more pronounced when we look at nation-states themselves. Whereas Sweden barely experienced any immigration in the middle of the twentieth century, today the nation of 9 million is home to 1.5 million immigrants and their children.[5] At last count, France was home to nearly 6 million Muslims, who now make up 8.8 percent of the population.[6] The Muslim population is predicted to reach around 14 percent of the population of France by 2050, and only slightly less in Germany.[7]

The United Kingdom, which has had a long history of welcoming persecuted people, saw a significant spike in the level of immigration over the past fifteen years. In 1997 net migration into the country was 48,000, but between 2005 and 2010 net migration reached on average 247,000 a year, and then continued apace.[8] Pew estimates that as of 2016 the United Kingdom had 4,130,000 Muslims, who make up 6.3 percent of the population.

That's a lot of new people to integrate culturally and economically in a continent of historically homogeneous nations. Even in the United States, the minority group that accounts for a larger percentage of the whole than Muslims do in Europe is

Latinos, who already have a long geographic and cultural rela-tionship with Americans. Juncker had, in many ways, summed up the conceit of the European Union's elite—one that's been adopted by so many Americans.

In the technocrats' conception of the world, people are au-tomatons, little scraps of GDP, who can be plugged into proper societal roles by their betters. The European argument for open borders might have been couched in compassion, but it ignored a fundamental, sometimes inconvenient, truth: Human beings have ideological, theocratic, and ancient baggage; principles, habits, rituals, outlooks, temperaments, hierarchies of morality, and numerous other societal arrangements have formed their worldview.

Why did Juncker, and so many of his colleagues, believe that millions of destitute and endangered Middle Eastern refugees had come to Europe in the first place? The borders, or at least the immense wealth and liberal values held within them, offered refugees safety from the horrors and degradations of tyrannical states and violent theocratic forces that dominate the contem-porary Middle East and Africa. The conditions in Syria, Iraq, Afghanistan, and Libya hadn't been created in a vacuum by a few nasty leaders, any more than Western European liberalism had sprung out of the ether.

Europe's Immigration Plan Is an Economic Disaster

Even if you ignore the negative externalities of the social dis-cord created by mass immigration, Europe's policies have been a failure on a purely economic front, as well. For decades, Eu-rope's elites argued that immigrants would be needed to replace the lack of organic population growth due to declining birth rates. One rationalization for allowing millions of newcomers to stream into Europe was that they would fill the manual-labor and low-entry positions that educated Europeans simply didn't do anymore.

That promise was not met. For one thing, as Europe was opening its borders, its economy was in the midst of deindustrializing. European nations had miscalculated the kind of foreign labor they would need in the coming years, attempting to solve a temporary problem by permanently changing the demographics of their countries. Aydan Özoğuz, a German commissioner for immigration, refugees, and integration, admitted that it was likely that three-quarters of new refugees streaming into Germany would still be unemployed after five years.[9]

Özoğuz guessed accurately. The reality is that unemployment among Muslim immigrants in Europe is skyrocketing. A 2017 study found that under 20 percent of Muslims in Europe aged sixteen to seventy-four were employed full-time.[10] In Britain, one of the continent's strongest economies, 53 percent of the general population was likely to hold a job, as opposed to only 38 percent of Muslims.[11] That number precipitously falls among newer immigrant groups. According to the Council of Somalis, for example, 90 percent of Somalis in the London boroughs of Kensington and Chelsea are now unemployed.[12] The study found a slew of predictable cultural factors causing this misfortune, including the inability to speak English, general illiteracy, and difficulty getting overseas credentials recognized.

We can transpose the same struggles to immigrant neighborhoods in most big cities in Western Europe. Turkish guest workers began to come to West Germany half a century ago. Nearly three million now live in Germany, clustered in neighborhoods like Kreuzberg and Neukölln in Berlin, struggling to integrate, with a large percentage unemployed and subsisting off generous social benefits, and with children still lacking the basic education required to break out of the economic trap.[13] (It wasn't exactly helpful that on a visit to Germany in 2011, Turkish prime minister Recep Tayyip Erdoğan told Germany's large Turkish community, "You must integrate, but I am against assimilation . . . no one may ignore the rights of minorities. Our children must learn German, but they must learn Turkish first.")

Slums dot urban and suburban landscapes in many major French and German cities. There is, of course, poverty in the United States, but there are very few, if any, permanent enclaves of generational immigrant poverty.

Europhiles will argue that this merely illustrates that we too should welcome larger numbers of immigrants and refugees. One of the triumphs of contemporary American integration has been creating stable communities that, after a generation or two, begin to melt into the suburbs and the great expanse of American life. We are not overloading the country with an influx from one place at one time.

The Europhiles who demand an open door for all the world's refugees happen to advocate for policies that disincentivize work, initiative, and thus acclimatization, undercutting the dynamics that make assimilation work.

The United States, for example, has a long-standing policy that—at least, in spirit, if not always enforcement—refuses entry to any noncitizen who may become a "public charge," denying them the ability to receive public assistance until they are citizens. When the Supreme Court affirmed the legality of the policy in 2020, the legal correspondent for *Slate* magazine called the decision a "human catastrophe."[14] Another columnist, in the *Washington Post*, likened it to Hitler-era policies, calling it "a weapon of racism and classism."[15] A writer at *The New Yorker* claimed it was "a throwback to the darker days of rejecting the neediest immigrants, be they Irish, Jewish, queer—or nonwhite."[16] This was the tenor across most of the American media.

These arguments aren't merely dishonest, they are bigoted. In the United States, Muslim Americans, many of whom have come from impoverished backgrounds, have a higher level of employment than the general population. There are around 5 million

Muslims living here, a number projected to reach 8.1 million by 2050,[17] and nearly a quarter report incomes that are $100,000 or higher—which is on par with, or better than, most minority groups.[18] The children of Muslim immigrants reach levels of education rivaling those of children whose parents are native-born. "Children growing up in America almost unavoidably assimilate American values," Paul Collier, an Oxford economist, once noted. "The same is far from true in Europe."[19]

A 2017 survey found that, even though Muslims were concerned about the presidency of Donald Trump, they still "believed that hard work generally brings success in this country and they were satisfied with the way things are going in their own lives—even if they are not satisfied with the direction of the country as a whole." Nearly 90 percent of Muslims said they are proud to be American and still have faith in the American Dream.[20]

Indeed, American Muslims achieved all this without cradle-to-grave welfare programs, without invasive private-sector unions, without high levels of regulations, without top-down economic planning—and without all the European-style safety nets American elites keep imploring us to adopt.

The success story of Muslim Americans illustrates that expectations of self-sufficiency are no barrier to success. Rather, they are the opposite. Just as it had been for the 26 million or so Irish, Italians, Jews, Scandinavians, and Germans—assisted by strong existing and Americanizing communities—who moved to the United States between 1850 and 1913, often poorer than most newcomers today, Muslim Americans can succeed with hard work.

Of course, the vast majority of immigrants do not enter the United States—or Europe, for that matter—seeking to become public charges. The economic data, however, is clear: Welfare incentivizes people to work less. It may seem benevolent to create an environment wherein impoverished refugees have unfettered access to the benefits of Western-style safety nets, but it is far more kindhearted and constructive to nudge people toward self-sufficiency for reasons that go beyond economic well-being.

Ethnic Islands Prevent Social Mobility for Immigrants

When the critically acclaimed film *La Haine* (Hate), which tells the story of three young immigrants living in a poverty-stricken suburb twenty miles outside of Paris, was released in 1995, it caused a sensation in France. It was among the first realistic depictions of the *banlieues*, the French housing projects. The movie's tragic story ends with two of the young immigrants being killed by police, and the third in a standoff, as a voice-over informs the viewer that they have just witnessed a "story of a society falling apart."[21]

More than half of France's North African immigrant population have been living in this type of neighborhood for generations. Many of the *banlieues* were erected in the 1960s to house the working-class families who were participating in the European postwar economic boom. As the expansion slowed and industry changed in the 1970s, the neighborhoods were specifically opened to house immigrants. Since then, these housing developments around France have been blighted by unrest and radicalism. In *banlieues* across France police are not welcome. No matter how soft the policing, any police intervention in *banlieues* runs the risk of starting a riot. French politicians regularly argue that sending police into these dangerous neighborhoods is counterproductive.[22]

The first major riot in a *banlieue* took place in 1981. Most of the rioters were French citizens of Arabic descent living in the Minguettes housing estates, located in Vénissieux, on the eastern outskirts of Lyon.[23] Minguettes contained forty towers, with

10,000 apartments and 35,000 crammed residents.[24] Rioting continued in urban developments throughout the 1980s as immigrants remained poor, unable to move to the middle class and out of their ghettos.[25] The 1990s continued to see riots, often leading to deadly encounters with police.[26] Chanteloup, as former mayor Pierre Cardo once noted, has a "crime-generating architecture."[27]

La Haine spurred calls for reform. None came. At least, none that were effective. Twenty-five years later, the *banlieues* are poorer, more segregated, and more violent due to the rise of political Islam.[28] Islam was not a major plot point in *La Haine*. Yet, if they were to produce a sequel, Islam would be *the* factor. The three immigrants depicted in *La Haine* all have different ethnic backgrounds: a black man, an Arab man, and a Jewish man. Such friendships are rare today.

In 2005, France saw another resurgence of riots perpetrated by second- and third-generation residents of these Paris suburbs, causing an estimated 200 million euros in damaged property. In all, 8,000 cars were set on fire and 2,900 people arrested.[29] Small-scale violence has become more targeted and more deadly. In one incident, sixty hooded and armed youths launched an attack on Chanteloup's police station as a reprisal for the death of a twenty-four-year-old shot by police after he took a hostage during a robbery.[30]

Riots again plagued the Paris suburbs in 2019.[31] Rather than spontaneous protests, however, much of this violence was preplanned ambushes that deliberately targeted the police. In one incident at Chanteloup-les-Vignes, police were attacked when they responded to a call about a fire in a trash bin. Bags full of stones and fireworks were thrown at them, before about thirty youths, some carrying batons, attacked. In another incident a community center was set on fire. A video posted to social media showed fireworks exploding all over Chanteloup with the words "The city is ours" and "Anti-police here."

Without work, immigrants often remain insulated from the broader culture, and are less likely to learn the language and adopt the customs of their hosts. Economic hardship brings, through necessity or desire, self-segregation.

When Sweden opened its country up to Kurds, Bosnians, and Somalis in the 1990s, they placed the newcomers in abandoned public housing units, immediately insulating them from the rest of the community.[32] These housing projects are often awkward for large families and typically far away from available work. In many cases, the reason the buildings were empty in the first place was that whatever industry they were built to support had already gone under and the native population moved elsewhere. Whether the state does it or not, warehousing immigrants in neighborhoods with high unemployment does not bode well for their future prospects, creating frustration and criminality.[33]

In November 2018, fifty cars were set on fire in a Swedish suburb of Uppsala in one of these predominately immigrant areas. It took the fire department three hours to show up—and when they did, police escorted them in full riot gear and carrying machine guns.[34] Things have eroded to the point that the postal service won't deliver to some neighborhoods and public libraries have had to close.[35] For the normally placid Swedes, the rise in this type of violence has been jarring, creating a political backlash that serves no one.

With the sudden influx of migrants, and shiftlessness spurred by unemployment, many European cities have seen a spike in crime, a resurgence of hate crimes, and political unrest. Though numbers are hard to come by, it is likely that Muslims made up 50 percent of the population of French jails.[36] Migrants make up 26 percent of Sweden's prison population and about 50 percent of those in prison for serious offenses.[37] One study found that two hundred foreign suspects were being arrested every day in London.[38]

Further, London's Metropolitan Police revealed that they held more than 72,500 nonnative suspects.[39] In Amsterdam, a city with a growing immigrant population, there has been an explosion of drugs, crime, and violence. In 2018, Arre Zuurmond, the city's ombudsman, set up a security camera in Leidseplein Square, which is surrounded by bars and clubs, and captured footage of nine hundred offenses in a single night. The area is so chaotic that police often don't even try to intervene, which only adds to the air of lawlessness.[40]

To put this in context, in the United States, even *illegal* immigrants are only half as likely to be arrested as the average American (though we should concede that they've broken the law by being in the country without permission).[41] In the United States, second-generation immigrants are more likely to commit crimes than the first, because the dark side of assimilation means newcomers are catching up with everyone else.[42]

As the author Christopher Caldwell, one of the sharpest social observers of contemporary Europe, noted, "ethnic islands" tend to reinforce the worst habits and ideas of newcomers. Such areas, he went on, "look like a seizure of territory rather than a multicultural enrichment."[43] These communities turn to theocratic associations untethered from European society to fill the void left by failed institutions. The emergence of mirror governments undermines the rule of elected bodies at the local level, which often explains why policing is difficult in migrant-heavy neighborhoods.[44]

The most obvious example of this is the no-go zones. While a number of conservative critics of immigration in the United States overstate the presence of segregated Islamic districts, they do exist. A 2018 poll indicates that most Germans fear no-go zones where they believe police are too afraid to patrol. Health Minister Jens Spahn said, "There are neighborhoods in Essen, Duisburg and Berlin where you get the impression that the state is no longer willing or able to enforce the law there."[45]

Even Merkel was forced to admit Germany was home to

growing segregated, largely autonomous areas, arguing that in a liberal nation "there cannot be any no-go areas, that there cannot be areas where no-one dares to go but there are such places." She added, "One has to call them by name and do something about it."[46] The remarks were widely criticized by other EU leaders for stirring up "nationalism."

But these neighborhoods are not figments of the imagination. Nor are they a peculiarity of Germany. Islamists have launched poster campaigns across the United Kingdom declaring Sharia law in enforcement zones[47] and members of a "Muslim Patrol" groups have stood on guard in the Tower Hamlet area outside the East London Mosque, harassing men who they claimed looked homosexual, women who did not dress conservatively enough, couples holding hands,[48] and people carrying alcohol.[49]

According to one report, there are twenty-five neighborhoods in the London area alone in which the British government believes violent Muslim extremism is percolating.[50] And according to another report, there were eighty-five Islamic Sharia courts operating in the United Kingdom.[51] These unofficial tribunals often apply Islamic law to resolve domestic, marital, and business disputes among themselves.

While religious courts are not unheard of in other nations, the creeping acceptance of Islamic jurisprudence over the principles in British law—an incursion on secular governance—is a corrosive reality. In 2008, the archbishop of Canterbury, Dr. Rowan Williams, noted that the adoption of certain aspects of Sharia law in the United Kingdom "seems unavoidable." It is a bad sign when the head of the Church of England argues that a shadow government must be embraced to maintain social cohesion and "the stark alternatives of cultural loyalty or state loyalty."[52] Such false choices, often offered implicitly but sometimes explicitly by many European leaders, are a concession that Islam and secular authority have a serious problem coexisting. Perhaps this is because Europe doesn't offer newcomers something better.

France, perhaps more than any nation, has struggled with disintegration.[53] As Dr. Emil Pain, professor at the National Research University–Higher School of Economics, noted, "Closed mono-ethnic, mono-religious or mono-racial neighborhoods and schools" have emerged in cities around the world.[54] One imam in the town of Roubaix told Martine Aubry, a well-known French politician, that she was not welcome to visit his town as it was now designated a Muslim area and covered by haram, which has a ban on Christian women.

In places like Sweden Muslim refugees start organizations with names like Young in Sweden or *Ung i Sverige*, which offer language courses in Persian and Dari *for* native Swedes. The group's Facebook page describes these classes as an "integration project," stating that Swedes must also "take responsibility to be a part of that society as well."[55]

Lack of Integration Leads to Radicalism

Secularism comes with other important advantages, namely, mitigating the damage of Islamic radicalism. To this point in history, only one nation had successfully acclimatized newcomers in that scale in a manner beneficial for both immigrant and host nation.

In recent years, bloody terror attacks in France, the United Kingdom, Italy, and Sweden have been directly connected to ISIS taking advantage of the refugee crisis to smuggle radicals into Europe.[56] The deaths themselves are tragic, but the turmoil, anger, and political disruption these events trigger are an even greater threat to liberalism and societal order.

Between January 2014 and May 2017, in the midst of the refugee crisis, there were 142 Islamist plots that took place across 15 different European nations.[57] These attacks caused 808 injuries and 189 deaths—with explosives, firearms, and vehicles.

The United Kingdom experienced 64 terrorist attacks in 2019, while France had 7 and Germany had 3. In 2019, 1,316 people were arrested for terrorism plots in the EU.[58]

In 2010, there were 200 Islamists on Stockholm's intelligence radar; as of 2018, there were 2,000. It's not all bad news, since Sweden saw 300 foreign fighters head back to Syria and Iraq as of 2018. As of 2018, Finnish authorities knew of 370 people connected to international terrorism. About 80 joined the conflict in Syria.[59]

Islamic terrorism, a rarity in the United States, is nearly a monthly occurrence in Europe. In October 2020, a Tunisian national stabbed three people in the Notre Dame basilica in the city of Nice, shouting "Allahu akbar."[60] In another attack that month, a French teacher was beheaded for showing cartoons of the prophet Muhammad to his students while teaching a class on free speech. His killer was eighteen-year-old Abdullakh Anzorov.[61]

In November, a major terrorist attack occurred in Austria, where several gunmen opened fire in six different locations on people eating out right before a second coronavirus lockdown. Four people were killed and twenty-two injured. Of the attack, Austrian chancellor Sebastian Kurz said the nation was engaged not in a battle between Christians and Muslims, he stressed, but "between civilisation and barbarism."[62] Kurz is right in the abstract. Terror is barbarism because of its brutality. They who kill in the name of Islam, however, are part of a worldwide, historic, ideological, and political movement that includes, to various degrees and various reasons, radicalized men and women from both great factions of the Muslim faith. They, like Juncker, might recognize that borders have much meaning, but they have civilization goals. Some of those adherents of this political Islam are now in Europe, which, unlike the United States, did very little vetting of those streaming into their continent from the Middle East.

There is a less conspicuous, though no less caustic, reper-
cussion to assimilation failures—and it is usually a price paid by
women.

A recent poll by the Policy Exchange found that though nearly
60 percent of British Muslims would prefer to live under British
law rather than Sharia, 28 percent choose Sharia. Many didn't
seem to understand the distinction. Half, for instance, believed
that homosexuality should be illegal. Nearly a third believed it
was acceptable for a British Muslim man to have more than one
wife. Nearly 40 percent agreed that "wives should always obey
their husbands." The most striking aspect of the survey was that
among those fifty-five and older, only 17 percent preferred Islamic law, whereas for those aged sixteen to twenty-four, the
number spiked to 37 percent.[63]

These communities are headed in the wrong direction. It
was long assumed that the oppressive religious habits regarding
women would soften through years of intermarriage and integration within European populations. Self-segregation has undermined this evolution, and sometimes reinforced bad habits.

For one thing, Muslim immigrants aren't marrying other Europeans. Oftentimes Islamic marriages are arranged or compelled
on young women, who either obey or see no other options. Various studies show that marriages have two purposes: to provide
foreign spouses with residency and to specifically resist integration into European culture. In Islamic enclaves in Norway, for instance, young girls imported for marriage are, as one researcher
called them, "living visas," and the situation they find themselves
in "a new form of human commerce."[64]

In some cases, young women come to Europe already married. Sometimes young girls are married off by parents in refugee
camps for their own protection and other times for dowries.[65] In
Denmark, a review found dozens of young girls living with older
men in asylum housing. Initially, authorities removed girls under
the age of eighteen from their husbands, and all girls under the

age of fifteen. But after two girls attempted to commit suicide, the policy was reversed.

Data in Germany suggests that there are thousands of immigrant marriages where one or both parties are under the age of eighteen. One such marriage, between a fifteen-year-old Syrian girl and her twenty-one-year-old cousin, has been playing out in Germany's court system. In this case it seems the Syrian girl wants to stay with her husband. This is often not the case. In Germany, a thirteen-year-old Kurdish girl was scheduled to marry a sixty-year-old man to become his second wife. Thankfully a teacher intervened and called authorities. The girl then had to live in a shelter because her family rejected her when she protested the marriage. This is a common story in Germany.[66]

Forced marriages are a big problem in Turkey and thus have become a big problem among the Turkish population in Germany. Some Turkish girls are brought to Germany specifically for the purpose of marriage. They are now referred to by activists as import brides. These young women are often tricked into coming to Germany, rarely speak the language, and are often isolated from the rest of society once they arrive.

While these marriages are immoral in and of themselves, they also halt the education of young women, leaving them wholly dependent on their husbands. Many Muslim girls also have no choice but to stay in a marriage even if it is abusive. Though most European countries have equal divorce rights for men and women, the same is not true for Islamic law.

Within many Muslim immigrant communities there is a general lack of respect for women by Western standards. Germans learned this the hard way during a mass sexual assault that took place on New Year's Eve in 2016. Leaked documents reveal that 2,000 men were accused of assaulting 1,200 German women in just one night in the German cities of Cologne, Hamburg, and others. Of the 120 suspects identified, about half were immigrants from North Africa who had only recently arrived.[67]

According to official complaints, groups of four to twenty young men formed circles around young women, groping them and stealing their possessions. In the very first hour of the New Year the police station nearest the train station received thirty to fifty complaints of sexual assault and theft.[68] This incident garnered international attention, but it was not an isolated one. In 2016, three girls, aged fifteen, sixteen, and seventeen, were assaulted over a two-hour period by a mob of thirty immigrants at a shopping center in Kiel.[69]

In Sweden, 58 percent of men convicted of rape and attempted rape from 2013 to 2018 were immigrants.[70] In Norway rape has become such a problem that the government started offering classes to migrants to teach them how to treat European women. Immigrants moving from conservative societies are often shocked to find women dressed in skimpy clothing and kissing men in public. Henry Ove Berg, who was Stavanger's police chief during the spike in rape cases, said "there was a link but not a very clear link" between the rape cases and the immigrant community in the city. Yet court documents reveal that seventeen out of the twenty men found guilty of rape were immigrants.[71]

Hanne Kristin Rohde, a former head of the violent crime section of the Oslo Police Department, said there was "a clear statistical connection" between sexual violence and male migrants from countries where "women have no value of their own." According to one African asylum seeker, even after taking the class he still struggles to understand that a woman can be raped by her husband. He explained that in his country of Eritrea, "if someone wants a lady, he can just take her and he will not be punished," at least not by the police. He noted that things were different in Norway, where women can do any job they want and have the right to relax in public without being bothered.[72]

In the United States, where there are few segregated immigrant communities, such marriages would be stigmatized. In Europe, authorities and leaders like the archbishop of Canterbury, if they don't look the other way, embrace relativistic politically correct rhetoric that debilitates society to forcefully condemn these nefarious societal habits for fear of offending minority groups. Americans, though moving in a similar direction, are not yet wholly constricted by speech codes.

Radicalism Leads to Right-Wing Backlash

Poorly executed policy creates barriers of entry for immigrants while also corroding faith among the host population. When the guardians of Europe fail, or refuse, to protect their borders and values by assimilating newcomers, they not only allow radicalism and theocratic ideas to fester, they also destabilize national cohesion, fueling anger, Islamophobia, and hypernationalism.

The pressure of the refugee crisis has created an explosion of populist movements across Europe that destabilized the Union itself. Merkel didn't merely open Germany's borders to mass migration, she demanded every member state participate in taking refugees. Germany pressured the EU into temporarily suspending laws requiring asylum seekers, who would go through virtually no background checks, to be returned to the first country they entered. Merkel said her country was showing the nation's "friendly, beautiful face" to the world.[73] Yet this was a clear case of *Vergangenheitsbewältigung*—loosely translated to mean "a struggle to come to terms with the past." For our purposes, it signifies a German overcompensation for the sins of the past.

Instead of a beautiful face, German policies reawakened, or at least revealed, the latent chauvinistic tendencies of her own nation. Whether it is mass protests, like the one that erupted in Chemnitz after a man was stabbed to death by two immigrants, where men flashed Nazi salutes and shouted, "Foreigners out,"[74] or the more significant rise of German and Austrian far-right parties, a lack of assimilation has stirred turmoil and fueled anger toward Muslims.[75]

One recent YouGov poll found only a mere 3 percent of respondents in Western Europe believed "all is well" on the migration front.[76] In another, 70 percent of Europeans said that the EU had botched the migration crisis. In yet another, a majority of Europeans now believe that immigrants imposed a burden, not a benefit, on their countries.[77]

The most dramatic backlash against German policies was Brexit, the withdrawal of the United Kingdom from the European Union, but Euro-skeptic movements have sprung up all over the continent. Many of them are genuine movements demanding self-governance, but some are openly xenophobic. From Germany's Alternativ für Deutschland to the Party for Freedom in the Netherlands to France's National Front to Portugal's Chega to a slew of Eastern European parties, there has been a proliferation of ethnocentric parties.

Italy provides a helpful example of how nearly unconstrained immigration has bolstered chauvinistic political movements in the form of the Northern League and Five Star Movement. From 2014 to 2018 Italy accepted 600,000 refugees—in addition to an already liberal immigration policy. Along with this surge came a dramatic political shift to the right. By 2018, Matteo Salvini of the Lega party adopted an "Italian first" slogan, campaigning against Brussels, international banks, and multinational corporations, and pledging to deport the 500,000 illegal immigrants in the nation. Under his leadership the Lega went from 4 percent of the vote to 18 percent and earned a place in the coalition government.[78]

Italy's national, cultural, and political battle over identity is playing out on a micro level in the region of Tuscany, the birthplace of the Italian Communist Party. The left hasn't lost an election in Tuscany for seventy years; until, that is, 2016, when nationalists won elections in towns across the region.[79] In the ancient city of Pisa—with a population of 90,000 people, 2,000 of whom are Muslim—the Northern League canceled the previous administration's agreement to even allow a mosque to be built. The town of Cascina, once famous for its furniture, has now closed down an already dilapidated migrant welcome center,[80] and insists that natives of Cascina be first in line for public housing and that migrants have documentation proving they own no property in their home country.

Much of this anger is brought on by German harassment. When smaller nations, overwhelmed by refugees, began balking at the prospects of open borders, the European Union began sanctioning them for adopting their own border policies—putting an end to the idea that this was a "community" of nations on equal footing.

Viktor Orbán, the nationalist prime minister of Hungary, was the most outspoken critic of mass Muslim immigration into the continent. Hungary had been the first place these refugees touched in the European Union when streaming from Turkey and the Balkans. The small nation had registered over 100,000 refugees in a few months during 2015, and it was encountering 3,000 new asylum seekers every day before it finally closed the border.[81] According to the Schengen agreement, once a refugee was in Hungary, that person was ensured free movement in twenty-six European countries—twenty-two of them in the European Union. There is no way that Hungary could possibly know who those migrants are, where they're going, or where they're from, much less have the ability to ferret out radicals among them.

The Hungarians weren't alone. The Czechs said no. Slovakia said forcing migrants on it would mean the "end of the EU."[82] Poland ignored the EU. The Court of Justice of the European Union found that all had broken EU law by controlling their own borders and refusing to take part in a mandatory refugee quota scheme.[83] "These member states cannot invoke their responsibilities with regard to the maintenance of law and order and the safeguarding of internal security in order to disapply a valid EU measure with which they disagree," said a statement from Eleanor Sharpston, an advocate general at the court.

But Orbán's real sin had been openly contending that he was protecting Europe's "Christian values" and "identity" by blocking a central route used by refugees.[84] In many ways, Orbán is a truly problematic leader who has destabilized many liberal institutions in his country. Yet, in modern Europe the mere mention of "Christian values" insinuates to elites some kind of xenophobic slight that disgraces all people living on a subcontinent built on, well, Christianity and "identity."

Despite the long-term project to do away with European borders, Hungarian culture still exists. Danish culture is a thing. The French aren't some artificial construct drawn up by social engineers. And though it is extraordinarily diverse and rich, European culture exists. It sometimes fails in the most violent and brutal ways, but, in the aggregate, human flourishing does better, by any measure, under this tradition than any other. There is a reason we have never seen Austrian or Swiss migration eastward toward Jordan.

Today, nearly every Christian-majority nation in the world still boasts of democratic institutions and high levels of freedom compared to nations in other parts of the world—with a few exceptions, like Russia. Certainly, there is no Muslim-majority nation with healthy democratic or liberal institutions or anything resembling religious or secular freedom. There are complicated ideological and historical reasons for this reality, but nonetheless, reality it is. The crush of immigrants had agitated an already tenuous political situation in Europe, further exposing the rickety edifice propped up by largely uninspiring notions of secular universalism and multiculturalism favored by American Europhiles.

That's not an identity or an ideal, but vacuous sloganeering.

The United States Is Far Better at Handling Immigration

The United States was on the receiving end of tremendous criticism from Europhiles for failing to follow the European lead in opening its borders during the refugee crisis that began in 2014 (and is still, in many ways, ongoing). It shouldn't be forgotten that Americans had sent $2 billion in humanitarian aid for Syrian refugees—for food voucher programs that fed hundreds of thousands, medical supplies, and education programs—more than any nation, or any five for that matter.[85] This is not even counting charitable organizations that raised hundreds of millions more. The United States had, until that point, resettled more refugees yearly for the decades preceding the Syrian War than the rest of the world combined.[86]

Even today, more immigrants live in the United States than in all of Europe. We could build a giant steel fence around the entire country, and the United States would still reign as the most welcoming place for foreigners that has ever existed. Accepting unlimited amounts of refugees, from the same place at the same time with the same ideas and the same problems, would lead to ethnic enclaves, poor assimilation, and the policy failures of Europe.

By the end of 2015, in fact, even Germany would see its mistake and try to put an end to the open flow of refugees, with Angela Merkel introducing a raft of restrictive border and asylum controls for "urgent security reasons."[87] The damage was likely irreversible.

That European nations felt a moral responsibility to aid and support refugees from the Middle East—and believe they will benefit economically—was commendable. It's an entirely Christian outlook, in fact. But so is preserving a culture that has provided the stability, freedom, and prosperity that has enticed so many people to enter your nation in the first place.

Once they opened the doors, Europe's most profound mistake was choosing a multicultural approach to immigration instead of the American melting pot approach. Civic integration is based on the idea that native or local culture can be complemented by a unifying culture. Unlike the acclimatization tactics of the eighteenth and nineteenth centuries, civic integration does not demand the suppression of an immigrant's own culture; rather it uses a series of incentives to encourage immigrants to adapt to their new country's codes, language, and customs. Immigration is quite often a positive force in society, and certainly it has been in the United States. Nevertheless, without integration and high levels of social capital—shared identity, values, trust, cooperation, and reciprocity—it promises to be destabilizing.

Trading in Western principles for vacuous universalism has been corroding European thought for thirty years, and a failure to assimilate is merely one of its consequences. In recent years, former British prime minister David Cameron, Angela Merkel, and French president Emmanuel Macron have admitted that "multiculturalism"—treating the distinct cultural or ethnic groups within a society as equally beneficial—is a perilous foundation for an open society. As the British writer Kenan Malik wrote in 2015, European "multiculturalism" has disintegrated from "an answer to Europe's social problems" to a fraught reality of "fragmented societies, alienated minorities, and resentful citizenries."[88] Majorities in every single member state of the European Union now believe, contra Juncker, that borders need better protection—with voters in Austria and the Czech Republic leading the way.

To this point in history, only one nation had successfully acclimatized newcomers on a massive scale in a way that is beneficial for both immigrant and host nation. It wasn't achieved by discarding the tenets of Western civilization because of an irrational need to coddle newcomers. During the refugee crisis in Europe, anyone speaking openly about the potential threats inherent in importing a new set of ideas—not people, but their notions—would be accused of fascist or bigoted tendencies. In secularized Europe, so-called liberals fear being labeled Islamophobic more than they fear the illiberalism of theocratic Islamic ideas.

Then again, there has never been an American "melting pot" in Europe. Perhaps there never will be. Though there have been golden ages in certain nations for rare minorities—Jews, for certain—it usually goes south at the first sign of economic or national turmoil. This can be attributed to Europe's geography, its hegemonies, and its long divisive history, but also to its contemporary policies.

Newcomers don't often internalize new values by osmosis. Some societies, like the United States, have adopted norms, policies, and civic institutions that are conducive for assimilating people. Some societies nudge or compel newcomers to embrace a new set of values. Europe does neither.

7

Richer Than You

In Europe one gets used to doing nothing. You sit on your ass and
whine all day. You get contaminated. You rot.

—*Henry Miller*, Tropic of Cancer

"What Can America Learn from Europe About Regulating Big
Tech?" asked *The New Yorker* in the summer of 2020. If one
paid attention to the mainstream American media, they might
wonder what Americans *can't* learn from Europe, a continent
perpetually on the cusp of overtaking the United States in a
range of industries and innovations.

Notwithstanding our superior achievements in growth,
wealth, and technology, whenever the European Union fleetingly
outperforms the United States on any economic data point, an
array of think pieces will appear in the financial press informing
readers that Europe has finally figured it out. And, of course, the
conventional wisdom among the Fourth Estate is that Europe
already has a firmer grip on how to properly wrangle the unruly
forces of capitalism.

This particular *New Yorker* piece was a pristine specimen of
a popular subgenre in media coverage in which hapless Americans are offered lessons on proper ethical policy from their Old
World cousins. In it we learn about an energetic woman named

Marietje Schaake, a former member of the European Parliament and the international policy director at the Cyber Policy Center, and who now teaches ethics to Americans at Stanford. Schaake, who marvels at the inequities and disorder of American life, offers readers "a forceful critique of Big Tech's extreme aversion to regulation" by championing Europe's more rational approach to lording over private-sector decisions. Various Europhilic voices are pulled into the story to reiterate that European lawmakers "have long outpaced their American counterparts" in creating regulatory regimes for tech companies. "I think it's incredibly important for not just Silicon Valley but the United States, in general, to become familiar with the European regulatory perspective," another Stanford law professor explains.[1]

Americans aren't above learning, adapting, and often appropriating good ideas from elsewhere. No rational person would believe otherwise. The conceit of the *New Yorker* piece, as with so many like it, however, is that our system is fundamentally unscrupulous and inferior. Which is confusing, considering the United States holds an immense advantage over Europe in technological advances that have made the world a better place.

Furthermore, America has a far more normal view of work than the complacent continent, American citizens are more content with and take more pride in their jobs, and the American meritocracy—contrary to popular belief—is growing more accessible to ordinary people as the years go by. The vast gap in technological achievement between America and Europe is one example of this cultural divide showing up in the results.

Europe, despite its wealth, its relatively stable institutions, its giant marketplace, and its intellectual firepower, is home to only one of the top thirty global internet companies in the world (Spotify), while the United States is home to eighteen of the top thirty. Of the top 154 technology companies in the world that appeared on the Forbes Global 2000 in 2019, 65 percent were American. The next-highest contender is China, with 20 percent. In a *Forbes* graph divvying up the origins of the world's top tech firms, Europe is relegated to the "other" category with Africa and South America.[2]

For that matter, only one European company appeared in the top ten corporate powerhouses in all world industries in 2020—an oil concern—and only seven in the top fifty.[3] Americans make up nearly half the list—despite having 500 million fewer people than Europe and 100 million fewer than European Union member states. Let's just say, all the top-selling smartphones and computers in Europe are made in South Korea and the United States, not in Norway or Spain.[4]

It should also be noted, incidentally, that despite the supposed lack of sexism in Schaake's enlightened Europe, less than 15 percent of start-ups are helmed by females.[5] One study found that Europe had the lowest female involvement in entrepreneurial activity of any region in the world "and the lowest gender parity." The leading nation in Europe for women was not a Western European one like France or Germany or Spain, but Lithuania. And the best nation for female entrepreneurship in the world is the United States, and it's not even close, with more than 35 percent of American entrepreneurs being female.

Americans—along with the Chinese—also dominate "unicorn" tech companies, start-ups that now have a valuation of over $1 billion.[6] A *Wall Street Journal* study found that Europe was home to fourteen such tech firms, while ninety-seven could be found in the United States.[7] The American venture capital market pumps around four times as much money into start-ups as all of Europe. Research and development spending by European technological firms makes up around 8 percent of the global total, as opposed to 77 percent for companies based in the United States.[8]

Since 1900, America has vastly outpaced Europe in the number of start-ups that have turned into big companies. And yet, Americans keep churning out more new ones every decade. It is this improvement of existing products, services, and models that is the leading driver of long-term economic growth and quality of life for Americans. The U.S. Department of Commerce says technological innovation has been responsible for 75 percent of the United States' economic growth rate since the end of World War II.[9] These inventions created prosperity *and* lifted mankind up.

Here are just a few examples of inventions that technologists and experts believe are the most important in the postwar era, in no particular order:

the internet
web browser
personal computer
laptop
mobile phone
smartphone
email
magnetic resonance imaging
microprocessors
noninvasive laser
robotic surgery
open-source software and information sites
light-emitting diodes
portable GPS systems
e-commerce
media file compression
nuclear power
Kevlar
social networking
robotic hearts
video games
the hard drive
graphic user interface

electronic car ignition

retinal implant

digital photography

the jet airliner

the microwave oven

blockchain technology

polio vaccine

genetically modified plants

bar codes and scanners

SRAM flash memory

anti-retroviral treatment for AIDS

3-D printing

high-density battery packs

Some of these inventions were devised in collaborative ways, and many are built upon advances and discoveries that stretch back hundreds of years into European society. But the vast majority were not only conceived in the United States, they were brought to market by U.S. companies.

None of this is an accident. In the United States, modernization is propelled by a system of limited state interference, a salubrious private sector that is devoted to spending on research, and a competitive free-market system that allows entrepreneurs and investors to keep, and reinvest, more of their money. It is a system that rewards risk and labor. The ideas that bolster this dominance were once widely championed by American policy makers and economists.

Nowadays, Europhiles show animosity toward all of them.

A Nation of Risk Takers

More than any policy initiative, or any leader, or any regulation, it is the ingrained American entrepreneurial spirit and work ethic that separates us from Europe. It's not because we are born smarter or wealthier or because, as many Europeans like to maintain, we are blessed with geographical luck and an abundance of natural resources. Rather it is that our behavior and expectations are different.

One of the most underrated traits we hold is our comfort with risk—a behavior embedded in the American ethos. It is true that most nations romanticize their founding, and, in many ways, we are no different. Still, it is hardly hyperbolic to contend that the United States was conceived in risk. While the Spanish and French crossed the Atlantic Ocean to extract treasure, the first British and German settlers, men and women escaping religious and political persecution, took immense personal risk not only by traversing the sea to land in North America but by building their communities in unexplored and potentially treacherous lands. They did this with the expectation that there would be little, if any, oversight or protection from their governments back home in Europe.

Americans, self-selected risk takers, created an individual and communal independence that engendered creativity. Early on, communities were creating a slew of innovations that nurtured self-efficiency in agriculture, home building, trapping, hunting, and self-defense. Later, the founders of the nation— many them entrepreneurs and inventors themselves—took great personal risk being branded traitors by the British Empire, even though they were already likely among the wealthiest and freest people on earth. The Americans who subsequently pushed west, and the ones who kicked off the first industrial revolution with interchangeable parts and mass production, also participated in this tradition. As did the great industrial enterprises of the twentieth century and the tech pioneers of Silicon Valley.

As does every man and woman who starts a small business today. Americans rarely delved into European-style romanticism or cynicism during the past century; rather they celebrated builders and innovators. Or, as the 1950s musical *Our Country 'Tis of Thee* put it, "There is no stopping a nation of tinkerers and whittlers, long accustomed to making, repairing, improving and changing." We might find such sentiments hokey today, but these notions remain.

One inescapable by-product of taking chances is failure. One of the reasons Americans are more willing to take on risk is that failing isn't seen as a humiliating or a career-ending event, rather almost as a compulsory ingredient to accomplishment. There is nary a tale of American triumph—not those of the Wright brothers, Alexander Graham Bell, Walt Disney, Steve Jobs, Thomas Edison, Ulysses Grant, or Henry Ford—that isn't buttressed by a slew of failures.

Even today, hundreds of self-help books assure people that failure is an event to be learned from and embraced. Failure is an ethos, even embraced in contemporary Silicon Valley culture. Data shows that somewhere around 1 percent of venture-backed companies end with a billion-dollar valuation.[10] A few years ago, in fact, the first conference devoted to failure, FailCon, was put on in Silicon Valley, where heavyweight CEOs like PayPal co-founder Max Levchin spoke of their repeated failures as the only way to achieving genuine success. "The one liberating thing with failure is that you start at like −5 the next time," Levchin explained. "Failure? I can fail tomorrow and I don't care, I'm failing now."[11]

"*Les misérables,*" read a recent headline in *The Economist*—the European voice of neoliberalism—which argued that "Europe's culture is deeply inhospitable to entrepreneurs" and that Europe has shown a "chronic failure to encourage ambitious entrepreneurs." The biggest problem, notes the magazine, is that "executives are extremely risk-averse" and intimidated by new ideas.[12] When European entrepreneurs were asked by Ernst & Young what they thought of their nation's entrepreneurial culture, the German, Italian, and French entrepreneurs were far less confident about the future of their country as a place for start-ups than those in the United States, Canada, or even Brazil.[13]

Start-up employees in the United States have twice as much upside exposure as their European counterparts. The benefits of labor in U.S. companies permit investors and CEOs, and employees, to amass that wealth. Because of a preoccupation with "inequality," European rules and taxation for stock option remuneration make it difficult for start-up employees to enjoy the benefits of innovation—and make it harder for new companies to attract talent. One CEO of a Berlin-based start-up recently noted that he "can't provide his people with a stake in the future of their venture without incurring crushing costs and hassle."[14]

European banks, incidentally, have on average a 6.7 percent return on capital, while among American banks the average is 14.4 percent.[15]

In many ways risk also comes with a lower downside in the United States, where companies that go bankrupt can renegotiate their debt, which offers innovators more space to take risks, without the threat of failure decimating their future. Nations like Ireland, France, and Germany have been attempting to adopt American bankruptcy rules, and the European Union has sent a directive to member states to reorganize their own.

European culture values stability over success, security over invention, and leisure time over work. A study of innovation around the world found that nearly 42 percent of Europeans between eighteen and thirty-five cited "fear of failure" as the barrier to creating a new business, which is not only far higher than in the United States but far more than in developing areas like sub-Saharan Africa and Latin America.[16] In another poll, 43 percent of European respondents said that they feared opening a new business because they worried it may bankrupt them, and 33 percent said they were averse to opening a business because it would mean "irregular income." Nearly 60 percent of Europeans would prefer to work as an employee rather than take on the risk of starting their own business.[17]

"In Europe, failure is regarded as a personal tragedy," Petra Moser, a German-born professor of economics at Stanford and its Europe Center, told the *New York Times*. "Here it's something of a badge of honor. An environment like that doesn't encourage as much risk-taking and entrepreneurship."[18] When asked "Suppose you were working and could choose between different jobs. Which would you prefer, a) being an employee; or b) being self-employed," nearly 70 percent of Americans chose to be their own boss but only 40 percent of the French. In the United States, over 50 percent of workers of all ages want to be the boss.[19]

"Worth" Ethic

In 2011, the chairman of the board of supervisors of China Investment Corporation, Jin Liqun, caused a stir in Europe by accusing the entire continent of functioning under "outdated" labor laws and a welfare system that left people "languishing on the beach" rather than working to the betterment of their continent. Jin went on to call Europeans "slothful" and "indolent," a people more reliant on safety nets than their own hard work.[20] While a representative of the communist regime in China has absolutely no moral authority to level such claims, it doesn't mean he didn't have a point. Europeans have a terrible work ethic. And not merely by American standards.

Much has been made by American journalists about the fact that Europeans work fewer hours than we do. *Americans never go on vacation! Americans eat at their desks! American take their work home with them! Americans are always on their phone!* Americans, they say, live to work while Europeans work to live.

Yes. *So what?*

It is true that large numbers of American employees do not

even take their allotted vacation time, while most Germans and French take every last second of it.[21] This only tells us that the American propensity to work long hours has a lot more to do with state of mind than any specific state policy or employee benefit problem.

As anyone who lives in the United States could tell you, in many ways the idea that Americans are wholly consumed by their work is something of a myth itself. We are certainly above average, not obsessed. Studies show that we work, on average, one hour longer than the average European per day. A recent OECD study of advanced economies found that under 12 percent of American workers regularly put in fifty or more hours every week at their job.[22] The United States fell in about average among industrialized nations in this regard.

Out of the twenty-seven nations in which employees worked less than in the United States, though, only three (Australia, Japan, and New Zealand) were not European. It would be more accurate, then, to say that Americans have a healthy work ethic and Europeans show a high degree of . . . well, let's call it complacency.

The first question is this: Why do so many Europhiles assume that more work is a drag on life? Many American pundits have argued that the "religion of workism"—as one Europhile in *The Atlantic* magazine put it recently[23]—makes us unhappy, causing dissatisfaction in our lives. When reading about the topic, journalists will often beg the question and try to figure out why Americans "need" to work more hours than Europeans, or why they feel "compelled" to put in long hours, though there's little evidence that these aren't simply personal choices.

Most polls show that American workers are perfectly happy with their jobs. In fact, most claim that work gives them meaning. When Gallup first asked employed adults if they were "satisfied" or "very satisfied" with their work in 1993, 86 percent responded in the affirmative. When asked the same question again in 2019, 92 percent said they were satisfied.[24]

It is not merely about wages, either. In a 2016 survey, Pew asked workers to best describe how they felt: 57 percent said it provided them with "a sense of identity," compared to 40 percent who said their job was just what they did for a living.[25] Americans were also "satisfied or very satisfied" with relations with coworkers, the flexibility of their hours, and their job security. Among other things, more than 70 percent were satisfied with their boss, their vacation time, and their chances for promotion. A recent CNBC study found that "meaningfulness" was the most significant overall component of happiness among American workers.[26] American men value wages, promotions, and bonuses more than women. Women value coworkers, social life, and work-life balance more than men.[27]

WHAT, THEN, IS THE REASON for European complacency? The British writer George Monbiot once noted, "If wealth was the inevitable result of hard work and enterprise, every woman in Africa would be a millionaire." Indeed. In Europe hard work is less likely to guarantee results, because policies that allow people to keep the fruits of their labor and compete matter far less. This is the future Europhiles see for the United States, because the most obvious motive for Americans' propensity to work longer hours is that there is a higher chance of a payoff. Europe's deficient work habits, conversely, are incentivized by generous social nets, powerful unions, and onerous labor laws that disincentivize initiative.

Freedom of contract is an important British principle adopted by Americans. European labor laws infringe on people's ability to decide who they will work for and in what conditions. The United States operates on an employment-at-will doctrine, meaning either party can choose to end the employment relationship for any lawful reason. In the EU, however, the employment contract means that an employer has to go through a long process to fire an employee. Wrongful termination laws are much broader in the EU, making the threat of being sued higher and thus the incentive for firing someone much lower.[28]

In the United States, less than 7 percent of the private sector labor force is unionized. Labor's decline happens to coincide with the largest boom in American history. And while regulations of working and environmental conditions exist, they are by every measure less onerous than in Europe. More economic freedom allows more movement of the labor force, both allowing workers to find the right fit and better success.

This does not prevent American Europhiles from lavishing praise on the European work model. "Europe could have the secret to saving America's unions," promised the website Vox, as if there were no debate about the efficacy of such an endeavor.[29] Furthermore, in Europe, entire sectors of the economy bargain with industry, rather than individual companies or individual workers, undercutting competition between business and workers themselves, which is the point of unions. Stricter hiring and firing requirements and regulatory hurdles, which Europhiles support, make it difficult to fire subpar, unproductive workers, and hire new blood.[30] This becomes a barrier for industrious workers, immigrants, and young people to enter certain vocations.

In many European nations, there is a two-tiered labor system, one where older workers are bestowed lucrative contracts that are almost impossible to lose, and a second where other workers are given temporary status and thus have almost no protections. Mario Draghi, former president of the European Central Bank, admitted, "In many countries the labor market is set up to protect older 'insiders'—people with permanent, high-paid contracts and shielded by strong labor laws."[31]

It is no bombshell, then, that during the financial crisis the youth unemployment rate in the EU increased from 16 to 26 percent—remaining high in many nations.[32] Europhiles like Steve Rattner, Barack Obama's auto czar, like to declare that the United States has fallen "behind many countries in Europe in terms of the ability of every kid in America to get ahead."[33] This is absurd. If that were the case, why do so many of Europe's best-educated young people keep moving from highly regulated nations to places in the United Kingdom, marginally better than most of the continent, or to the United States? Europeans rely on immigrants to do their menial labor, but fail to offer them the same opportunities. Pre-coronavirus European unemployment among the young was dangerously high. French youth unemployment, for instance, was at 19.9 percent, while in the United States it was at 3.7 percent. The only nations in Europe with higher youth unemployment are Greece, Spain, and Italy, which have similarly stringent labor laws. In France, the youth unemployment rate has consistently remained around 20 percent.

"France Lets Workers Turn Off, Tune Out and Live Life," a *New York Times* headline recently explained.[34] The problem, though, isn't that laws *allow* French workers to tune out—Americans can tune out whenever they like, after all—it's that they force them to tune out.

In France, the legal length of the working week for most companies can't exceed 35 hours. No working day can exceed 10 hours. And no employee can work more than 4.5 hours without a break even if they want to (though, no doubt, many ignore these regulations). These kinds of rigid protections do not comport with the contemporary knowledge-based society and internet economy. Still, American journalists can't stop praising the policy.

"When the French government instituted a policy that will allow employees to disconnect from work email while they're not in the office, effective at the start of 2017, many American workers may have looked across the ocean with jealousy," claimed one recent *Time* magazine piece.[35] Anecdotally speaking, I don't know of a single person who's ever looked upon France and been jealous of their institutionalized laziness, though perhaps there is such a faction. In fact, I suspect the author of the article worked from home, emailed outside her designated work hours, and toiled more hours than allotted a French employee by their own volition.

The new French law *Time* was speaking about established a workers' "right to disconnect," requiring companies with more than fifty employees to have hours when staff would not have to answer emails. French legislator Benoit Hamon, speaking to the BBC, described the law as an answer to the travails of employees who "leave the office, but they do not leave their work. They remain attached by a kind of electronic leash—like a dog."[36] In the United States the very idea that a legislator could dictate how long you should work or when you can use your phone to work would still, despite the growing Europhilic inclinations of so many politicians, be overstepping the acceptable bounds of legislation.

France's complex labor laws, incidentally, run somewhere around 4,000 pages. On top of the 35-hour workweek, employees are also given 27 days of paid annual leave, though some companies, like EDF, which is 85 percent state-owned, have written into some employee contracts that employees can have an additional 27 to 31 days on top of the 27 already given. All of this coupled with France's high minimum wage means it is no wonder the country is in financial trouble.[37] Every time there is talk of reforming labor laws, protests—often violent—break out. If the French put as much effort into working as they did into marching, perhaps their economic problems would be fixed.

IT MUST BE STRESSED ONCE more that, though European leaders have ensured that their economic futures are interlocked, the people have illustrated different weaknesses and strengths. As the left-wing politician Joschka Fischer complained, "Germany is a problem because the Germans are more diligent, disciplined, and more talented than the rest of Europe (and the world). This will always lead to 'imbalances.'"

European languor is unsustainable in the long run. As the continent's economy grew more productive and wealthier, it began producing more leisure time, more lavish safety nets, and fewer opportunities for upward mobility.

This isn't simply an argument about hours—after all, the most productive workers in Europe can be found in places like Ireland, where they work about the same hours as Americans. It's about laws that inhibit flexibility and new technologies and jobs that require that flexibility. The Europhiles aren't clamoring for Ireland's new work ethic, they are idealizing and pining for the French model. And that would be disastrous for the United States economy, and more important, incompatible with its work ethic.

Bootstraps

"Americans, like human beings everywhere, believe many things that are obviously untrue," Kurt Vonnegut Jr. wrote in his classic *Slaughterhouse-Five*. "Their most destructive untruth is that it is very easy for any American to make money." Kurt Vonnegut was both right and wrong. It certainly isn't easy for an American to make money. It just happens to be easier here than anywhere else.

One of the most destructive untruths of the Europhile is his contention that the meritocracy doesn't even exist. To convince people of this, the Europhile will fearmonger about growing poverty, a shrinking "middle class," and the rise of inequality.

Europeans have traditionally been far more class-conscious

than Americans, and they remain so. According to the World Values Survey, 70 percent of Americans believe that the poor can escape poverty if they work hard enough. Only 35 percent of Europeans share this view. Europeans also believe that the wealthy are undeserving of their riches, which, because of high regulations and rent seeking, are mostly from birth and awarded on privileges. They believe that social mobility is low and that an American Dream in their country is illusory.

That has not been the case in America. Politicians still strain to paint their lives as a hardscrabble tale filled with failures and fortitude, and finally success and redemption. Europhiles are far more enamored of technocratic top-down economic planning. They tend to mock the idea that Americans can bootstrap their way to success as a convenient mythology, which strengthens their argument for tighter controls and safety nets over spontaneous technological and market competition.

Europhiles tend to see celebration of the meritocracy as a jeremiad against the poor rather than a national aspiration. Every economic failure is, to them, de facto evidence of the system's fundamental shortcoming, and they often ignore the evidence that risk taking means failure. It is challenging these days to find any journalist arguing that American life is still largely meritocratic. Here, for instance, is a recent sampling from our media: "American Meritocracy Is a Myth," by Rajan Menon, a professor of international relations at the City College of New York; "The Myth of Meritocracy," by bestselling author and former secretary of labor Robert Reich; "Has the Myth of Meritocracy Killed the American Dream?" a discussion of elites at the Aspen Institute (yes, was the answer); "The False Promise of Meritocracy," by Marianne Cooper, a sociologist at Stanford; "The Myth of American Meritocracy," in *American Conservative* magazine; "Five Myths about Meritocracy," in the *Washington Post*; and books like *The Meritocracy Trap*, *The Tyranny of Merit*, and *The*

Meritocracy Myth (a college textbook). There are dozens more just like them.

When Congresswoman Alexandria Ocasio-Cortez, the socialist darling of the media, lamented that it was a "physical impossibility to lift yourself up by a bootstrap. . . . It's physically impossible. The whole thing is a joke," she claimed that 60 percent of wealth in America was inherited.[38] As most bootstrappers know, one of the primary reasons to accumulate wealth is to ensure that your children have a better life. But still, it is unclear where exactly Ocasio-Cortez came up with the 60 percent number, though it is likely taken from the work of the Marxist economist Thomas Piketty, who often makes this claim.[39]

More reliable information tells us something very different. One recent study of the wealthiest people in the world found that nearly 70 percent of Americans were self-made, while nearly 24 percent had a combination of inherited and self-created wealth. Only 8.5 percent of global high-net-worth individuals had inherited the majority of their wealth.[40] If anything, because of the rapid economic changes, poverty elimination, and the full of socialism, society has become more meritocratic—and no place is more meritocratic than America.

Most wealthy Americans earn their money. In one long-term study, titled "Family, Education, and Sources of Wealth among the Richest Americans, 1982–2012," economists Steven N. Kaplan and Joshua D. Rauh investigated the behaviors and backgrounds of the four hundred wealthiest individuals in the United States over thirty years as reported by *Forbes*.[41] They found that the share of the self-made wealthy had risen from 40 percent in 1982 to 69 percent by 2011. Similarly, an analysis by finance researchers for the libertarian *Cato Journal* determined that half of the wealth in the Forbes 400 has been "newly created in one generation."[42]

According to another study, by the Peterson Institute for

International Economics, half of European billionaires had inherited some of their wealth, while only a third of billionaires in the United States did. More telling, perhaps, is that around 20 percent of Europe's inherited fortunes go back four or more generations, while only 10 percent do so in the United States.[43]

The BMO Financial Group found that two-thirds of the highest-earning Americans were self-made, compared to only 3 percent who inherited the majority of their wealth. And among those self-made high earners, nearly a third were first-generation Americans or born elsewhere.[44]

As we'll soon see, for the average person, the economic opportunities of American life outpace any other place in the world. Operation Warp Speed, the public-private partnership initiated by the U.S. government to facilitate and accelerate the development of COVID-19 vaccines, was run by a Moroccan-born Belgian American immigrant named Moncef Mohamed Slaoui. And despite stereotypes, a recent survey found that, of the top 1 percent of American earners, less than 14 percent were involved in banking or finance. Around a third were entrepreneurs or running nonfinancial businesses. Another 16 percent were doctors or other medical professionals.[45] Nearly 70 percent of wealthy Americans grew up in middle-class or lower-income households. Only a third of people with assets in excess of $5 million grew up wealthy.[46]

These are hardly new Gilded Age aristocrats. Not only hasn't the American meritocracy failed, but in numerous ways we've actually become more meritocratic.

Smarter Than You

On the educational front, the system benefits from generous government research grants, but in America the state doesn't play an outsized role in deciding the focus of research. This is good, because politicians and governments, no matter where they are in the world, are by nature risk averse and people pleasers. Innovators are contrarians who invest their time in ideas that are often seen as lost causes.

The top five most innovative universities in world are in the United States—as well as eight of the top ten and forty-six of the top one hundred. And it's not just Ivy League schools. Among the most innovative universities are UNC Chapel Hill, USC (Southern Cal), the University of Texas, Caltech, and the University of Florida. Germany is second best on the list with only nine schools. France has eight. That these American universities and research labs pull human capital is critical to this success. If you're interested in learning about culinary arts or the Fauvists, you might go to France. If you're forging a future of science and tech, you want to go to the United States to work and do your research.

In the past century, there have been 383 Nobel laureates from the United States—by far the most in the world.[47] What makes it even more impressive is that United States winners are often immigrants. Nearly 40 percent of the Nobel Prizes won by Americans in chemistry, medicine, and physics were awarded to people born in other nations.[48] In 2020, every Nobel Prize was awarded to either an American, a team of Americans, or a team with an American member.[49]

In 2020, there were one million international students—mostly from Asian nations—studying in the United States. The vast majority of them focused on engineering, math and computer science, and business and management. Around 340,000 Americans study abroad every year, usually for a semester, in programs set up by American universities.[50]

European higher education isn't academically subpar, but they have a different set of priorities that are far less accommodating to transformation. Despite endless criticisms about funding (from the left), the ideological disposition of professors (from the right), and cost (from everyone), American science and research institutions remain the envy of the world. American schools vigorously compete for students. The United States remains the leading place that top young minds come to to learn from all over the world, and it is a great exporter of innovative talent. The reasons are obvious. Schools foster environments of scientific freedom. In many top universities, students can create their research projects for academic credits and work on patent applications and build start-up companies.

American institutions of higher education promote entrepreneurship ideas that hatched within their walls and were taken to the market. The idea for Google was first researched at Stanford, the spreadsheet at Harvard Business School and the Massachusetts Institute of Technology, the nicotine patch at the University of California, seat belts at Cornell University, Gatorade at the University of Florida, and plasma screens at the University of Illinois, just to name a few. Some schools, most notably Stanford University, have opened commercial licensing so that they can partake in the bounty of the inventions devised on campus, making them, in essence, business partners. The results of this program have seen advances in "gene splicing," a boon to mankind in both agriculture and medicine, a process for the remediation of contaminated groundwater, a Global Positioning System accurate enough to permit fully automated landing of airplanes, fiber optic amplifiers for telecommunications networks, and injectable collagen for plastic and cosmetic surgery, again to name just a few.[51]

There is no parallel cultivation of American schools in Europe. In French *grandes écoles*, schools of higher education, which produce most of the nation's top engineers, very few have graduates that have any interest in starting up their own businesses. Most have secure jobs waiting for them that they may never relinquish. Marie Ekeland, a French venture capitalist, told the *New York Times* in 2019 that the "digital world is all about sharing and working together, experimenting and failing. This is the opposite of the grandes écoles."[52] Similar attitudes prevail in the government-funded *Mittelstand* vocational schools in Germany—home of Europe's most vibrant economy—which are "very slow, very risk averse," explains Christian Miele, another big investor. Only 2 percent of Germans between fourteen and thirty-four years old have started a business, compared with 9 percent of U.S. young people.[53] No advanced nation comes close to the United States.

Nevertheless, Europhiles argue that the entire system is rigged because poverty and destitution are driven by the excesses of capitalism and lack of a proper European-style safety net and regulation. Anytime there is a ripple of a possible economic downturn, experts like Thomas Piketty, Paul Krugman, and Joseph Stiglitz, the "inequality"-obsessed progressive economist, will take to the pages of major American periodicals to implore citizens to embrace the European social models to save us. "Three decades of neoliberal policies have decimated the middle class, our economy, and our democracy," Stiglitz recently asserted. In *Scientific American*, of all places, Stiglitz declared, "The American Economy Is Rigged" and the "notion of the American Dream—that, unlike old Europe, we are a land of opportunity—is part of our essence."[54]

One of the pillars of the Europhile's argument is that the American middle class is shrinking. We must concede that the middle class has been "shrinking" for a while, not for the reasons critics of the United States contend but rather, unlike in Europe, because more people are moving from the middle class to the upper middle class. In 1979, around 38 percent of families in the United States were in the middle class, compared to only 32 percent in 2014.[55] When Stephen Rose, of the left-leaning Urban Institute, adjusted thresholds for inflation going back to 1979, he found that those moving into the middle class—defined as any household of at least three earning $100,000 to $350,000, or at least double the U.S. median household income—had "grown substantially," from 12.9 percent of the population in 1979 to 29.4 percent in 2014, while the percentage of poor and near poor had fallen from 24.3 to 19.8 percent, as had the lower middle class, from 23.9 to 17.1 percent.

When the economist Mark Perry dove into the numbers, he found that American households earning $100,000 or more per year have tripled since 1967, from 9 percent to 29.2 percent. At the same time, lower-income households, those making $35,000 a year, fell over the same period of time by five percentage points. None of this is to mention that the lower middle class today probably has a materially better existence than the upper middle class of 1979.[56] All of this undermines the claims of a Eurocentric political movement that feeds the anxieties of millions, by promising to save it by bringing an administrative state and social safety net that underperforms the American economy.

It has been, despite all the social programs and economic interventions, a mixed bag for Western Europe's biggest economies since 1990, with shares of adults living in middle-income households increasing in France, the Netherlands, and the United Kingdom, but shrinking in Germany, Italy, and Spain.[57] Overall, the middle-class share of the adult population fell in seven of the eleven Western European countries, according to a study by Pew. Though inequality—a largely meaningless statistic—hasn't risen at the same pace as in the United States, most Europeans aren't moving into the upper-middle-class expansion of the lower-income class. "The progress of the middle class has halted in most European countries," said Daniel Vaughan-Whitehead, a senior economist at the International Labor Organization in Geneva. "Their situation has become more unstable, and if something happens in the household, they are more likely to go down and stay down."[58]

Concerns over inequality have led Americans to believe we are poorer than we actually are. The media constantly makes sure to create that impression. "Why America's 1-Percenters Are Richer Than Europe's," NPR recently explained to its audience. "The wealth of the top 1% of Americans has grown dramatically in the past four decades," the story went on, making the highly debatable claim that inequality was "squeezing both the middle class and the poor. This is in sharp contrast to Europe and Asia, where the wealth of the 1% has grown at a more constrained pace."[59]

A recent *New York Times* editorial, headlined "Please Stop Telling Me America Is Great," made a similar claim, noting that the United States was just "okay." "Comparing the United States of America on global indicators reveals we have fallen well behind Europe—and share more in common with 'developing countries,'" wrote Taige Jensen and Nayeema Raza, adding that "the myth of America as the greatest nation on earth is at best outdated and at worst, wildly inaccurate."[60]

As a subjective matter, a person is free to believe that America is "great" or not. Conservative populists were not urging citizens to make America "great *again*" only a few years ago. I should reiterate, as well, that this book is not making the claim that the United States isn't in need of improvement. But the *Times'* contention that "America is the richest country" in the OECD, "but we're also the poorest, with a whopping 18 percent poverty rate—closer to Mexico than Western Europe," is not only subjective and largely irrelevant, it is also highly misleading. It speaks to a flaw of Europhiles when comparing the fate of Americans and Europeans and others in the world.

For one thing, the United States has the highest per capita wealth in the world, rising 13 percent in 2019—the year before the COVID-19 pandemic—to $245,000.[61] Americans also have one of the highest median incomes in the world—allegedly outpaced only by smaller European nations.[62] Median income is a somewhat misleading statistic, as it measures the earning power of an individual but doesn't take into account the accumulated

personal wealth of older Americans. Nor does it take into account the income disparity once we start subtracting taxes and
other fees. And, as numerous economists have pointed out,
European industry and earning benefits from the spillover of
American wealth.

Sometimes, especially when one hasn't experienced any other
life, it is challenging to contemplate the scale of American wealth
in comparison to the world. When Pew analyzed the 111 nations
that accounted for 88 percent of the global population, they
found that middle-income range translates to an annual income
of $14,600 to $29,200 for a family of four. The U.S. average
household income is over three times the amount. Nearly nine
in ten Americans find themselves substantially above the global
middle-income standard, which is to say that by global standards
there are virtually no poor people in the United States. And
the contention that we have more in common with "developing
countries" than Europe is little more than clickbait for the Europhilic readers of the *New York Times*.

Though the United States constitutes less than 5 percent of
the world's population, Americans generate and earn more than
20 percent of its income. It has the largest economy in the world;
its share has remained basically unchanged since 1980, when it
accounted for 25.2 percent of the world GDP. Today, despite the
rise of China and India and other developing economies, its share
is 23.91. During that same time, the European Union's share of
the world economy fell from 34.6 percent to 22 percent.[63]

While national GDP growth matters, it doesn't tell us the
full story, either. Simply because developing economies like
China and India are experiencing a larger percentage of growth
doesn't mean citizens in those nations are better off. There is,
after all, only so much room for traditional powerhouses to
expand. A better measurement in evaluating the prosperity of
individuals is the change in the value of real GDP per capita.
On this front, the United States has outperformed all European

nations. From the pre-coronavirus years of 2016 to 2019, Americans saw $3,413 in real GDP growth per capita, while the next-best Western nation, Finland, saw $2,309 in growth, and most experienced under $1,500 in growth.[64]

Now, by American standards, there are plenty of poor people among us. We shouldn't pretend otherwise or demean their struggles. Yet, when Europhiles make claims about the United States' high poverty rate, they are almost always comparing low-income Americans to the median income of other Americans. As a domestic concern this is an objective method of measuring poverty, but as a global concern, not so much.

To put it in perspective, it's likely that if all of the United States' poor revolted and formed their own new nation tomorrow, they would enjoy higher standards of living than the vast majority of nations in the world, and that includes the majority of European nations. Because once all income, charity, welfare benefits, and social benefits are calculated, the poorest 20 percent of Americans consume about as many goods and services as the relatively wealthy nations of Italy, Spain, and Britain.[65]

America's lower-income population also benefits from:

EASY MOVEMENT: There are those who gravitate toward vocations and lifestyles that fulfill them in ways that higher earnings may not. The schoolteacher and nurse may not make as much as the lawyer or the stockbroker, but it doesn't necessarily mean they are unhappier. Nor is wealth an easy thing to quantify. For example, a family who lives in a suburb of Boise or Nashville may be less wealthy than the family that lives in the suburbs of New York City or Washington, D.C., but that doesn't necessarily mean that their quality of life is more wanting.

Still, culturally speaking, it's a lot easier for an economically disadvantaged New Englander to move to Arizona or Florida and make a life for himself than it is for a Hungarian or a Pole to move to Luxembourg or Denmark to seek his fortune.

Freeing states to craft tax codes, union laws, legal structures, environmental policy, and regulatory burdens allows them to lure new residents and corporations. States entice newcomers by funding their research universities or entice locals by offering them in-state tuition. They entice retirees and low-income Americans with low property taxes or no state income tax altogether.

This jumble of laws and guidelines grates against the sensibilities of central planning Europhiles. This happens to be the very reason corporations and businesses are fleeing high-regulatory and high-tax states like California and New York for Texas and Florida (though sadly many bring their bad policy ideas with them). Perhaps after hemorrhaging workers—and revenue— California and New York will be impelled to embrace reforms. It would be the pressure of the economic competition that would impel them to do so. That's the sort of dynamic that is often missing in integrated European economies—and the EU as a whole.

LOWER TAXES: Though American corporate tax rates remain high—even compared to many European nations—the state is still less onerous and less expensive. According to the OECD, outlays of spending in the United States at the federal, state, and local levels total 38 percent of the GDP. The average, where the larger welfare and entitlement state must be fed, is over 50 percent—led by France, which spends around 57 percent.[66]

The United States already has a budding welfare state, but Europhiles incessantly demand more spending and pretend that the wealthy can foot the bill. Since, inevitably, consumers pay all taxes—either by being charged more for goods and services or slower economic growth—it makes sense that European governments charge household income heavily and directly.

Unlike Americans, who are prone to tax revolts every decade or so, Europeans are quite pliant on the matter. For example, Germany's *second*-highest marginal income tax is 42 percent. It kicks in for a married household earning around $124,000. An

American couple pulling in the same income would pay 22 percent of their income—and wouldn't pay the top marginal tax rate of 37 percent until they earned $612,350.[67] On average, a European making two-thirds their country's average wage, or around $37,000 a year, pays a 50 percent marginal tax on every additional dollar they earn.[68]

In France, the highest tax burdens fall on the middle and working class, with marginal tax rates as high as 70 percent. In France the average worker labors three and a half months longer than an American worker to pay his taxes. The average European workers have to work on average more than two months longer than Americans to pay the taxman.

On top of this, Europe also imposes a value added tax of around 20 percent on almost all consumption. European law *requires* that the standard VAT rate must be at least 15 percent. In some cases, consumption taxes account for up to a quarter of total government revenue in many countries.[69] And as lower-income households allocate a larger percentage of their income to consumption than the wealthy, the tax is regressive.

Since Americans live in relatively low tax rates compared to Europeans, they earn and invest—incentivizing more work and entrepreneurship. More work means more wealth means more production means more investment and more savings. Consequently, Americans are more likely than any other people to save money and invest their money. Nearly 30 percent of Europeans said in 2017 that they have zero savings, and among those who have managed to squirrel away some cash, just under 40 percent have three months' take-home pay banked. Germany is one of the worst nations in this regard, with 34 percent of those answering one poll saying they have no money put away. On the other hand, just 16 percent of Americans say they don't have a penny saved.[70]

AFFORDABLE ENERGY: The United States, unlike Europe, has yet to institute burdensome centralized regulatory schemes to intentionally inflate carbon energy prices in an effort to fight climate change. What has resulted is a boom of natural gas production—which has helped curb carbon emissions by allowing the country to move away from dirtier coal—just as most European nations banned fracking *and* moved away from cleaner nuclear energy production.[71] While consumers and American businesses enjoy plentiful, and relatively inexpensive, energy, low-income Americans also benefit by being able to heat and air-condition their homes and use their cars.

While the United States is near the bottom in energy costs in the industrial world, Germany has the highest global electricity prices per household in the world, followed by Denmark, Portugal, and Belgium—eight of the top ten of the world's priciest energy markets can be found in Europe.[72] When added up, state fees and taxes make up more than 52 percent of the energy cost to the average German consumer.[73] The difference between what Americans pay and what Europeans pay is stark. On average, Americans paid 12.7 c/kWh, while Europeans averaged 26.6 c/kWh.[74]

In the United States, the average federal tax on gas is 18.40 cents per gallon while the average tax on diesel is 24.40 cents per gallon. The average state tax on gas is 29.86 cents per gallon while the average diesel tax is 31.76 cents per gallon.[75] By contrast the average gas tax in the EU is $2.48 and the average tax on diesel is $2.00 per gallon.[76]

It does not look like things will be getting better for the transportation industry anytime soon in the EU. The auto industry makes up 14.6 million jobs within the EU while another 20 million people work in agriculture. Together these two industries account for 25 percent of the EU's overall carbon emissions.[77] To bureaucrats in Brussels, turning carbon emissions into a crisis so that they have an excuse to regulate these two industries even more is an opportunity too good to pass up. If passed, the European Green Deal is sure to regulate the European auto industry out of business if they can't transition to electric cars quickly enough. There is no clear answer to what they are going to do about cows, though.

European Union elites seem to be under the impression that regulatory homogeneity and centralized economic policy is the only way to compete with the United States. This is confusing since the United States is still home to perhaps the most diffused political and economic system in the world, one that allows states to compete for industry, small business, workers, and capital, rather than a conformed federalized infrastructure.

Many progressive Democrats, most notably Elizabeth Warren, have championed "accountable capitalism" based on the European model of corporate governance and trade policy, championing the nationalization of certain sectors of the economy, including health care and energy. Though Europhiles rarely speak of trade-offs, the price for fighting inequality and alleged capitalistic excesses would be diminished economic growth and personal freedom, which would make not only businesses poorer, but families as well.

8

The End of Faith

Liberty cannot be established without morality, nor morality without faith.

—*Alexis de Tocqueville*

There is no starker illustration of the decline of Europe's once-great Christian culture than the fate of its brick-and-mortar institutions. Hundreds of once-glorious churches, some of which took communities decades to erect and became great centers of civic life for hundreds of years, are being shuttered and decommissioned every year due to waning spiritual interest. Many of these beautiful architectural achievements, odes to the culture of Europe, with their dramatic vaulted ceilings and magnificent stained-glass windows, have been converted into concert halls and libraries, but supply is quickly outstripping demand. Christianity is being replaced, quite physically, by secularism, consumerism, multiculturalism, and Islam.

Why does it matter? Americans are far more devout, and yet also freer and wealthier than Europeans. They have larger families and exhibit more concern toward their communities. The relationship between this communal health and conviction isn't an accident.

In places like Arnhem, the Netherlands, the Church of St. Joseph, where only a few decades ago more than a thousand Roman Catholic worshipers would show up on Sunday for mass, was converted to a skate park so that scruffy teenagers could perform toe-flips underneath images of a weeping Mary. As of this writing it lies dormant. Many other houses of worship will follow. It is estimated that around 1,600 Roman Catholic churches and 700 Protestant ones will likely be closed in the Netherlands within the next five to ten years, fated to become grocery stores, gyms, and bars.[1]

The Netherlands is not alone. The century-old Church of Santa Barbara in Llanera, Spain, has been revamped and transformed into a skateboard park called Kaos Temple—and with sponsorship from the energy drink company Red Bull, a celebrated local artist covered the ceilings and walls with modernistic geometric figures. The Martyrs Free Church in Edinburgh, Scotland, once a thriving Lutheran house of worship, is now a bar called Frankenstein, where flimsily dressed bar dancers entertain bachelor party guests. St. Paul's Church in Bristol is a school that trains people for a career in the circus and "physical theatre."

The Church of England has been forced to close around twenty houses of worship every year for the past decade. In Germany, the Roman Catholic Church has closed down more than five hundred churches in the past decade. Around seven hundred of Holland's Protestant churches are expected to be closed in only the next few years.[2] The best chance for a church to survive these days is by becoming a tourist attraction.

It should also be noted that not all churches have the ignominy of being transformed into skate parks or goth dance clubs. In 2018, the Nur Mosque was inaugurated in Hamburg, the second-largest city in Germany, after a Muslim investor bought the former Christian place of worship and donated it to the city's Islamic center. The same fate befell the Dominican church in

Lille and Saint Joseph Church in Paris. The Al Fateh Mosque in Amsterdam, the Sultan Ayoub Mosque, and the Osman Ghazi Mosque in the Netherlands were built in former churches. There is great demand for mosques in Europe. While one might not believe that there is anything wrong with importing large numbers of people whose traditions may not comport with yours, it might be more problematic if their faith is also replacing yours.

There are likely four times as many Muslims praying in mosques in Britain on any given Friday as there are Anglicans in church on Sunday. Islam is the fastest-growing religion in Europe—it may triple in size within three decades.[3] Actually, at this point, it is the *only* growing traditional religion in Europe.

Christianity is all but dead in Europe. In twelve out of twenty-two major European countries polled in a recent Pew study, over half of young adults between the ages of sixteen and twenty-nine did not to identify with any religion or denomination.[4] Nearly 80 percent of young adults in places like Estonia, Sweden, and the Netherlands say they have no religion at all. Germany, a country with one-quarter the population of the United States, is home to ten times as many atheists.[5]

This is not merely a trend in Western Europe, either. The survey of sixteen- to twenty-nine-year-olds found the Czech Republic was the least religious country in Europe, with 91 percent of that age group saying they have no religious affiliation. The six "most Christian" nations are all historically Catholic-majority countries like Ireland, Portugal, and Austria, and in Central Europe like Poland, Lithuania, and Slovenia. And all of them are on the same path, as well. Christianity is no longer the norm in Europe. Like the gods of ancient Rome and Greece, Jesus is nearly a relic of another time.

The decline of Christianity, especially in Western Europe, is likely deeper than the top numbers even suggest. One can look at the growing group of "believers" who are nonreligious—often referred to as "nones." Nearly 50 percent of the British population, for instance, identify as "nones." By 2009, "nones" had already outnumbered all Christian denominations put together in Europe.[6] Even those nonpracticing Christians are more numerous than those who attend services monthly in every Western European country but Italy.[7] Perhaps even Europeans who claim to be nominally Christian do virtually nothing to participate in communal religious life, or in the traditional continuity that makes that life important to a society. In places like France, only 4 percent of practicing Catholics regularly attend Sunday mass.

Like in Germany and the United Kingdom, around a quarter of Americans identify as "nones," but this statistic is misleading. Several important measurements of religious commitment illustrate that even "nones" in the United States are as religious as, or even more religious than, self-identifying Christians in Western Europe. "It is not just a 'nominal' identity devoid of practical importance," Pew researchers noted. "On the contrary, the religious, political and cultural views of non-practicing Christians often differ from those of church-attending Christians and religiously unaffiliated adults." Twenty percent of "nones" in the United States still pray daily, but only 6 percent of Christians in Britain do so. Twice as many American "nones" as German Christians believe in God with absolute certainty.[8]

Americans are also more likely than Europeans to believe in three traits that are commonly associated with Christian notions of God—around 62 percent of Christians in America say that they attend religious services once or twice a month, around three times as many as Europe, but the same percentage believe God "loves all people regardless of their faults," "knows everything that goes on in the world," and "has the power to direct or change everything that goes on in the world." Around 60 percent of Americans say that God is all-powerful, while the median in Western Europe on this question is 25 percent.

The decline wasn't inevitable, nor tied in any way to the rise of prosperity, as so many secular atheists and Europhiles like to contend. Christian self-identification, in fact, had largely remained the same in postwar Europe, and had even risen slightly in recent history, from 75 percent in 1970 to 78.6 percent in 2010—most likely fueled by the end of communism in Eastern and Central Europe. It is only in the past two decades that Christianity in Europe has collapsed by around 75 percent.[9] To put this in context, 84 percent of the world's population identify with a religious group, and they are generally younger and have more children than those who have no religious affiliation. The world, as a whole, is getting more religious.[10]

A Religious People Is a Patriotic People

"It is not just religion that has disappeared from Europe—so has the memory of what religiously ordered, or even a religiously inclined, society was like," Christopher Caldwell observed.[11] The more committed a person is to their faith—the more they go to church—the more likely they are to believe in preserving the Constitution as written, and the more likely they are to believe that America plays a special God-given role in history.

As I mentioned before, the death of religion in Europe alters the moral and societal fabric of community. Religion's effect in America is obvious in the habits of her people. When it comes to patriotism, for example, evangelicals, the most faithful group, also report the most intense feelings toward the nation, with more than two-thirds saying they are "extremely proud" to be an American.[12] They are followed by mainline Protestants (56 percent), minority Christians (49 percent), Catholics (48 percent), and religiously unaffiliated Americans (39 percent).[13]

Americans are still an idealistic people. The Declaration of Independence famously announced, "We hold these truths to be self-evident, that all men are created equal, that they are endowed by *their Creator* with certain unalienable Rights, that among these are Life, Liberty and the pursuit of Happiness." This founding document informs the Constitution, which restricts the state from meddling in our lives because liberty is not bestowed by a king, some social scientist at a think tank, or any governmental body. It is the providential nature of these rights that has made them a bulwark against European-style governance—whether it be fascism, socialism, bureaucratism, or whatever ism comes next. It is the providential nature of these rights—the rights that Europhiles find hopelessly unsophisticated—that has girded the most successful national project mankind has ever attempted.

So rigid, almost religious, is our belief in natural rights—borrowed from secular European thinkers who were functioning under long-held Christian belief systems—that it has survived the vagaries of democracy, elite opinion, rhetorically gifted presidents, transnational pacts, and all sorts of cultural trends. Even the least religious Americans once acted as if these rights were divinely inspired. I write this as an atheist who believes we should act as if liberty is handed down by God himself.

"If God did not exist," Voltaire, the eighteenth-century French Enlightenment philosopher and critic of the church, once wrote, "it would be necessary to invent him." Well, many who latch on to this quip like to think Voltaire was launching a broadside against faith. But the idea that man needs to believe that there is something better and greater than himself—not merely the kings or politicians who rule them—is tethered to the foundational notions of American freedom. Many of the Founders believed faith and liberty were not only compatible but intricately linked. James Madison argued that the Constitution required "sufficient virtue among men for self-government," otherwise, "nothing less than the chains of despotism can restrain them from destroying and devouring one another." John Adams noted, "Our Constitution was made only for a moral and religious People. It is wholly inadequate to the government of any other."[14] Numerous denominations treated the idea of the United States as a heavenly gift, something akin to the new Zion. In the Episcopal Church's national convention in 1786, it resolved that "the Fourth of July shall be observed by this church forever, as a day of Thanksgiving to almighty God for the inestimable blessings of Religious and Civil Liberty vouchsafed to the USA."[15]

On one side of the contemporary cultural divide, the idea that God tells us anything anymore is deemed childish, or worse. To take just one recent example, it's why the hosts of popular shows like *The View* can openly mock people of faith. "I don't know that I want my vice president, um—speaking in tongues and having Jesus speak to him," Sunny Hostin said of the evangelical Mike Pence. To which another host, Joy Behar, responded: "It's one thing to talk to Jesus. It's another thing when Jesus talks to you. That's called mental illness, if I'm not correct, hearing voices." Behar would later apologize—one assumes *The View* has a sizeable audience in the heartland—but the tone of our cultural elites has become dismissive about God having any tangible role in human affairs.

That's why you see many Europhiles react with confusion and contempt when citizens demand adherence to rights that were codified in the eighteenth century. More gratingly to them, however, it is the religious person's *lack* of reverence for progressive ideas and technocratic institutions, a stubborn clinginess to inherent and long-standing rights of religious freedom, for instance, that makes faith not just annoying, but problematic for the Europhile. For those who believe the primary source of human decency and fairness springs forth from The Hague or a government program, the idea that a magical being has conferred the birthright of individual liberty on people is now seen as destructive. Why won't these stubborn people get on board? Catholic legal scholar Robert P. George put it best when he explained that those embracing religious virtue can't be "counted on to trade liberty for protection, for financial or personal security, for comfort" or "for having their problems solved quickly."

Once you view natural rights embedded in the Constitution as merely "man-made" (like, say, a gun control bill or Medicaid expansion), then surely contemporary experts, bureaucrats, can fix them, whittling away what's wrong, and concoct new "rights" whenever something troubles them. When citizens treat the ideals of the Enlightenment as if they are inalienable natural rights rather than a pliable set of guidelines perpetually bending to accommodate the vagaries of contemporary life and secular politics—as has been the case in Europe and increasingly on the American left—they do a better job of protecting individual liberty and fostering stability. Putting man above God as the final arbiter of "rights" is a haughty and perilous enterprise, as witnessed by Europe's tragic recent history.

Religion Doesn't Make Americans More Bigoted and Cultish

One of the aspects of American life most scoffed at by cultured Europhiles is the sincerity and persistence of religious Americans. The nation's most Europhilic president, Barack Obama, once rather infamously noted Americans in the heartland "get bitter (and) cling to guns or religion or antipathy to people who aren't like them or anti-immigrant or anti-trade sentiment as a way to explain their frustrations." One can forgive Obama, who like many Europhiles views American "exceptionalism" as merely a subjective notion rather than an objective truth, since he was always quick to find personal failures in those who did not vote for him. He was, however, wrong about the faithful in America.

To some extent, of course, human beings suffering from the strains of economic downturns and creative destruction—and

Obama made his remarks in 2008, on the heels of a severe recession—will want to lay the blame for their tribulations on outsiders, and thus turn to more isolationist economic policies that they believe will protect their livelihoods and traditions. That's human nature. Religious Americans, though, have shown no more inclination toward "frustration" or bitterness or hatred or clinginess than other people. Probably less.

Now, happiness is a complicated sentiment to measure, but most studies illustrate that Americans are as happy and content as anyone in the world—and this is especially true of its religious citizens. When the Pew Research Center compared the lives of those who actively participated in church congregations and those who did not, the former were found to be more contented by almost every measurement. While religiously active people were more satisfied in their spiritual and family lives, they were also more "civically engaged" in their communities. They were more inclined to vote, join the Rotary Club, or start a book club. Those who are involved in congregations also made healthier lifestyle choices—smoking and drinking less than those without a faith.[16]

In another study, Harvard researchers found that 28 percent of people who attended a religious service weekly were "extremely satisfied" with their lives, compared to only 19.6 percent of people who never attended services. "We think it has something to do with the fact that you meet a group of close friends on a regular basis, together as a group, and participate in certain activities that are meaningful to the group," the head of the study noted. "At the same time, they share a certain social identity, a sense of belonging to a moral faith community. The sense of belonging seems to be the key to the relationship between church attendance and life satisfaction."[17]

The sense of belonging also makes us more charitable. Europhiles love to portray America as a cartoonishly greedy nation driven by a hyperindividualistic and capitalistic nature that exhibits little concern regarding the common good or others around the world. This idea even pervades our own culture.

When asked to describe themselves, 68 percent of Americans came to the word "selfish" as the top negative trait (though higher levels saw themselves as "patriotic" and "honest").[18] "Is Narcissism the Cost of Being an American?" asks scholar Gordon C. Nagayama Hall in *Psychology Today*.[19] "Americans Really ARE Selfish: Study Finds Individuals Are Only Motivated by Self-Serving Acts," says the British tabloid the *Daily Mail*, in an article about a Stanford University study that makes the claim that Americans "aren't driven by a sense of community." Europe's greatest champion in the United States, the *New York Times*' Paul Krugman, who has noted our alleged national obsession with self-interest on countless occasions, says, "The cult of selfishness is killing America."[20]

Europhiles of the Krugman variety, keenly interested in coercing everyday people to participate in large-scale collective actions *they* deem the "common good," often confuse—or ignore—the distinction between self-reliance and selfishness. The most prominent European observer of American habits, Alexis de Tocqueville, remarked that in the American disposition, "every one [is] the best judge of his own interest" and thus "every individual possesses an equal share of power."[21] It is a system that, at its best, encourages and helps facilitate personal achievement, creating a more peaceful society that makes room for free coexistence rather than compelled collectivism. It is undeniable that Americans who embrace this rather confident egalitarian outlook, one that tells them they can achieve anything, seem arrogant and self-obsessed. As the British comedian Ricky Gervais put it, "Americans are brought up to believe they can be the next president of the United States. Brits are told, 'It won't happen for you.'"[22]

By nearly every measure, Americans are more generous with their money and time than Europeans. Indeed, American char-

itable giving exceeds the entire GDP of most European countries. And this is not a matter of giving because we are taxed
at lower rates (though that fact surely incentivizes our giving).
According to the *Almanac of American Philanthropy*, Americans
donate around *seven* times as much as continental Europeans to
charitable causes per capita.[23] Per person, even after adjusting
for differences in household income, Americans donate twice
as much of their income as the Dutch, three times as much as
the French, five times as much as Germans, and ten times that
of Italians.

Then not only are Europeans stingier than Americans in
their personal charity, but they are stingy compared to people in
poor countries like Indonesia, Kenya, and Myanmar, all of which
rank higher per capita in giving of themselves than Europeans.[24]

Only 14 percent of American donations come from foundation grants, and another 5 percent from corporations. More than
80 percent of charitable giving, however, is done by individuals.
And this charity is found wide and deep within society. Every
year, six out of ten households in the United States donate to
a charitable cause, and the typical household gives somewhere
around two to three thousand dollars. The entire nation is altru-
istic, though the more religious the population, the more it gives.

In the United States, the generous can be found among the
wealthy *and* the poor. As a percentage of income, Americans in
lower income brackets are just as generous as the wealthy, and
more generous than most of the middle class. Unsurprisingly, in
absolute dollars the rich give the most, with the top 1 percent of
the income earners donating a third of all charity. And the richest 1.4 percent are responsible for nearly all charitable donations
made at death.[25]

Despite stereotypes about the selfishly rich, the more the nation struggles, the more the wealthy Americans pitch in. During
the coronavirus crisis, for example, the nonprofit arms of major
investment houses saw huge increases in charitable giving from

wealthy Americans.[26] Grants to food banks and other food assistance programs were up 667 percent nationally—800 percent in the hardest-hit mid-Atlantic states. Middle- and working-class people continued to give to their local charities, even as they struggled—one report tallied over 750,000 transactions to more than 100,000 charities in the first three months.[27]

One often hears critics of the United States arguing that charity can be given to religious causes, unlike sophisticated European efforts. This is also a myth. The three most popular causes Americans contribute to are household basic social services, "combined purpose" charitable organizations like United Way or Catholic Charities—which help the poor—and health care.[28]

Americans are also quick to respond to emergencies—both here and abroad. After the Katrina and Rita hurricanes hit the Gulf Coast in 2005, Americans donated $6.47 billion to the cause within weeks. When the 2004 Indian Ocean earthquake and tsunami hit, 25 percent of American households donated to the relief efforts through their churches, schools, and other newly formed charities, raising $2.78 billion within weeks. Corporations donated another $340 million and foundations another $40 million.[29] When a magnitude 7 earthquake devastated Haiti's capital of Port-au-Prince, killing hundreds of thousands of people, Americans donated some $519 million within weeks. There is no other nation that does this kind of instantaneous and worldwide giving.

This disparity between the United States and Europe extends to volunteering with one's time, an undervalued method of charity. In 2019, 63 million Americans donated by volunteering their time and talents to charitable organizations.[30] From 2009 to 2018, researchers asked respondents around the world if in addition to donating money they had done either of the following in the last month: helped a stranger or someone they didn't know who needed help or volunteered their time to an organization. The United States of America had occupied first place for more than a decade.[31]

WHY DO WE SEE THIS disparity? Surely Europeans aren't innately selfish. The biggest predictor of charitableness is religious belief. Among those Americans who self-identify as religious, 65 percent give to charity regularly. Religious Americans are also far more likely to give to nonreligious charities—around 75 percent of people who regularly attend religious services gave to congregations, and 60 percent gave to religious charities or nonreligious ones. By comparison, fewer than half of people who said they didn't attend faith services regularly supported any charity, even a secular charitable cause.[32]

Now more than 40 percent of secular Americans give to charity, still better than most European nations. A culture and the habits formed over two hundred years of American life have created a society that both values and leans heavily on charitable causes. This is driven by the pressures of being within groups that treat charity as a duty.

Second, the American disposition is to rely far more on the communal and local help than Europeans, who rely on government to do their charity for them. The internet has made Americans even more charitable over the years. For example, as riots swept through Minneapolis after the killing of George Floyd in the summer of 2020, the Scores Sports Bar was looted and vandalized, and ultimately destroyed by rioters. The owners, a local firefighter named Korboi "KB" Balla and his wife, Twyana, had poured their life savings into the project, which hadn't even opened its doors because of the coronavirus pandemic. The couple had no insurance. No way to save their livelihood. Twyana began posting pictures of the bar on her Facebook page, noting that the business was now little more than a pile of bricks.

That Friday, a desperate Balla launched a GoFundMe campaign for his rebuilding efforts. By Sunday afternoon the couple had raised $873,000.[33] There are tons of similar stories to be told over the years. This kind of grassroots charitable effort might be possible on a larger scale because of digital and information technology, but its traditions are firmly embedded in American cultural habits going back to the first Puritan communities of New England. American historical self-reliance, still ingrained in our DNA, was both born of necessity and propelled by a new American virtue. The first settlers left behind central governments and dominant churches and were left to deal with problems locally.

Tocqueville noted in the 1830s that unlike the Europeans, Americans would often spontaneously cluster into local associations, including philanthropic ones, to fix their problems. It is almost as if he was writing about GoFundMe campaigns:

> Americans of all ages, all conditions, all minds constantly unite. Not only do they have commercial and industrial associations in which all take part, but they also have a thousand other kinds: religious, moral, grave, futile, very general and very particular, immense and very small; Americans use associations to give fetes, to found seminaries, to build inns, to raise churches, to distribute books, to send missionaries to the antipodes; in this manner they create hospitals, prisons, schools. . . . I often admired the infinite art with which the inhabitants of the United States managed to fix a common goal to the efforts of many men and to get them to advance to it freely.

Then there is the entrepreneurial impulse in Americans that generates new wealth that is paired with a performance-based ethic that makes even the most-wealthy American feel an obligation to their neighbors. Europeans will, no doubt, argue that they already give charity in high taxes that fund big social safety nets. The data shows, however, that in overall spending, there isn't much difference between the United States and other developed nations—each redistributing 20 percent of GDP. Once added in with the massive amount of charity, there is no comparing American generosity—the only difference is that most of ours is not a state obligation.

American Separation of Church and State Has No Equivalent in Europe

It might seem ironic to Europhiles that Americans have transposed their orthodoxy about God to their notions about governance, since the Founders had famously erected a wall of separation between the two. But it is exactly this arrangement that allows a unifying system to make space for faiths to coexist peacefully. It was as Madison argued: "The purpose of separation of church and state is to keep forever from these shores the ceaseless strife that has soaked the soil of Europe in blood for centuries."[34] His goal—the cessation of religious conflict rife in Europe at the time—has for the large part been averted in the United States. It is worth remembering that until Christianity began petering out on the continent, there were still religious conflicts in places like the Balkans and Ireland. For centuries, people of different faiths have found it virtually impossible to live not only with each other, but near each other, in Europe.

Here in America the state doesn't endorse or support or favor any particular denomination or prop up any particular church. In countries where faith is dying, like Austria, Denmark, Finland, Germany, Sweden, and Switzerland, citizens still pay "church taxes" to keep religious institutions afloat. In Denmark and Greece there are still official state religions (Sweden severed official ties in 2000). In places like Ireland, Greece, Poland, Germany, and Slovakia, religion is specifically mentioned in their legal structures. In Great Britain there are two state churches:

the Anglican Church of England and the Presbyterian Church of Scotland. In many of these situations the church and politics have been intertwined in ways that have helped undermine faith. Moreover, state-funded churches, like state-funded anything, become lethargic and ineffective.

In many ways, the United States looks to be on a similar trajectory to Europe. When the *Wall Street Journal* and NBC News asked hundreds of young Americans in 1998 what values were important to them, by wide margins they said hard work, patriotism, commitment to religion, and having children. These four values had dominated polling since the question was first posed. When asked the same question in 2019, the number of those who valued patriotism and religion most had fallen by 20 points.[35] Whether we like it or not, the fates of American patriotism and faith have always been entwined. We can see what happens when a civilization forgets its foundational moral beliefs. It is likely that once we follow Europe's lead, our near-religious adherence to liberal values will begin to putrefy as well.

There are, of course, downsides to *blind* faith. The question is, who is practicing it in the United States these days? Those wedded to top-down, state-run solutions as the answer to all the nation's tribulations, or those who believe that millennia of philosophy and tradition, and two centuries of relative stability, should not be dispensed with so easily?

Nor can one force people to be religious, of course. There is no government program that can impel people to go to church and believe in the Lord Almighty. We can, despite the best efforts of Europhiles, protect religious freedom and institutions that make faith matter in the United States. As religion continues to decline in the West, the social bonds of faith communities that used to tie social communities together begin to decay. Europe also gives us an example of what happens when you can't find any worthwhile values to replace the old ones. The fascism and communism that dominated European life in the second half of the twentieth century were a shot at replacing faith. We all know how that turned out. Today Europhiles advance a utilitarian credo that is devoid of idealism or fidelity to tradition that is reminiscent of ways they lost faith in the past.

"In the old world, personal autocracies, except for perhaps brief periods, had been limited, or at least qualified, by other forces in society," the historian Paul Johnson wrote about the rise of communism in the early twentieth century, "a church, an aristocracy, an urban bourgeoisie, ancient charters and courts and assemblies. And there was too the notion of an external, restraining force, in the idea of a Deity, or natural law, or some absolute system of morality." Secular society, led by Europe, is slowly finding itself without these restrictions on the state. It is not, of course, to say that European commissioners are like the commissars of the Soviet Union. But a moral slippery slope exists in a society that's lost its moral lodestar.

9

Thought Police

My own opinion is enough for me, and I claim the right to have it defended against any consensus, any majority, anywhere, any place, any time.

—Christopher Hitchens

In the fall of 2020, the *New York Times Magazine* published a sprawling 8,600-word essay by the writer Emily Bazelon, arguing that it was time for the United States to rethink its zealous adherence to the First Amendment.[1] "It's an article of faith in the United States that more speech is better and that the government should regulate it as little as possible," Bazelon noted. "But increasingly, scholars of constitutional law, as well as social scientists, are beginning to question the way we have come to think about the First Amendment's guarantee of free speech. They think our formulations are simplistic—and especially inadequate for our era."

Bazelon went on to argue that scholars have been making the case for "something that may seem unsettling to Americans: that perhaps our way of thinking about free speech is not the best way. At the very least, we should understand that it isn't the only way. Other democracies, in Europe and elsewhere, have taken a different approach. Despite more regulations on speech, these countries remain democratic."

Do they? Are nations that do not allow open debate truly "democratic"? Or are they merely majoritarian? The ability of Americans to express themselves without ever worrying about the state is unique in history, and even in the world today. The amendment to the Constitution that offers them this unqualified protection is an individual right that protects us *from* the state, rather than allowing us to enjoy it under the state's discretion. "Congress shall make no law . . . abridging the freedom of speech," it says. This is still a radical idea.

Everyone else, including Europe, does it the "other way." The European Union ostensibly protects free speech in Article 10 of its Convention of Human Rights. You can tell immediately that the protection won't be particularly useful because it's two paragraphs long. The First Amendment, in contrast, ensures freedoms of religion, speech, press, petition, and assembly in a single, highly serviceable (or, as some Europhiles might say, "simplistic") sentence.

Article 10 of the European document begins well enough, promising: "Everyone has the right to freedom of expression. This right shall include freedom to hold opinions and to receive and impart information and ideas without interference by public authority and regardless of frontiers. . . ." But the Europeans don't really mean it, as the second paragraph makes clear:

> The exercise of these freedoms, since it carries with it duties and responsibilities, may be subject to such formalities, conditions, restrictions or penalties as are prescribed by law and are necessary in a democratic society, in the interests of national security, territorial disorder or crime, for the protection of health or morals, for the protection of the reputation or rights of others, for preventing the disclosure of information received in confidence, or for maintaining the authority and impartiality of the judiciary.

Free speech in Europe is contingent on the vagaries, conditions, and restrictions connected to concerns over "national security," "territorial disorder," "crime," and protections of "health
or morals" of the state—which are all flexible notions that em-
power government to impose arbitrary limits on expression as
long as the majority of the European Union approves. Article 10
is worse than useless, in fact, because it creates the false sense that
a legitimate, enduring liberty can exist in Europe under these
malleable notions.

And sadly, it's not just American "scholars of constitutional
law" and "social scientists" who advocate that we adopt European speech restrictions, but high-profile television personalities
with law degrees, like CNN's anchor Chris Cuomo, who not
long ago claimed that "hate speech is excluded from protection"
under the First Amendment.[2] It is members of the American Bar
Foundation like Laura Beth Nielsen, who argues in major newspapers like the *Los Angeles Times* that citizens should be barred
from expressing offensive words in the public square.[3] Nielsen
says "hate speech" should be banned because it has "been linked
to cigarette smoking, high blood pressure, anxiety, depression
and post-traumatic stress disorder, and requires complex coping strategies." One of the many problems with this argument
is that European nations have had hate speech laws for decades,
and yet they smoke more[4] and have higher levels of suicide and
depression.[5]

Journalist Richard Stengel, a former managing editor of the
once-powerful *Time* magazine, and now a member of the Joe
Biden administration, argued in the *Washington Post* that the
government should begin policing speech because the United
Nations diplomatic corps simply can't comprehend why we allow
unfettered speech. "Even the most sophisticated Arab diplomats
that I dealt with did not understand why the First Amendment
allows someone to burn a Koran," Stengel recollected.[6] Even the
most sophisticated Arab diplomats are working for theocratic

states that not only fail to protect basic civil liberties but also occasionally behead, hang, and flog people for crimes against the Koran.

What Stengel should have told his sophisticated Arab friends is that free speech is a neutral principle, and that burning a Koran, like burning an American flag, is a political statement. What he should have told his diplomat friends is that the First Amendment doesn't "let" us do those things; it protects our inherent right to express ourselves in any manner we please.

Stengel, and other Europhiles, also worried that unregulated discourse of American life was responsible for allowing Moscow "to slip its destructive ideas into our media ecosystem." Distressed at Donald Trump's presidency, many Democrats accused Vladimir Putin of benefiting from our system of open speech. Perhaps he did. Only a few months before Stengel's piece, the Duma had passed a law criminalizing speech that "disrespects" Russian society.[7] Adopting Putin-like speech restrictions to stop people like Putin would be a weird way of illustrating how much you love American values.

Nearly every censor in the history of mankind—including the Europhiles and Putin—has argued that speech should be curbed to balance out some existential threat. And nearly every censor in history, sooner or later, expands the definition of "harm" to undercut the rights of their political opponents.

We can already get a glimpse of how this works by watching groups like the Southern Poverty Law Center, for years the gold standard for identifying racist organizations, turn into a partisan outfit that regularly accuses mainstream conservative civil rights groups they disagree with on policy of perpetuating "hate."

Even the American Civil Liberties Union, an organization that once so rigidly adhered to the principles of the Constitution that it famously defended the right of a neo-Nazi group to march through the Jewish-heavy Chicago suburb of Skokie, now explicitly endorsed the European view that free speech should be curbed because it can hurt "marginalized" groups. "Speech that denigrates such groups can inflict serious harms and is intended to and often will impede progress toward equality," the ACLU declares in new guidelines governing case selection, "Conflicts Between Competing Values or Priorities."

This kind of qualified view of expression has crept into places like the U.S. Patent and Trademark Office, which argued that "hate speech" was not protected by the Constitution, after it refused to register the inflammatorily named band the Slants a trademark on the ground that it might be demeaning to Asian Americans. (The band, incidentally, consisted of Asian Americans.)[8] The Supreme Court took the side of the band, but the growing call to view speech as a competing value rather than an inherent right is growing.

Throughout history, authoritarians have made the claim that liberty should be subdued because of the uniqueness of the perilous moment society faces. Despite the assertions of Bazelon and her experts, the First Amendment is not "especially inadequate for our era." We are now experiencing fewer wars and less violence than perhaps at any time in human history. Even if this weren't the case, as we'll see, regulations on speech haven't made Europeans any safer. They haven't changed human nature. With all its laws regulating speech, hateful ideologies have a far longer tradition, and more traction today, in European nations than they do in the United States, where a person can say whatever they like.

Europeans, as history unfailingly demonstrates, have far greater deference to authority and to the state than Americans. And perhaps no people in Europe have shown more submissiveness to government power than the Germans, who are now on the forefront of another misguided attempt to undermine free expression at home and abroad.

Whereas once Germany enacted strict laws banning Nazi symbols and Holocaust denial—*Volksverhetzung* it now prohibits any kind of hate speech or incitement, both of which are constantly evolving concepts. Citizens can be imprisoned for up to five years and face huge fines for breaking these laws. This works to undermine open discourse in ways small and large.

Germans, it seems, believe restrictions on expression will temper the ugly nationalistic inclinations that tend to pop up. The postwar Austria and Germany justifications for controlling speech have changed somewhat, but the principle remains the same: There was widespread belief that laws against Holocaust denial and hate speech should, in part, be instituted to stop fascist movements from growing and destabilizing governments and societal order. But if the only way to stamp out illiberalism is through authoritarian and illiberal means, maybe it's not the speech that's the problem but underlying societal morals and values.

Are we susceptible to the same ugly inclinations? Intellectuals who advocate for speech restriction in the United States will often bring up Karl Loewenstein, the German Jewish intellectual who traveled to America in the late 1930s to make the case that some speech codes were necessary to save democracies from the menace of fascism. Loewenstein, often held up as a prophet of the coming implosion of Europe, argued then, as do Europhiles like Bazelon today, that "legislative limitations of abstract notions of liberty" were needed to control man's most nefarious instincts.[9] Then, as today, many technocrats believed laws restricting dehumanizing expression would help avert threatening results. But Loewenstein was mistaken in two important ways:

First, the United States did not fall to fascism nor to communism, even though it never engaged in any systemic regulation of speech (it is true that once war broke out, the FDR administration did put considerable pressure on media to shut down dissenting voices). Americans would later act as if there was unanimity in its opposition to Hitler, but it was not so. Less than six months after the attacks on *Kristallnacht*, a Nazi rally took place at Madison Square Garden, organized by the German American Bund, which twenty thousand people openly attended to hear fascist speakers. There were a number of radio talk show hosts, most famously the popular Charles Coughlin, who spent years praising European fascism and spreading hateful ideas about immigrants and Jews. Those perceptions would change once Americans learned more about the crimes and aims of the Third Reich.

It is precisely that we do not have "abstract notions of liberty," but a constitution with a quite strict definition of them, woven into the social fabric of the country, in good and bad times, that helps us avert a national corrosion of principles. The relentless attack by Europhiles on the ideals that gird that stability and idealism makes it far likelier for authoritarianism to gain a foothold. It's undeniable that Americans have an imperfect history when it comes to speech—and much else   but it is this very optimism regarding liberty that helped propel the national effort to defeat fascism.

Second, Loewenstein was also wrong about Europe, where hate speech laws existed and failed to stem the tide of European fascism—in fact, in some marginal ways these laws may have buttressed its rise. As Flemming Rose, the editor of *Jyllands-Posten*, the Danish newspaper that published the Muhammad cartoons in defense of free expression, told *The New Yorker* in 2015, speech restrictions didn't even work in pre-war Germany:

> I found that, contrary to what most people think, Weimar Germany did have hate-speech laws, and they were applied quite frequently. The assertion that Nazi propaganda played a significant role in mobilizing anti-Jewish sentiment is, of course, irrefutable. But to claim that the Holocaust could have been prevented if only anti-Semitic speech and Nazi propaganda had been banned has little basis in reality. Leading Nazis such as Joseph Goebbels, Theodor Fritsch, and Julius Streicher were all prosecuted for anti-Semitic speech. Streicher served two

prison sentences. Rather than deterring the Nazis and countering anti-Semitism, the many court cases served as effective public-relations machinery, affording Streicher the kind of attention he would never have found in a climate of a free and open debate. In the years from 1923 to 1933, *Der Stürmer* [Streicher's newspaper] was either confiscated or editors taken to court on no fewer than thirty-six occasions. The more charges Streicher faced, the greater became the admiration of his supporters. The courts became an important platform for Streicher's campaign against the Jews.[10]

Speech restrictions both undermine debate and make martyrs of the worst elements of society. This is what Europeans are doing today, in both small and large ways.

Fake News

None of this even takes into account mission creep. In Germany, laws that begin with the aim of shutting down Nazis end by turning half-literate cartoonists working in their basements into martyrs. Not long ago, police raided the homes of at least thirty-six people accused of posting "illegal content" online.[11] Most of the offending speech was indeed ugly, but also quite puerile. The German government created a "Streisand effect," a social phenomenon that occurs when individuals or groups try to hide or censor speech; it often has the unintended consequence of publicizing that information. "The still high incidence of punishable hate posting shows a need for police action," Holger Münch, president of the Federal Criminal Police Office, said at the time. "Our free society must not allow a climate of fear, threat, criminal violence and violence either on the street or on the internet."

Which creates a bigger climate of fear in society, one wonders: unknown internet trolls without any power spreading ugly sentiment among a few hundred followers on social media, or the German police empowered to break down doors of citizens for speech crimes?

The difficulties with allowing humorless bureaucrats to run operations dictating expression were on display after a popular German magazine, *Titanic*, sent out a tweet mocking German police for trying "to appease the barbaric, Muslim, rapist hordes of men" because they communicated in Arabic. The account was immediately suspended at the behest of the state. Prosecutors opened an investigation into whether their words amounted to incitement or hatred. As it turned out, the satirical magazine was mocking a politician, Beatrix von Storch, a member of the right wing Alternative for Germany.[12] When an American tech giant is banning German political satire at the behest of the government in Berlin, it tells us something is wrong.

When an ugly anti-Semitic flier was being passed around in Cologne, in an effort to bring awareness to the situation, the Jewish community shared it on Twitter. The mayor of Cologne retweeted it. Both were prosecuted under hate speech laws by the government.[13]

Thousands of Germans are convicted and fined for personally insulting someone in public every year.[14] In 2020, German lawmakers made destruction of foreign state flags—including those of authoritarian states—or the denigration of national anthems punishable by up to three years in prison.[15] It wasn't until 2017 that a law barring the insulting of foreign leaders was finally repealed—and only because it opened up the prospects of foreign dictators shutting down domestic speech, a practice on which the German government holds a monopoly.[16] Namely, Turkish strongman President Recep Tayyip Erdoğan. Unable to arrest journalists who mock and criticize him, Erdoğan spends a lot of time using European laws to try to censor them.

As of this writing, the Stockholm Center for Freedom lists 165 journalists who have been arrested in Turkey; 88 are serving their convictions, and another 167 are wanted.[17] Two Turkish journalists face possible life sentences because they are alleged to have sent "subliminal messages" on television encouraging a government coup.[18]

Turkey, of course, is waiting for its accession into the European Union. It may never happen, but if it does, Erdoğan would simply be able to rely on constricting EU speech regulations to clamp down on criticism. It is a good reminder of how easy illiberal laws founded on good intentions can be appropriated by illiberal forces with bad ones. And how quickly internalizing ideas about censorship can grow into a societal norm.

In 2008, Germany pressured the European Union to pass a decision aimed at "fighting racism and xenophobia," which compelled every member state to institute tougher hate speech legislation and criminalizing certain speech. All twenty-seven nations have since incorporated such restrictions into their national legislation. Any statement that an individual might perceive as insulting to a group to which he belongs becomes punishable by law. And since it is virtually impossible to track and root out all hateful thoughts, much less tamp down on thought crimes, Germany and other European powers have begun to impel businesses to do it for them.

Germany imposes fines on social media companies of 50 million euros for failing to delete online "hate speech" or defamatory "fake news" within twenty-four hours of being notified.[19] Such laws are tantamount to the state censoring speech.

France soon moved to follow Germany's lead, passing its own law giving internet companies like Facebook, Google, and Twitter only twenty-four hours to remove "hateful" speech or face fines of $1.4 million per violation—charges that would quickly add up to hundreds of millions of dollars.[20] France, ostensibly the protector of European liberal order, has long acquiesced to censorship using a number of rationales we hear from Europhiles in the United States. When speaking in front of the Congress in 2018, French president Emmanuel Macron called for a global war against "fake news," declaring that "democracy is about true choices and rational decisions. The corruption of information is an attempt to corrode the very spirit of our democracies."[21]

The speech was widely applauded by American elites, who've become paranoid that open discourse corrodes "democracy." Of course, limiting speech and threatening companies that allow for it neither offers "true choices" nor allows for "rational decisions." There is no universal definition of "fake news," any more than there is a universal definition for "hate speech." Over the years many stories deemed "fake news" by those in power including by President Trump and the Democratic Party's congressional leaders—have turned out to be quite real and important. Allowing those with the most power to define what we see and hear and define what is important portends disaster.

Apparently, there is no global definition for "democracy," either, because the French parliament passed a law that allows the state national broadcasting agency to suspend the licenses of television channels it deems irresponsible. It empowers judges to determine the veracity of news and order media to take down "fake news," and shut down access to websites and social media accounts that spread stories it deems untrustworthy. "Only authoritarian regimes try to control what the truth is," said senior conservative senator Bruno Retailleau. Freedom of expression carries risks, but that's better "than the temptation to control minds," he went on to note in his scathing speech.[22]

Indeed, forcing major companies into censoring free expression has undermined the ability of the most democratized engine of free speech ever invented by man, the internet. Companies that face hundreds of millions in fines for allowing impertinent speech to remain on its platform will become overly cautious and begin shying away from allowing any kind of contentious debate and political speech, creating an environment that undercuts healthy interactions, independent reporting, and oversight by stemming the open flow of information.

We saw as much when Twitter blocked a French government voter registration campaign on the grounds that the country's new internet regulations are too difficult to obey, so the platform tried to be entirely clear of French political content.[23]

These kinds of laws also engender corruption. When Alexandre Benalla, Macron's security officer and deputy chief of staff, was caught on camera beating up protesters in Paris in May 2018, he was fired from his job. Later, it was reported that despite the Macron administration's public distancing from Benalla, he retained his diplomatic passport and continued to speak for the president. *Le Monde*, France's largest newspaper, discovered that, before officially distancing itself from the wayward security aide, the president's allies had illegally obtained a police video of Benalla's attack on protesters and spliced unrelated violence into those videos and spread it through a number of anonymous Twitter accounts in an effort to make the aide appear justified in his attack. They did this during an election.

No government judges were there to take it down. No censor saw it as an intrusion into the election. The normal person is barred from making his own discerning choice about news, but government can always manipulate censorship laws. Maybe not the one in power today. But maybe the next one. Which is why Americans have defined ideas about rights, not "abstract notions of liberty."

Digital Control

The attempt to control speech has manifested in numerous corrosive ways, including the codification of do-it-yourself censorship—another idea Europe has tried to export.

In 2014, the European Court of Justice concocted a modern "right to be forgotten," allowing citizens to petition search engines like Google and Yahoo!, forcing them to remove articles from their search results for a wide variety of reasons. Cloaked in fears over privacy, nearly a million individuals have requested to change and revise history and erase events. As of this writing, Google has received nearly a million requests to delete a total of 3.3 million URLs. The search engine giant has granted the requests approximately 55 percent of the time.[24]

As is often the case, regulations create more hurdles for smaller companies and individuals than they do for the wealthy and big corporations. Something like 20 percent of all specific requests came from only 1 percent of the requesters—many of them "reputation management services" and law firms working for the well heeled. Here are a few examples of pieces that were either targeted or removed from the internet by Google at the behest of the European Union:

- A story about a schizophrenic patient who was found guilty of murdering a man after escaping from a mental hospital.[25]

- An article about a British politician seeking reelection who wanted to delete mentions of his past corrupt behavior in office.[26]

- Two men, Wolfgang Werlé and Manfred Lauber, who murdered a German actor in 1990, sued Wikipedia to remove mention of their crime as they had already paid their debt to society.[27] (German's highest court has already granted other murderers their privacy.[28])

- Numerous doctors have asked for negative reviews from patients to be removed.

- Google was forced to remove seven articles that reported on a person's aiding and abetting an attempted terrorist attack. The tech giant was also forced to remove a story about a former minor's murder of "a close family member."[29]

- A Belgian newspaper was forced to scrape its archives of a 1994 article about a doctor's drunk driving in which he killed two people.[30]

- A former bank clerk wanted articles removed about a conviction for stealing money from elderly customers' bank accounts.[31]

- A pedophile convicted of possession of child sexual abuse imagery had links to pages about his conviction removed.[32]

"Right to be forgotten" laws in the digital age are nothing but an Orwellian attempt to revise history. Alas, like most European ideas, it is gaining favor among Americans. A number of progressive groups support the idea of government monitoring internet speech on numerous levels.[33] And regrettably, according to a Pew poll, a large majority of Americans support keeping information about themselves outside the purview of online searches. Given the option, 74 percent of Americans say it is more important to be able to "keep things about themselves from being searchable online," while 23 percent say it is more important to be able to "discover potentially useful information about others."[34]

As with many issues, the problems of the reality will often undercut the theoretical. New York State politicians introduced a right-to-be-forgotten bill in 2017 that would have required the removal of any items judged by bureaucrats to be "inaccurate," "irrelevant," "inadequate," "excessive," or "no longer material to current public debate or discourse," without "any disclaimer [or] takedown notice." Failure to comply would make the search engines or journalistic institutions liable for statutory damages of $250 for every offense, plus attorney's fees. Imagine the insanity of allowing the state or even individuals to remove information that is alleged to be no longer "current public debate or discourse."

It would have allowed politicians and CEOs and criminals to retroactively diminish the ability of Americans to learn about their histories. We have no idea what kind of debate, or what history, will be relevant tomorrow. And yet this idea is almost surely going to be revived by American Europhiles as soon as the court is more willing to entertain such intrusions. Allowing states to force companies to revise history, as they do in Europe, would allow the powerful to stop the flow of open information in a free society.

Other than Europhiles themselves, perhaps the most precarious threat to freedom of online expression in the United States is the European Union itself. Because while tyrannical regimes like China crush free speech for its own people, it is the Europeans who have attempted to force U.S. companies to adopt their limitations on speech globally, by suing tech companies in international courts. France, for instance, has on numerous occasions tried to impose the European Union's "right to be forgotten" rules on the entire world by compelling American tech giants to adopt censorship regulations.[35]

Google, appropriately, has argued that such an obligation could easily be abused by authoritarian governments, including those in European nations like Turkey and Russia, to attempt to cover up human rights abuses and control news output. World leaders and bad actors could sue social media companies in European courts and require them to remove content that was critical of their leadership. In the United States, the "right to be forgotten" is a clear violation of the First Amendment. Now whether Google actually cares about authoritarianism is up for debate. The fact that authoritarian governments would benefit from such regulations might be a clue that the regulations themselves are highly problematic.

Still, there are many such cases. One of the most well known concerned a former Green member of the European Parliament from Austria, Eva Glawischnig-Piesczek. The European Union forced Facebook to remove critical comments about her, but more, the Court of Justice advocate argued that the EU be granted the right to suppress free speech globally. As the European Union's tech companies, he noted, "do not regulate the territorial scope of an obligation to remove information disseminated via a social network platform, it does not preclude a host provider from being ordered to remove such information worldwide."[36] Or in other words, Austrian courts wanted to compel a massive social media platform to ban speech that was critical of hypersensitive Glawischnig-Piesczek in the United States, as well.

It should also be noted that Europe already has far stricter laws governing slander and defamation than the United States. They have even less need for expurgation of speech. Nearly twenty European Union nations have criminal "insult laws" on the books, and journalists can still be charged under criminal defamation. Currently, journalists in Italy can face imprisonment for up to three years for defamation, and the penalties get worse if the statement is directed at a political, administrative, or judicial figure.

In six European Union member states, defaming a public official is more severely punishable than defaming a private citizen. The opposite is true in the United States, where celebrities and political figures have a tough road in trying to shut down or intimidate their critics.

The words and ideas that governments regard as "hateful" may well be nothing but uncomfortable thoughts used in political discourse. Neither in Europe nor anywhere else for that matter has there been an authentic or lasting definition of "hate speech."

Now, obviously, there are universally hateful things to say. Some taboos on speech are governed by organic ways and stigma, but government-induced taboos are dangerous because they undermine free discourse. It shouldn't need to be said that innocuous and uncontroversial speech doesn't require defending. Once Europe normalizes the idea that offensive speech is illegal, it will have chipped away at one of the most imperative liberal values in an irreparable way. The importance of speech has been knocked down. In the hierarchy of important values in the guise of protecting the weak and promoting justice, it does neither.

We simply can't trust politicians who are often ruled by the caprices of the mob, or of their own power, to define our values when it comes to speech. One wonders if the title of this book could be considered hateful in Europe. It is the sensitivities of those in power that will always win out. In the world, not only is it difficult to define bad speech, it is almost impossible to control it.

In the United Kingdom, where at various times "insulting" speech has also been defined as hate speech, twenty-one-year-olds from Oxford University were being arrested by police for making juvenile "homophobic comments" like, "Excuse me, do you realize your horse is gay?"[37] and sixteen-year-olds are prosecuted for holding up a placard with the words "Scientology is a dangerous cult."[38] In 2018, British police opened investigations into people for tweets that criticized gender reassignment surgeries for children.[39]

In England, police departments are increasingly asking the public to report on neighbors, not merely over "hate incidents" motivated by prejudice or hostility but ones that might be "perceived to be so."[40] Criminal investigation into allegedly hateful words can be launched without any evidence other than the fact that someone's feelings were hurt. In the United Kingdom "expressions of racial hatred, which is defined as aversion against a group of persons by reason of the group's colour, race, nationality (including citizenship) or ethnic or national origins," are illegal.

From 2014, when Hate Crime Operational Guidelines began allowing police to keep an eye out for "non-criminal hate incidents," to 2019, the British police compiled 119,934 incidents. The guidelines allowed the authorities to collect the names and speech incidents deemed motivated by hostility, "irrespective of whether there is any evidence to identify the hate element." Without any due process, without the ability to face one's accuser or to offer contravening or dispositive evidence—as if anyone in a free nation should have to do such a thing, anyway—the police logged those non-crimes into a database that could often be seen by potential employers doing background checks.[41] The authorities in Britain, whose traditions of free expression we adopted centuries ago, keep lists of people who say mean things.

In an interview discussing the Black Lives Matter movement in the summer of 2020, the highly regarded bestselling British historian David Starkey told popular podcaster Darren Grimes, "Slavery was not genocide, otherwise there wouldn't be so many damn blacks in Africa or in Britain, would there? You know, an awful lot of them survived."

Whether slavery is genocide or not, this was a deplorable way to talk about human beings. Starkey immediately apologized after the interview, though it did not save his career. Starkey had spent decades publishing and writing without any hint of racism, but with this one comment on a podcast, his publisher immediately dropped him. He was forced to resign his honorary fellowship at Fitzwilliam College at Cambridge. Canterbury Christ Church University fired him as a visiting professor. The seventy-five-year-old's career was finished.[42]

Perhaps Starkey deserved this ignominious fate; perhaps he deserved another chance. Whatever the case, what happened next was far worse, with the British authorities chilling speech. Not only was Starkey investigated by the Metropolitan Police for his slavery comments—in the end, nothing but an opinion—the twenty-seven-year-old Grimes was also investigated for merely publishing the interview on his YouTube channel as a possible violation of the 1986 Public Order Act's prohibition on stirring up "racial hatred."

Unnerving and unpopular topics and arguments are a mainstay of healthy public discourse. They help societies either come to terms or dispense with ideas. It is obvious, of course, that widely popular opinions and innocuous words don't really need any protections. Not long ago, the legalization of gay marriage in the United States would have been considered an obscure and offensive position to the majority of Americans. Today the position is the law and the norm. "Hate speech" is often subjective, and laws dictating what we can say are abused by those in power to chill speech. That is why treating free expression as a neutral principle is so vital in maintaining the liberal order.

Treating adults as children is a corrosive element of European society. In Britain, the Committee of Advertising Practice is tasked with censoring ads that chafe against whatever fashionable grievance culture is pumping out. They will ban, among others, commercials in which family members "create a mess, while a woman has sole responsibility for cleaning it up," ones that suggest "an activity is inappropriate for a girl because it is stereotypically associated with boys, or vice versa," and ones in which a man "tries and fails to perform simple parental or household tasks." If you believe this kind of thing is the bailiwick of the state, it's unlikely you have much use for the Constitution.

The Real Hate Speech

Bazelon is right about one thing: When compared to the rest of the world, the United States has an exceptionally high bar for censoring speech—even if we sometimes fall short. One of the most famous cases in this regard was a 1969 U.S. Supreme Court decision reversing the conviction of Clarence Brandenburg, who gave an incendiary speech at a Ku Klux Klan rally. Only speech that incites "imminent lawless action" can be shut down. This has nothing to do with "hate."

Nor does it, as many Europhiles—and some Europeans—like to claim, have anything to do with shouting "fire" in a crowded theater. This infuriating analogy, issued by Oliver Wendell Holmes in *Schenck v. United States* and subsequently repeated by untold thousands of censorship apologists, was at the heart of one of the most egregious violations of free expression in American history. The unanimous *Schenck* decision allowed the Wilson administration to throw antiwar socialists, some of whom had fled czarist Russia and other European oppression, into prison for violating the Espionage Act of 1917. The alleged "harm" of these antiwar activists—who were, in every sense, engaging in legitimate political expression—was undermining recruitment efforts for the war raging in Europe. Whether the United States should have joined World War I is still being rigorously debated. That it has become the guiding light for Europhiles on speech restrictions is telling on many levels.

In my experience, most Europeans don't fully grasp the American concept of neutral principles. They simply see no upside in believing that hateful, even evil, speech should be protected as a democratic value. In almost every poll, Europeans will tell you that free expression is an important right for them, but they have a vastly different understanding of what it entails.

When Pew specifically asked people in six major European Union nations if they would approve of censoring speech that minorities found offensive, nearly 50 percent were fine with it. The number was 70 percent among Germans, 62 percent among Italians, and 50 percent of Poles. In Scotland, only 5 percent disagree with the statement "Free speech is an important right," and yet 21 percent, in the same poll, say it should be a criminal offense to say that someone born biologically male cannot become a woman—and 40 percent under the age of twenty-five believe so.[43] It's not surprising that the recent Hate Crime Bill proposed in overhauling the Scottish law would have allowed police to threaten people who "stir up" hatred with a maximum seven-year jail sentence.[44]

Polls, alas, also show an increasing openness to hate speech laws in the United States. A recent survey found that 40 percent of millennials are okay with limiting speech offensive to minorities.[45] Another found that 50 percent of Democrats have warmed to the idea of banning "hate speech."[46] A study by the First Amendment Center a few years back found that nearly 40 percent of Americans said the First Amendment "goes too far" in guaranteeing rights—a record high.[47] In 2018, more than 40 percent of Republicans said that "the president should have the authority to close news outlets engaged in bad behavior."[48]

While many of these polls seem to elicit answers that are politically situational—what does "bad behavior" mean?—the outlook of millennials is most concerning. In polling—and most anecdotal evidence—American millennials are far more likely than older generations to say that speech that offends them is tantamount to "violence" and place opaque concepts of "fairness" and "tolerance" above free expression in the hierarchy of important values. The European outlook is increasingly gaining currency. This is untenable as society can't expect a handful of people to shoulder the peril associated with free speech or defend the most unpopular words and thoughts. And once you surrender, it will never be enough. That is the case in Europe, where censorship is both internalized and legislated. And it might well be the case in the United States soon enough if Europhiles get their way.

10

The Future Must Not Belong to Those Who Slander the Prophet

Two things form the bedrock of any open society—freedom of expression and rule of law. If you don't have those things, you don't have a free country.

—Salman Rushdie[1]

After the publication of his novel *The Satanic Verses* in September 1988, the British author Salman Rushdie was thrust into one of the most consequential literary controversies in history. Because of the book's purportedly impertinent treatment of the prophet Muhammad, it was banned in Rushdie's native India and dozens of other nations—including every Muslim-majority country in the world. Though Rushdie would later become a powerful advocate of free expression, initially he turned on his own book, apologizing numerous times for its contents. "I profoundly regret the distress that publication has occasioned to sincere followers of Islam," he said in one statement.[2] He declared his allegiance to Islam, asking his publisher to hold back release of the paperback edition of the book. As a matter of self-preservation, his position was certainly understandable.

It was all to no avail. Iran's supreme leader Ayatollah Khomeini issued a fatwa against Rushdie, contending that even if the author "became the most pious man of all time" it was the duty of every Muslim to "employ everything he has got" to murder the writer.[3] For the first time in postwar history, there would be widespread protests and terrorism aimed at suppressing free expression in the liberal Western world.

In the United States, two bookshops in Berkeley, California—home of the free speech movement of the 1960s—were attacked. A small newspaper called the *Riverdale Press* in New York was firebombed after publishing an editorial defending the right to read the novel and criticizing the bookstores that pulled it from their shelves.

In Europe the situation was even more destructive. The Italian translator of *The Satanic Verses*, Ettore Capriolo, was stabbed to death in his apartment in Milan.[4] The Norwegian publisher of Rushdie's book, William Nygaard, was shot three times in 1993, but survived.[5] In Belgium two imams were murdered for expressing moderate positions regarding the affair.

England would become the center of the most sustained violence and protests. Two big booksellers in London were firebombed in April 1988, and there were two more explosions connected to the selling of the book that May. Unexploded devices were found in three other bookstores around the country. Numerous booksellers eschewed carrying the novel for fear of reprisal. Rushdie was forced to employ round-the-clock protection by bodyguards, compelled to spend the next decade in hiding. The fatwa still stands today. In fact, the bounty has risen to over $4 million.[6]

It is not Europe's fault that Islamic radicalism exists. It is, however, Western Europe's fault that it bends to the will of those who threaten her. Would any major publishing house in Europe today release a book comparable to *The Satanic Verses*? Doubtful. Not because of any "hate speech" laws prohibiting the publication of such a book—though, as we've seen, plenty of laws do exist—but rather because the European cultural norm is now to maintain social harmony by avoiding controversy and placating fundamentalists. It is a toxic merging of multicultural progressivism and Islamism. This position has gotten Europe neither more freedom nor more harmony. What it has done is given theocrats a heckler's veto.

As author Kenan Malik noted not long ago, the lasting legacy of the Rushdie fatwa was that Western Europe had "internalized" censorship. "Rushdie's critics lost the battle—*The Satanic Verses* continues to be published," he wrote. "But they won the war. The argument at the heart of the anti-Rushdie case—that it is morally unacceptable to cause offence to other cultures—is now widely accepted."[7]

Many Europeans would, no doubt, argue that self-constraint shouldn't be considered "censorship" at all. For them the word is reliant on some form of state-compelled restrictions and interference. In the most literal sense, they are accurate, but it is also true that a proscriptive cultural environment that inhibits open debate and bows to the extortions of the least liberal element undermines the spirit of open expression and is functional censorship. It is often equally as dangerous—if not more. And it is often difficult to come back from this outlook once it is engaged.

Before the release of author Sherry Jones's novel *The Jewel of Medina*, a fictional retelling of the life of one of Muhammad's wives, including the six-year-old Aisha, Random House's publicity department approached a professor of Middle Eastern studies at the University of Texas, Denise Spellberg, to get her views on the book. Needless to say, the professor wasn't a fan, reportedly finding the book "incredibly offensive" and a "very ugly, stupid piece of work," claiming that the "explosive" contents would inspire Islamic violence.[8]

Everyone's a critic, right? But the professor then reportedly warned a colleague, Shahed Amunallah, who brought the book's topic to the public's attention. There were immediate demands for an apology before the book was even released. The onetime publisher of *The Satanic Verses* immediately bowed to the pressure and canceled *The Jewel of Medina* over fears of violence in Europe. Rushdie called the incident "censorship by fear."[9] Jones herself, on a speaking tour of the United States—not Europe, where her life would have been in danger—made the case for the importance of defending the freedom to offend readers, even suggesting that Muhammad would have agreed with her decidedly liberal outlook on free expression.[10] Color me skeptical.

No other major publishing house would touch the Jones book. When a small English publisher, Gibson Square, took a chance, its London offices were firebombed.[11] Writing in London's *Daily Telegraph*, the radical English Muslim cleric Anjem Choudary—some Europeans are, it seems, still afforded the ability to air their grievances without concern of violent backlash— noted that the British should be "aware of the consequences they might face when producing material like this. They should know the depth of feeling it might provoke."[12] The only reason that Choudary believed that Islamic law had any bearing on the publishing world or how European secular society acted was that it did.

Jones's novel wasn't the first or last work that would be censored. In the age of democratized media, fully censoring anything is going to be difficult. (European governments, as we've seen, are working to rectify that problem.) But self-censorship and capitulation to threats of violence are now an embedded feature of European existence. That attitude filters upward and codifies into cultural norms and laws.

When a Danish publisher put the call out to find an artist willing to contribute cartoons for a volume in a series of innocuous children's books explaining the world's religions, including Islam, it led to embassy burnings across the Muslim world and in Europe. In London, protesters outside the Danish embassy held signs saying, "Freedom go to hell" and "Behead those who insult Islam."[13] The publisher pulled the book.

When the Danish newspaper *Jyllands-Posten*, less innocuously, published cartoons of the prophet Muhammad to make a point about self-censorship, it sparked a worldwide crisis and condemnation from European leaders. One of the Danish cartoonists, Kurt Westergaard, was inundated with death threats. Four years after publication of the cartoon, a Somali refugee broke into Westergaard's home, where he was with his wife and five-year-old granddaughter, with an axe and a knife. The three escaped.

In 2018, the German division of Random House, citing fears of "stirring up Islamophobia," framed self-censorship as a means of preserving decency against extremism rather than as an act of capitulation to radicals, and canceled a book by bestselling left-wing immigration critic Thilo Sarrazin. The economist had already been chased out of his position at Germany's central bank, the Bundesbank, for his heterodox views.[14] No one should be guaranteed a job or a book, of course. The act of folding to pressure, however, is an illiberal one that incentivizes more threats and more violence, and in reaction, more Islamophobia.

Few people are interested in dealing with the perils of such controversy. This is why the Deutsche Oper in Berlin felt compelled to cancel performances of Mozart's opera *Idomeneo*. Not only because it offended the sensibilities of Muslims in Germany, but because it had become an "incalculable security risk" for people to go see it.[15] It is the reason the Royal Court in London canceled performances of Aristophanes's *Lysistrata*. It is why the Manchester Art Gallery[16] and London's Whitechapel Art Gallery[17] removed works of art featuring naked women. The same people who often scoff at the puritanism of Christians will avoid insulting some Muslims by censoring their own venerable cultural sensibilities to ensure harmony. It is a pitiful and counterproductive surrender.

Je Suis Charlie

Twenty-seven years after the Rushdie fatwa was announced, two French Islamists forced their way into the Paris editorial offices of the satirical newspaper *Charlie Hebdo* and began shooting. The journal's offices had been moved to an unmarked building after they were firebombed in 2011 in response to the publication of a satirical cartoon of the prophet Muhammad. The shooters managed to kill twelve people. A related attack soon followed in a nearby kosher supermarket, where four Jews were murdered by a friend of the assailants.

Even today, the paper's editor, who had published offensive caricatures of popes and rabbis and politicians, lives under police protection for the crime of satire against Islam. *Charlie Hebdo* is an ill-mannered equal-opportunity slayer of sacred cows. No such publications really exist in the United States. France once had a vibrant history of provocative, irreverent, and transgressive cultural writing that spared few. It is a dying breed.

And for a brief moment after the attack, the free world rallied around *Charlie Hebdo*. "Je suis Charlie" became a global rallying cry. The massive march through the streets of Paris that followed included virtually every major world leader, among them many hypocritical European heads of state who are happy to clamp down on free expression in their own nations (though not the Europhilic then-president of the United States, Barack Obama).

But the parade hid a sad truth. Free expression is dying in Europe. Not merely because there are laws that inhibit it—though there are plenty, as we've seen—but because it is not valued and venerated as a liberal value anymore. Though criticism and mockery of Islam might be distasteful, they are a completely legitimate form of political speech, as is criticism of Catholicism, Mormonism, Judaism, and Scientology, all of which *Charlie*

Hebdo had satirized in its pages. In a free nation we have no responsibility to "respect" anyone's ideas about the world, or the afterworld, nor do we have any right to expect to live in a world free of offense.

Or, at least, this is the American ideal of free expression. The threat of political violence—something that despite our numerous disagreements hasn't been much of a concern for the average American in a long time—hangs over the head of many Europeans in ways we couldn't imagine.

Charlie Hebdo marked the beginning of a trial over a murderous attack on its newsroom in 2015 by republishing the blasphemous cartoons of **Muhammad that** prompted the original assault. Again, violence broke out, in the streets of Paris, at a church in Nice, and elsewhere in France. There was no widespread "Je suis Charlie" this time.

Around the same time, a forty-seven-year-old history teacher named Samuel Paty was beheaded in a Paris suburb by the father of one of his students after he showed cartoons of the prophet Muhammad during a civics lesson teaching the importance of free expression.

Terror in France is commonplace. But this wasn't a case of a rogue killer. French authorities arrested eleven people in connection with the murder, including at least four family members who had recently been granted ten-year residency in France. "Last year, a student told me that it was completely legitimate to kill someone who failed to show respect to the Prophet [Muhammad]," Fathia Agad-Boudjhalat, a history teacher in Paris, told French radio the week of the attack. "It comes from what they hear in their families."[18]

After the beheading of Samuel Paty, the larger French public began to recognize and vocalize the reality that much of Islam's value system does not comport with French values of secularism and freedom of speech. Philosophy teacher Alexandra Girat heard from her students after the *Charlie Hebdo* attack that "they deserved it. . . . They shouldn't represent the Prophet that way."[19] It's clear that European liberal democratic values are getting lost in translation.

These extremist views, for example, are not the norm among most Muslims in the United Kingdom, but the more insulated communities are from Western cultural norms, the more dangerous they become. Today, 27 percent of British Muslims say they have some sympathy for the motives behind the attacks on the *Charlie Hebdo* shooting in Paris and 45 percent believe that Muslim clerics preaching violence against the West can be justified.[20]

This speaks to one of the primary problems with Muslims not integrating into Western culture. "Secularism, as it's understood and practiced in Europe," points out American intellectual Shadi Hamid, "is not value-neutral." Secular governance "asks conservative Muslims to be something that they're likely not."[21] Political Islam makes no space for criticism, and it is not separated from public or political life.

Again, crowds gathered in France to pay tribute to Paty. President Emmanuel Macron said all the right things about peaceful coexistence under secular governance. Thousands descended onto Paris's Place de la République carrying signs that read, "I am Samuel" and "I am a teacher." But are they? How many teachers will be willing to risk their lives teaching the importance of free speech to immigrant populations? There are nearly six million Muslims—the largest in the European Union—who must embrace the French principle of state secularism, *laïcité*, which is the foundation of France's national identity.

You can see idealism cratering. After the attacks, *Politico Europe* ran an op-ed by a French intellectual, Farhad Khosrokhavar, titled "France's Dangerous Religion of Secularism," in which he noted that defenders of blasphemy "invoke freedom of expression, but what blasphemy does, in fact, is trap France in a vicious cycle of reactivity to jihadist terror that makes it less free and less autonomous." The Associated Press asked: "Why does France incite anger in the Muslim world? Its brutal colonial past, staunch secular policies and tough-talking president who is seen as insensitive toward the Muslim faith all play a role."

The proper response to political disputes over words, as one might expect the Associated Press to know, is to go to the ballot box or write a letter to the local newspaper editor. It is not to behead schoolteachers. Contra Khosrokhavar, there is no vicious cycle of "reactivity" between jihadist terror—or even orthodox Islam—and secular liberalism, because in democracies only one of those two has legitimate claim to governance. The surrender of European institutions to champion the moral standing of liberalism is at the center of Europe's conundrum.

Not one reporter or pundit complaining about radical secularism asked why *Charlie Hebdo*, which viciously lampooned popes and Hasidic Jews, never experienced other forms of religious violence. It's not as if Jews had a rosy European history.

One of the serious tribulations facing Europe, as we'll see, is a lack of, or a slow-moving, ideological assimilation of many Muslim newcomers, who are less inclined in Europe than in the United States to shed old ideas regarding governance and adopt new more liberal ones. One opinion poll ordered by a "free speech commission" found a large majority of Danish Muslims, for example, were in favor of banning "criticism of Islam." More than 76 percent of not only immigrants themselves, but descendants of immigrants from Muslim-majority countries like Turkey, Lebanon, Pakistan, and Somalia, the four biggest immigration groups in the nation, believed that secular government should make it illegal to criticize Islam.[22]

Where would immigrants get the idea that such infringements on discourse could even be entertained in a free nation? Well, European cultural and political leaders are the ones who create those expectations. Those who surrender to threats against speech are the ones who create those expectations. Elected and unelected cultural leaders and experts who, with great specificity, lay out the contours of acceptable speech to spare the feelings of select groups are the ones that create those expectations.

In 2016, a dozen Christian street preachers were arrested in London for disturbing the peace by quoting—verbatim—from the Saint James Bible.[23] The citations were deemed Islamophobic and homophobic hate speech. One might have chalked up these arrests to overzealous policing, but when London's popular mayor Sadiq Khan was asked whether Christians should be able to openly read from the Bible in public without fear of arrest, he replied: "There's not an unlimited right to freedom of expression or free speech."[24] When Khan appeared at an event in Austin, Texas, he encouraged Americans to join the European effort to force-censor this kind of hate speech and force tech companies to adopt European standards or face fines for violations. He was, predictably, warmly received by attending Europhiles.

European leaders can claim that curtailing politically incorrect discourse is largely about hindering the spread of ugly ideas among nationalists and extremists, but it clearly has a chilling effect on society and the general population.

A recent survey conducted by the Institut für Demoskopie Allensbach found that a mere 18 percent of Germans felt free to express themselves in a public space.[25] Only 17 percent felt comfortable expressing their view on the internet. And only 31 percent felt free to speak about their opinions about controversial topics *among friends*.

Sooner or later, of course, the internalized inhibitions manifest in law. European nations are increasingly accepting of censorship, meant to punish those who make intemperate comments and preemptively dissuade anyone away from engaging in debate in the first place. The mission creep regarding "hate speech" grows, because once a society abandons the principle of free expression the idea becomes malleable and arbitrary.

The European Commission for Democracy Through Law—

better known as the Venice Commission—is the kind of agency technocratic Europhiles salivate over. An advisory body of independent "experts" in the field of European "constitutional law," it advises on the government extent of freedom of expression. These experts have decided that "gratuitously offensive" speech should be unprotected in Europe. Religious freedom, they have also decided, includes the right *not* to be insulted. The commission's latest fifty-six-page set of speech guidelines makes it clear that they believe authors, publishers, editors, and journalists should all be open to the possibility of criminal investigation and prosecution for unacceptable speech. "The mere fact that forms of expression are considered to be insulting is not sufficient to justify the imposition of penalties," the document says. "However, the intensity of the speech and its effects on the reputation of the person concerned are a factor to be taken into account."[26]

It's difficult to imagine, even with the inroads made by Europhiles, that Americans would ever allow bureaucrats to adjudicate whether speech is too intense or not. But this kind of pernicious attack on open discourse filters upward. It infects every alleged ideal of speech: journalism, fiction writing, and academic freedom.

When a woman named Elizabeth Sabaditsch-Wolff was fined 480 euros by an Austrian court for having "disparaged" the prophet Muhammad, almost no one in Europe came to her defense. Sabaditsch-Wolff's sin was holding two seminars, during the course of which she discussed the marriage between Muhammad and six-year-old Aisha. Sabaditsch-Wolff had directly quoted from the Koran and other Islamic religious texts. So the core of the prosecution focused on offhand remarks she had made during breaks.

In the end, a Viennese court found Sabaditsch-Wolff guilty of the Orwellian crime of deliberately seeking to degrade Muhammad by accusing "a subject of religious worship of having a primary sexual interest in children's bodies." Her comments had "a malicious violation of the spirit of tolerance," since they had been "capable of hurting the feelings" of Muslims and threatening peaceful coexistence.

Sabaditsch-Wolff appealed her case to the European Court of Human Rights—where non-Austrians would decide her fate. That court upheld the previous ruling, declaring that she had no right to say offensive things about "objects of veneration," ruling that Sabaditsch-Wolff's right to freedom of expression was less important than the right of Muslims not to have their "religious feelings" hurt. Needless to say, mundane speech is rarely in need of protection, since no one will object to it. Speech that targets "objects of veneration" is in special need of safeguards.

When Austrian politician and parliament member Susanne Winter argued that "in today's system" Muhammad would be considered a "child molester," referring to his marriage to Aisha, she was convicted of "incitement." Winter was also prosecuted for claiming that Austria faces an "Islamic immigration tsunami." She was ordered to pay a huge fine and received a suspended three-month prison sentence.[27] The Austrians fined someone not only for merely restating what was in the Koran but for engaging in an important contemporary debate over Muslim immigration.

In Denmark, once a bastion of free expression, journalist Lars Hedegaard, president of the International Free Press Society, was forced to stand trial in Copenhagen *three times* for an incident in which he criticized Islam. During the trial Hedegaard was forbidden from entering historical or scholarly evidence backing his criticisms (not that such things should even be relevant in a trial over speech rights). Hedegaard was acquitted, but only on the technicality that he had not known that his words, expressed in a private conversation, were being taped.

Denmark's speech laws are wholly subjective and allow for the suppression of individuals holding minority or controversial views. Here are some highlights:

Anybody who offends another person's honor by insulting words or actions or by stating or disseminating charges, that are suitable for reducing the insulted person in the esteem of fellow citizens, will be punished by fine or ordinary imprisonment.

Anybody who publicly mocks or insults the religious doctrine or worship of any religious community lawfully existing in this country will be punished by fine or imprisonment for up to 4 months.

Even with the growing popularity of a European style of censorship in the United States, allowing government to punish those who *offend another person's honor* might seem like an alien idea. But that is the endgame. In Denmark there can be no open discussion about faith. Even if they were so inclined, most Danes, one imagines, would rather avoid debating contentious issues than be thrust into a Kafkaesque legal battle over their opinions. Those with politically indecorous opinions about immigration take themselves out of the debate, as far-right nationalists fill the vacuum.

The Importance of Protecting Unpopular Speech

Europhiles, who either struggle with the concept of neutral principles or don't very much care for them, will wonder why anyone would feel the need to defend an academic who is fixated on Muhammad's young wife—and I certainly wouldn't vouch for the reasoning of any of the people above. But this ignores the most important problem with instituting speech codes. Once the state can decide what you can say, it is imbued with a power to lord over everything you say. Europhiles will often argue that we shouldn't valorize free speech for its own sake. But why not?

For one thing, the argument that we should afford a subset of citizens—in this case Muslims—special protections from open discourse is bigoted. It says you don't believe Muslims can handle one of the foundational concepts of liberalism that others can. And this attitude is increasingly pervasive in Europe, both culturally and systemically. Speech codes undermine assimilation and modernity. We also shouldn't forget that hate speech codes and the self-censorship that goes on in Europe also compromise the liberal Muslim voices in the Middle East and elsewhere attempting to reform blasphemy laws and speech restrictions in their own nations.

For another thing, a lack of respect for the objective rights of people will lead to a corrosion of the rights of all people. After an Islamist extremist went on a shooting spree in Vienna in 2020, Austrian chancellor Sebastian Kurz blamed the incident, rightly, on the presence of "political Islam."[28] The legislation Kurz sent parliament in reaction to the shooting allowed authorities to ban membership of designated "Islamist" organizations, the power to preventively arrest people, the power to close mosques deemed radical, and the power to strip Muslims of their citizenship.

The vast majority of Muslims who live in the United States have no expectations that a secular nation would uphold speech laws to protect them, because we have a tradition that does not engage in these kinds of special protections. Then again, in past years the United States has been infected by this European authoritarian impulse to dictate rhetorical etiquette and appropriate political speech. The idea of passing hate speech laws, long a norm in Europe, has been aggressively normalized in the United States. Even more alarming is an embrace of the proposition that Americans should be protected from things that offend them.

Free expression can't be defended by a few people; it must be shouldered by an entire society. In this regard, Europe is failing. Indeed, the most important forms of European self-censorship are likely the ones we never hear about.

How many works of literature have been abandoned before even coming to fruition? How many writers and artists shelve ideas because they know no one will publish their work? How many important but contentious arguments are vetoed by the mob before they are even taken up? How many academic theories aren't pursued because of fear of career-ending backlash? How many are fearful of defending unpopular ideas on principle? In Europe you're not only on your own; the state and society will work against you.

11

Europe as Retirement Home

Here the past was everywhere, an entire continent sown with memories.

—*Miranda Richmond Mouillot*

Historically speaking, Europe's population tends to contract due to genocide, violent internal ethnic conflict, and bloody transnational wars. This time around, the arrangement is far more peaceful, and likely to be far more permanent. Europe is in the midst of what the historian Niall Ferguson calls "the greatest sustained reduction in European population since the Black Death in the fourteenth century," and there is little prospect of turning back.[1]

For the most part, alas, the continent's depopulation isn't the doing of any plague. Rather, Europe is systematically committing suicide. Right now, the birth rate in every one of the twenty-seven European Union nations is below replacement level—which requires an average of 2.1 children per woman to perpetuate from one generation to the next.

The median age of a European is now forty-three, which is around five years older than the average person in the United States and around twelve years older than the rest of the world.[2] Of the top fifty oldest nations in the world, thirty-two are on the

European continent.[3] If this trajectory continues, and there is no reason to believe it won't, Europe will become, both culturally and economically, an anemic shell of its former self within only a few decades. It is destined to have wealthy enclaves surrounded by either empty buildings or tens of millions of newcomers. It is a potentially catastrophic societal equation.

Unless Europeans can magically change the immutable laws of economics, they are in trouble. The number of working Europeans, those between twenty and sixty-four years old, peaked in 2010. By 2020, there were nearly twelve million fewer of them, even with the most robust immigration ever padding those numbers. By 2035, there will be about fifty million fewer people of working age in all of Europe than in 2010. The retired populations in places like Italy are soaring, with estimates of the proportion of people over sixty-five rising to 20 percent by 2050.[4]

Years ago, the conventional wisdom was that fertility would always be higher among Catholics—for, among other reasons, the church discourages contraception. Today onetime Catholic-majority nations are some of the worst performing in Europe. In 1965, more than one million babies were born in Italy. By 2020, it was less than half of that total.[5] Southern Europe has exceptionally low fertility rates, with Portugal and Spain joining Italy in the top-ten world economies with the lowest number of births per woman. France, bucking the trend, is home of the highest fertility rates in the European Union, but even it is well below replacement level.

Weddings have fallen to historical lows in once-Catholic-majority nations like France, Spain, Italy, Ireland, Poland, and Portugal. In Italy, weddings have fallen to under 200,000 per year, the lowest number since World War I. For years, Europeans have pointed to the 2007 recession as the reason for declining fertility rates, but they have not stopped since.[6]

This trend is not unique to Western Europe. Eastern Europe,

where denizens experience more economic and personal liberty today than they ever have in history, are seeing their biggest population contraction since World War II. In nearly every postcommunist nation, deaths now outnumber births. While women in Eastern Europe were having an average of 2.1 children when the Soviet Union fell in the late 1980s, only a couple of decades later the average had fallen to 1.2. Of the twenty most rapidly shrinking countries in the world, eighteen are in Europe, but fifteen are either former Warsaw Pact nations or formerly communist nations.[7]

Even in Germany, it is the former East Germany part of the nation that is experiencing the sharpest decline. The childless rate of the nonreligious is about double that of religious Catholics and Protestants in German-speaking areas of Europe. In those same areas, Muslims are not only the most religious denomination, they marry younger, and almost all marriages produce at a minimum the replacement rate.[8] Then again, the Muslim fertility rate in Europe is at 2.6—or a full child more than the average non-Muslim European.[9] In France, French women have 1.7 children each, but foreign-born women have 2.8 children each. In Austria, for example, the birth rate for Catholics is 1.32, for Protestants it is 1.21, for secular Europeans it is 0.86, and for Muslims it is 2.34. According to demographers from the Vienna Institute of Demography, this means that Islam could be the majority religion for Austrians under the age of fifteen by 2050.[10]

Though the focus of the debate over demographics and immigration typically, and for good reason, centers on Middle Eastern newcomers, there's also a trend of Europeans moving from east to west within the continent. Incentivized by the European Union's allowance for open movement, millions of Eastern Europeans have migrated to wealthier nations with more economic opportunities and generous social safety nets. Half a million Poles, for instance, have permanently moved to Britain alone over the past two decades.[11] More than three million Romanians have moved to Western Europe since Romania joined the European Union in 2007.[12] Between 2013 and 2016, around 230,000 have left Croatia, a country of only four million, to live in Western Europe.[13] Latvia has lost about a fifth of its people since joining, or more than 18 percent of its population, while Lithuania has lost 17.5 percent.[14]

THERE IS A HUGE ECONOMIC cost to these demographic trends.

By the year 2060, Germany's population is expected to plunge from around 80 million people to 67 million.[15] While the nation's population hit an all-time high of 83.2 million in 2020, or around 200,000 more than the previous year, this number was entirely gained through the addition of Middle Eastern and Eastern European immigrants. By 2050, the percentage of people aged sixty years or over is projected to hit nearly 40 percent of the population.[16]

In other words, Germany, the most economically powerful nation on the continent, is old. Really old. Unsustainably old. And it's getting older at an increasingly alarming pace. After Japan and the city-state of Monaco, in fact, it is the oldest nation in the world. While part of this trend can be attributed to increasing life expectancy, bolstered by technological advances, much of it has to do with people not having children anymore.

Under Chancellor Otto von Bismarck, Germany became the first nation in the world to adopt a progressive social insurance program, in 1889. Such programs have become a hallmark of German life since. The rest of Europe has followed and built increasingly top-heavy and bloated social institutions. As with many industrial countries, Germany will see increasingly fewer people entering the job market, leaving the rest of the population unable to finance the generous pensions and social programs that a growing retired population will need, producing a looming disaster to the grandchildren they do have. By 2030, the United Nations predicts that the percentage of Germans in the workplace (this, before the COVID-19 pandemic) will precipitously drop to around 54 percent of the country's population. If the demographic trends continue, one in five pensioners in Germany will be threatened by poverty in the next twenty years.[17]

To offset the labor shortage, Germany, for example, would need to import somewhere around 500,000 new immigrants every year for decades just to keep up.[18] We've already seen what an influx of newcomers means to societal cohesion. It is perilous for any nation to rely on immigration as the sole means of growth. And, of course, newcomers also age, and also bring with them older relatives and their own set of problems. As Nicholas Gailey, a demographer at the International Institute for Applied Systems Analysis in Austria, points out, even if every European Union member adopted more open migration policies, adding over 100 million new people by the year 2060, the average age in Europe would still continue to climb.[19]

A number of European nations have begun linking retirement age to life expectancy, but it is unlikely to be enough. It won't matter what the pension age is if you have no one left to foot the bill. One study estimated that the retirement age in Europe would have to be raised to seventy-seven years to fix the pension shortfalls that are coming.[20] Most Western European voters do not react well to the trimming of benefits.

"The equation is clear: to meet its workforce deficit and maintain its economic dynamism, Europe needs migrants," then–United Nations secretary-general Ban Ki-moon said in Brussels in 2015.[21] As we've seen, Europeans struggle mightily to assimilate newcomers. In any event, the number of migrants needed to maintain present economic growth would mean replacing a large chunk of its population in a short span of time. It is true that without a constant stream of migration many European economies would already be in trouble.

An aging population in Europe will have a far harder time adjusting to this new reality than the United States should we follow the continent's lead. Indeed, the United States also relies on immigrants to replenish the workforce, and declining fertility rates and longer life expectancy will be bad economic news for programs like Social Security. Despite the best effort of Europhiles, however, Americans are still far less dependent on the welfare state, and the massive tax revenues needed to fuel it, for their retirements.

An Anti-Child Society

European secularism is depressing levels of fertility and making it more difficult to be a parent for those who do want children. Indeed, even in the United States, government programs championed by Europhiles have begun to crowd out churches, charity, and local civic organizations that once offered the kind of vibrant communal setting that made children more enticing. Civic society—religious institutions, neighborhood associations, and nongovernmental institutions we voluntarily join and grow—provides communities with a self-governing self-reliance that fosters an environment in which families can thrive. In American life, unlike that of Europe, that civic society preceded the state. Europhiles want to reverse this equation.

In the United States, certainly, it is still true that the more socially conservative one's community, the larger one's family. In the 2016 and 2020 presidential elections, the Republican Donald Trump won the top ten states (sixteen of the top seventeen) with the highest fertility rates, while Democratic Party candidates Hillary Clinton and Joe Biden won the bottom ten states in fertility. Indeed, the decline in faith correlates almost exactly with the decline in children. In the United States, Mormons are the most likely to have bigger families (3.4 children), followed by

Protestant denominations favored by African Americans (2.5), evangelicals (2.3), and Catholics (2.3). Those below replacement levels are least religious: Jews (2.0), mainline Protestants (1.9), and atheists (1.6). Those who can't make up their minds about anything—agnostics—bring up the rear at 1.3.[22]

So, it is no revelation that the more devout a European, the more likely they are to have a larger family. Even more: regularly attending a place of worship is proven to incentivize parents to have more children. A study published by the British Royal Society suggests that the social bonds formed by religious communities give public support that differs from secular communities. Mothers who received help from members of their church congregations had higher fertility rates, because, among many reasons, the support they found in their places of worship cut the typical costs of having a larger family.[23]

Strong social bonds, not government programs and goodies, entice humans to have more children. And European governments often send conflicting messages. Even while everything in the culture either stigmatizes or disincentivizes having children, the state implores people to reproduce, since the present trajectory isn't economically sustainable.

Some nations, like Denmark, fund public relations campaigns reminding young Danes that their biological clocks are ticking, trying to press them to have more kids. Denmark is one of the wealthiest countries in Europe and parents are afforded all kinds of perks—twelve months' paid family leave and highly subsidized day care, among other goodies. Women under forty can get state-funded in vitro fertilization. The entire society is set up to make child-rearing easy. But Denmark's fertility rate is still only at 1.7 births per woman, on par with the United States—which is at its lowest number ever—though it employs very few state-induced incentives (other than a tax break for every child).

According to the United Nations, two-thirds of European

nations have introduced measures to try to increase fertility rates, which sometimes includes cash payments for babies and state-funded or impelled paid parental leave. The outlier, and successful in this pursuit, if we're to believe its internal statistics, is Russia, where there are programs that incentivize baby making, and the birth rate has risen to 1.48 children per woman from its 1999 low of 1.16. It is quite possible that the rise from that kind of disastrous low might simply be an organic rise. We shall see.

In other places similar programs have failed. In 2015, Italy started handing cash to women for every child they had, and its fertility rate, one of the lowest in the European Union to begin with, remains at around 1.3 children per woman.[24] Poland and Hungary have nationalized IVF clinics. The latter has been the most aggressive in implemented measures to incentivize women to have more children, offering waivers on personal income tax for women who raise at least four children for the rest of their lives and subsidies for large families to buy cars and houses. Grandparents are eligible to receive a state-provided child care fee if they look after young children. All of this has hardly made a dent. Hungary hasn't seen an increase in its population since 1980. Back then 10.7 million people lived in the nation; today it has a projected population of 6.5 million by 2100.[25]

All of this has a lot to do with the decline of the institution of marriage. After a temporary spike in the early 1990s, marriages in Western Europe, especially in German-speaking places, are now at historic lows. There is a rise in nonmarital partnerships. But those unions have a far lower chance of lasting, and people who aren't in long-term committed relationships rarely have children. The fact is that religious people marry more often and earlier and have more time for children. Marriage has been in decline in the United States—though it has plateaued since the mid-2000s. Yet our nuptials are at a far higher rate than in the European Union. There are around seven marriages per thousand people per year in the United States, while only four per thousand in the European Union.[26] Outside of Nevada and Hawaii, two states that have a thriving nuptial industry, the top states for marriage are Arkansas, Utah, and Tennessee[27]—all three rank in the top ten "highly religious states."[28]

Many Europhiles, in their quest to convince voters to adopt social safety nets, blame the dropping fertility rate on the lack of a robust welfare state. In Vox, one of the nation's leading champions of Europeanization, Caitlyn Collins, a professor of sociology and gender studies at Washington University in St. Louis, says, "Leaving it to individual women to find private market-based solutions is insufficient, and it's part of the explanation for why we're seeing continuing declines in fertility in the US."[29]

There is, of course, no evidence to back up this contention. Setting aside momentarily the pros and cons of European-style socialized medicine, women in the United States have higher fertility rates than women in most European nations, and yet most are on some form of private insurance. Poor families are already eligible for Medicaid. Countries and communities with poorer populations often have higher fertility rates than wealthy ones, whether the state has instituted a single-payer system or no discernable system whatsoever. And states with more robust American-style private-oriented insurance markets—Texas and South Dakota—have some of the highest fertility rates in the United States. "American women became mothers last year at rates that were inversely proportional to family income," Jeremy Carl, a research fellow at the Hoover Institution at Stanford University, said. "The birth rate was almost 50 percent higher for those with less than $10,000 in family income than for those with family incomes of $200,000 or more."[30] It is the wealthy who are having fewer children.

Is Infertility Simply an Inevitable By-Product of Industrialization?

Is this kind of decline inevitable in the wealthy nations of Europe—and the United States—whether the population remains tethered to some Abrahamic faith or not? When researchers looked at the Swiss census, for example, they found that nonreligious but well-off Swiss mothers were having only 1.11 children, while women who identified as having a religious denomination, and were similarly situated economically, were having nearly double as many births as the nonaffiliated. So it seems indisputable that organized religion makes us more communal. A pair of researchers recently called Europe's demographic decline "an outgrowth of an individualistic and egocentric society," the kind that inevitably leads to the rapid aging we are seeing now.[31]

Then again, there are other factors. Most obviously, the role of women has evolved in liberal societies, with huge numbers entering the labor force in the second half of the twentieth century. For the first time in history, women became the majority of the workforce in the United States in 2020.[32]

Now, it would be easy to blame secular feminists. Some, after all, do promote the idea that the childless life can help one escape from a patriarchal world fashioned around the twin roles of marriage and motherhood. But the lack of children among Europeans is disconnected from the desires of its women. At least, that's what they tell pollsters.

Around 87 percent of women in all European Union member states say that their ideal family size personally is two or more children. Around 57 percent say that two is the ideal, and 30 percent say three or more is ideal. Around 92 percent of respondents offered pollsters a specific numerical ideal, while others said things like "it depends" or "I don't know." Around

87 percent of men also said their ideal family would include two or more children.[33]

It seems more likely that many of those women are delaying adulthood. After attending college and committing to careers, women have either put off having children for later in life, limiting the size of their families, or have forgone having them altogether. The West has a pervasive problem with delayed adulthood in general. One European study found that half of people aged eighteen to thirty on the continent still live with their parents. Not the most opportune place to make children.[34]

That said, delaying adulthood also often means believing in childish ideas. There are other, perhaps less corrosive, but no less illogical, reasons for European demographic decline. One is the near-religious conviction for environmental alarmism, which, for now at least, attracts a far more devout following in Europe than America. For that matter, the environmentalist creed likely attracts a far more devout following than any other faith in Europe, where it is more probable for a young person to believe in a coming ecological End of Days than a theological one. And Malthusians—those who believe humanity has a moral responsibility to inhibit population growth so that population does not outstrip the means of subsistence—are a growing and dangerously persuasive faction on a continent that can't afford it.

The European media offers a steady stream of commentary and news coverage warning that having children is a crime against Mother Earth. It's unsurprising, then, that a growing reason European couples have cited in recent years for remaining childless is the state of the environment. One in seven adults under thirty-five who don't want children say they believe the world has too many people, with one in ten saying children would add to climate change pressures.[35] Though some of these Europeans are likely offering ad hoc justifications for not having children, if one in seven adults in Europe who are under thirty-five and felt they couldn't have kids because of the environment changed their minds, Europe would largely be saved from a barren future.

Whether you believe that climate change is an imminent or existential threat or not, there is little evidence that having fewer children is a solution to the problem. For one thing, developing nations in Africa and Asia, unwilling to eschew families, are growing at a pace that makes Europe's constriction essentially irrelevant. A 2017 study published in the *Proceedings of the National Academy of Sciences of the United States of America* gamed out various scenarios by adjusting fertility and mortality rates and found that even if a worldwide one-child policy or some "catastrophic mortality event" hit the world, that still would not significantly reduce the global population by 2100.[36] So the world population isn't going down anytime soon—therefore, pursuing other ways to fight climate change besides eschewing children would be more wise.

On the other hand, according to the World Bank, because of the spread of trade, technological advances, and plentiful affordable energy, the number of people around the world living in extreme poverty has now fallen below 10 percent.[37] There has been no correlation between poverty and fertility, as some of the wealthiest places are also some of the densest. Despite continued high fertility rates in developing nations, we have fewer hungry people than ever in the world; we have fewer people dying in conflicts over resources, and fewer dying from extreme weather. So, while the idea of having fewer children might be growing in popularity among wealthy American Europhiles, the evidence to back life choices is drying up. Then again, doomsayers have been ignoring human nature and ingenuity since the eighteenth century, at least.

Nevertheless, one can see American media and academic landscapes now littered with alleged experts making the case for European-style anti-natalism. As one recent *Science* magazine piece pointed out, "By choosing to have one fewer child in their family, a person would trim their carbon footprint by a whopping 58.6 metric tons—about the same emissions savings as having nearly 700 teenagers recycle as much as possible for the rest of their lives."[38] In 2020, more than 11,250 scientists, the majority of them from Europe, signed a declaration stating that our planet is in the midst of a "climate emergency" and the best thing anyone can do is have fewer kids.[39]

In a tone that implied journalists were reconciling themselves to hard truths, stories about the letter ran across mainstream American media. The popular congresswoman Alexandria Ocasio-Cortez, whose entire oeuvre is a washed-over Euro-style socialistic sloganeering, claimed (falsely) that "there's a scientific consensus that the lives of children are going to be very difficult. And it does lead, I think, young people to have a legitimate question: Is it okay to still have children?"[40]

That's a shame. It has now become fashionable in the United States to ape European movements, like BirthStrike, in which British women pledge not to procreate until the problem of climate change—around since . . . well, forever—is permanently fixed. The founder of this popular movement, a musician named Blythe Pepino, says, "I love my partner and I want a family with him but I don't feel like this is a time that you can do that." The committed environmentalist might have taken the sacred vows of poverty, obedience, and chastity, but it seems that only one is followed through on regularly.

Americans are now starting up similar anti-natalist orders. "When we first started this project, I didn't know anybody who had had any conversations about this," said Meghan Kallman, a cofounder of Conceivable Future, which the *New York Times* euphemistically refers to as an "organization that highlights how climate change is limiting reproductive choices." One misguided member of this infertility cult notes, "I don't want to give birth to a kid wondering if it's going to live in some kind of 'Mad Max' dystopia."[41] Why would she think such a thing? The women's magazine *Marie Claire*, which peddles itself as a periodical for "Beauty Tips, Celebrity, and Career Advice," recently featured a puff piece about the upside of a childless world, in which one philosopher noted that the "optimal population of earth is zero."[42]

Now, perhaps as a Darwinian matter, it's a net positive if those who believe their children will be plunged into a dystopian hellscape refrain from procreation, but sadly, the nation can't afford it. Increasingly, it seems we are adopting this European attitude. In 2019, a poll found that a third of American men and women aged twenty to forty-five cited climate change as one of the factors in their decision to have fewer children. The younger they were, the more likely they were to lean on this rationalization.[43] It too is a shame. Over the past forty years, when Americans were having as many children as any Western nation, our water and air have become cleaner, and crime rates and poverty have both fallen. What Malthusians never take into consideration are the efficiencies and technology we don't have yet, which continually amaze us and undermine their dark vision of humankind's future. What they never consider is that perhaps the child they're not having might invent a solution to one of environmental issues. In Europe the chances of this happening shrink by the day.

Surrendering the Future

The dwindling family is an abdication of societal responsibility to both the future and the past. The future, in its most crude terms, is a numbers game. The more people that exist, the more advanced science we invent, the more wealth we create, the more taxes we collect, the easier it is for an aging workforce to enjoy retirement. On a deeper level, a salubrious and vibrant society is most often a young one. The benefits of having children are numerous and exist on both the personal and societal levels. A refusal to establish new generations to perpetuate your society, its ideals, its hard-won culture, is suicide. Having children reflects having faith in your society. A lack of them causes not only economic decline, but also, as we've seen in numerous nations in Europe, political instability.

Europeans don't trust their society with the future—and judging from their ugly past, perhaps there is reason for them to be skeptical. Whatever the case, low fertility is a manifestation of many of the other problems discussed in this book.

The symptoms of this deterioration have already started to materialize in the United States. Though still in better shape than most European nations, outside of a short reprieve during the mid-2000s, birth rates have been falling for the past three decades. Part of this decline can be attributed to modernity, but part of it is a societal attitude that degrades the importance of family and children.

In many ways, though, the United States is better situated to stabilize fertility rates than Europe, because of stronger rural and growing suburban communities where children are generally more desired, and stronger religious institutions that create the social relationships that make it easier and parenthood seemingly more fulfilling.

The good news is that most women here say that, ideally, they would still like to have more than two kids as well. Gallup shows that American women wanted 3.5 kids in the 1930s until the 1960s. But by the 1980s they wanted around 2.5, and that number has remained stable since.[44] In the United States total fertility rates among the married have not changed very much over the last fifteen years. According to the Centers for Disease Control and Prevention, childbearing has risen eightfold among women in their late thirties and early forties. As technology makes that a safer and more realistic option, perhaps birth rates will steady or even rebound. Over the past decade, 86 percent of women ages forty to forty-four have become mothers, reversing decades of declines. Today, 55 percent of never-married women ages forty to forty-four have at least one child, up from 31 percent two decades ago.[45] We must avoid a European decline, because it's clear that serious demographic collapse is exceptionally difficult to reverse.

Europe has already given up. The United States doesn't need to follow.

12

The Sanctity of Life

Neo-paganism locates happiness in the unlimited satisfaction of desires, which means the suppression of all prohibitions.

—*René Girard*

The abandonment of Judeo-Christian ethics has left a vacuum in Europe. When you combine this moral fecklessness with a state empowered to make life-and-death decisions for individuals, you have a slow-moving disaster on your hands. While personal and communal benefits that personal faith provides individuals are important, they are also a counterforce to political forces that corrode the sanctity of life. Without faith, and without the foundational guardrails of traditional liberalism that had sprouted from the Christian belief system, European culture increasingly relies on self-serving scientific paganism.

The debate over euthanasia is a complex bundle of ethical issues concerning the end of life, suffering, and personal autonomy. No one should diminish the arduous set of excruciating choices families face when making decisions related to the sick and elderly. But there is a moral hazard now posed by the state-sanctioned killing of the sick when it sees no effective pushback from the weakened or virtually nonexistent European religious institutions.

It is here we see the biggest danger in normalizing and socializing the oxymoronic idea of "death medicine," which puts a monetary value on life. Such calculations make for a bleak society. Yet this thinking has become increasingly popular in the United States as well, led by the ugly crackpot theories of Australian "moral philosopher" Peter Singer—a regular on the editorial pages of American newspapers and magazines—who praises the European models and argues that "hedonistic utilitarian[ism]" and "the traditional view of the sanctity of human life" will be obsolete by 2040, and that "only a rump of hard-core, know-nothing religious fundamentalists will defend the view that every human life, from conception to death, is sacrosanct."[1] Others, like the bioethicist (and sometime high-level Democratic Party bureaucrat) Ezekiel Emanuel, who offers watered-down versions of the same antihumanist outlook that treats people like walking portions of the GDP, argue that people offer society little past the age of seventy-five.[2]

The United States still features a relatively vibrant and hard-core block of know-nothing religious fundamentalists who push back against anesthetized scientific value judgments regarding the value of human life. The same can't be said of Europe. Perhaps it never could.

Even so, a wide-ranging majority of Americans believe that doctors should be legally allowed, at a patient's and a family's request, to end a terminally ill patient's life using painless means.[3] The European model allows for a person to take their life for basically any reason they want—and often at the discretion of the state alone.

In 2002, Belgium became the third nation on the continent to legalize doctor-assisted suicides, after Luxembourg and the Netherlands. In the decade that followed Belgium's legalization, the number of "patients" using the suicide program rose nearly eightfold.[4] From 2003 to 2013, despite increasing life spans, the majority of "patients" deciding to end their lives with the help of a doctor were younger than eighty. According to researchers, some of the largest increases in this time period were among those who did not have terminal cancer and those who did not expect to die in the near future.[5] Then again, the Belgians show little regard for the well-being of their most vulnerable populations. One can certainly be critical of America's policy in reaction to the COVID-19 pandemic, but Belgian authorities purposely "abandoned" thousands of elderly people to die in nursing homes and denied many of them hospital treatment, according to an Amnesty International investigation.[6]

Belgian law allows anyone who feels "unbearable *psychological or physical suffering*" to choose death by government. And the European medical establishment has evolved from the view that the procedure should be used only as a necessity to relieve the physical suffering to being used to relieve emotional suffering. In 2013, in fact, Belgians amended their laws to allow the death of children, so you can imagine that the number of people who use "death medicine"—which is often kept purposely opaque—will likely be growing.

While studies show that euthanasia for non-life-threatening psychiatric disorders is still not the norm in Belgium, its prevalence has also risen since 2008. Wim Distelmans, one of the nation's leading advocates of euthanasia, put to death a forty-four-year-old who was depressed over a botched sex-change operation and forty-five-year-old deaf identical twins who said they had lost the will to live.[7] These, like the suicide of Paralympic champion Marieke Vervoort[8]—who wasn't facing a life-threatening disease, either—are high-profile cases. Most, however, are not.

Of the one hundred people who showed up at a single Belgian clinic between 2007 and 2011 suffering from non-life-threatening ailments such as depression, schizophrenia, and

Asperger's syndrome, forty-eight were given the option of a lethal injection because doctors decided that their conditions were "untreatable" and "unbearable." Thirty-five took the lethal injection.[9]

In Belgium, doctor-assisted suicide is a basic service, included in your government-mandated health service, which anyone in the European Union can access. These are real-life "death panels"— a phrase made famous in the United States by Sarah Palin in the 2008 election campaign, warning against state-run health care—in places like Belgium. The bureaucracy that decided who can take their own life has the Orwellian name Federal Control and Evaluation Committee on Euthanasia. In theory, a doctor must meet certain criteria and complete and submit a registration form within four working days after killing through euthanasia. An evaluation committee then reviews the form and determines whether the killing was performed in accordance with all the legal requirements. There is virtually no oversight from any other organization or civilian group. Though thousands of cases flow through the bureaucracy every year, not one doctor has ever been reported for breaking the law. And only a small minority of doctors, all of whom presumably take the Hippocratic oath seriously, refuse to offer the service.[10]

To put all of it in perspective: Murdering someone in Europe won't get you a lethal injection—as of 2019, the death penalty has been abolished in all countries other than Belarus—but being depressed about your heinous crimes might. In 2014, a serial rapist and murderer named Frank van den Bleeken, who was facing thirty years in prison for a slew of horrifying crimes, sought to end his life, citing his violent impulses and the depression that overcame him by the prospect of being locked up for the rest of his life. Belgian officials agreed to grant him the right to die—though van den Bleeken backed out.[11]

Indeed, one of the reasons euthanasia is increasingly common is that the expansion of state-sponsored suicide in one Western

European nation makes it legal in all of them. When a 2005 EU directive allowed medical qualifications to be recognized in another EU member state, it also meant it would be easier for doctors to accompany a suicidal patient. Now "euthanasia tourism" is thriving. Europeans travel to Switzerland for assisted suicide—221 people killed themselves in the nation in 2018; 87 of them were from Germany, 31 from France, and 24 from the United Kingdom. According to one emergency doctor at Belgium's Brugmann University, 7 out of 15 people who ended their lives in his institution were French.[12] At the Jules Bordet Institute in Brussels—named after the Nobel Prize winner whose lifesaving work was in immunology—nearly a third of all euthanasia consultations are obtained by the French.[13] Why? Because it's cheaper to kill yourself in Belgium than the Netherlands or Switzerland, and because ending your life is covered by the European Union's health insurance plan. Your French health care provider will pay for your demise, as well. The entire arrangement is quite the money saver. Every member of the European Union is complicit.

As is the culture. The people who push this kind of nefarious ideology are often minor celebrities. They include Philip Nitschke, an Australian who became the first physician in the world to administer a legal voluntary lethal injection to four terminally ill patients. In 2019, he was in Amsterdam, hawking a new machine called Sarco, short for "sarcophagus." This sleek suicide pod seats one, and using nitrogen, it gives the passenger a pain-free death through asphyxiation. All one needs to do is press a button. It is at least, as far as I can ascertain, his fourth insta-suicide design. He is, according to the European press, working on "an elegant gas chamber" in Switzerland.

"We've got a number of people lined up already, actually," Nitschke told *The Economist*. The woman he speaks of is not terminally ill, but she does have macular degeneration. "She's also got an ideological, philosophical supportive commitment to the idea," Nitschke went on. "She's coming from a long way because she likes the concept and she sees it as the future." *The Economist*, which covers Nitschke as a Silicon Valley tycoon who has invented some kind of solar-powered motorcycle, notes that the nefarious death merchant has "PR-savvy pizzazz."

In the trailblazing Netherlands, both euthanasia and assisted suicide are legal if the patient is enduring a malleable and subjective mental "suffering," whether or not their life is in any danger or they are in any physical pain. Any person from the age of twelve can request to be killed, but parental consent is required if a child is under sixteen. The slippery slope has been a huge moral and ethical disaster. "The process of bringing in euthanasia legislation began with a desire to deal with the most heartbreaking cases—really terrible forms of death," said Theo Boer, a professor of ethics and one of the biggest (and few) critics of the Dutch methods. "But," he goes on, "there have been important changes in the way the law is applied. We have put in motion something that we have now discovered has more consequences than we ever imagined."[14]

Dutch doctors killed more than six thousand people in 2017—psychiatrists alone killed eighty-three of their mentally ill patients, up from twelve in 2012.[15] Some of their stories are simply horrifying.

In 2016, Marinou Arends, a now-retired Dutch doctor, euthanized a woman who was suffering from dementia but had never specifically acceded to being killed. In fact, the patient struggled to stay alive. Arends first drugged the woman's coffee to knock her out. When the woman awakened prematurely and struggled, her family held her down as the doctor administered the lethal injection. Arends was charged by local authorities, who presumed such coercion would be, at least, considered manslaughter. Though the patient had never specifically conceded to the needle, or the time of her demise, the verdict at a court in

The Hague found that the doctor had met "all requirements of the euthanasia legislation."[16]

In that same year, a Tilburg couple named Monique and Bert de Gooijer gained worldwide notoriety by acceding to let their son, an obese and mentally slow thirty-eight-year-old named Eelco, kill himself. Hundreds of people wrote to the local newspaper in support. The letter the de Gooijers said was the most touching came from a woman whose daughter had walked in front of a train and ended her life. "She envied us," Monique told the reporter in front of her husband, Bert "because she didn't know why her daughter had done it. She said: 'You were able to ask Eelco every question you had. I have only questions.'"[17]

The Dutch procedure for "unbearable suffering" began to be stretched and loosened. Between the years 2007 and 2017 the number of state-sponsored euthanasia cases spiked from 2,000 to 6,600. Dutch statistics show that more than 400 patients who never asked for euthanasia were also likely killed by doctors—"termination without request or consent" is the official term for "mercy killings" in the Netherlands—though it is technically illegal.[18] When we add in the incredible 32,000 Dutch who died under palliative sedation—"in theory, succumbing to their illness while cocooned from physical discomfort, but in practice often dying of dehydration while unconscious," as one article explained—we find that nearly a quarter of all deaths in the country were induced by doctors and paid for by the state.[19]

Even in the United Kingdom, the director of public prosecutions has drawn up a list of situations in which assisting someone's death is justified. Others have floated the idea of "assisted suicide tribunals" at which terminally ill people could make their case for dying. Talk about death panels. The campaign to legalize assisted suicide has become bound up with society's broader inability to value and celebrate human life today. During the coronavirus pandemic, old-age homes in Britain were handing an abundance of do-not-resuscitate orders to residents, often for potentially avoidable deaths.[20]

Don't Worry, It's Eradication, Not Eugenics

In 2020, a Dutch Christian group (yes, a few still exist) produced a documentary, *De Laatste Downer* (The Last Downer), which explored the lives of the last Europeans afflicted with Down syndrome. In one episode, a young man with the genetic disorder named Sjoerd visits the Dutch National Institute for Public Health and the Environment, a research institute that forms government policy, to ask experts to calculate the cost of his life. Rather than informing Sjoerd that a decent and humane society never puts a dollar amount on a life, the government researcher begins making calculations on the whiteboard and answers that those with Down syndrome cost society "48,000 Euro per year approximately."[21]

The narrator then asks how the cost of Sjoerd's life compares to that of "normal persons." The researcher's answer is 5,000 euros a year "per person." Are "Downers" the most expensive human burdens on society? asks the narrator. The researcher responds that the cost of "Downers" is "very comparable to people who stay in nursing homes (and) elderly patients with dementia" who require institutionalization and "24-hour care 7 days a week."

And we all know what can happen to elderly patients with dementia in Europe.

One could chalk this episode up to a clueless pinhead academic simply forgetting that a human being was standing in front of him. The sad fact is that there is a general dehumanizing of those with genetic defects in Europe. They are unwanted. Ninety-nine percent of women who receive positive tests for Down syndrome in Europe end up aborting their pregnancies. In Denmark, 98 percent of unborn children with Down syndrome are aborted. Italy, Germany, France, Switzerland, England, and Belgium now all have rates exceeding 95 percent.[22] Most Down syndrome births seem to be a result of parents receiving inaccurate test results.

Not long ago in Europe, Nazis required doctors to register all babies born with Down syndrome. And the first humans they gassed were children under three years old with "serious hereditary diseases" like Down syndrome. Most often the disease isn't hereditary, of course, but for many, these children are still considered undesirable although most are born with only moderate cognitive or intellectual disabilities and may live full lives. The average life expectancy for a person with Down syndrome is now between the ages of fifty and sixty, with some living into their seventies. The ugly reality is that somewhere around 99 percent of Europeans, many of whom are in their later childbearing years, simply don't view such a child as worthwhile.

If there had been DNA tests in the 1930s and early '40s, the Nazis would almost certainly have compelled German citizens to rid themselves of those with Down syndrome. Now, I am not arguing that European governments have adopted National Socialist policies or that citizens of the European Union believe in the same crackpot theories about racial and genetic inferiority, or that they desire to eliminate people on anything approaching the scale of the Nazis. One imagines that most women carrying babies with genetic disorders didn't opt to abort because they harbor hate or revulsion toward Down syndrome children. One also assumes they had other justifications, including the desire to give birth to a healthy child and avoid the complications that the alternative would pose. Nor is this a book to debate the morality of abortion. *However,* we can't ignore the fact that many of the underlying societal rationalizations—and inherent questions about how a decent society treats its sick—have some similarities. Europe, after all, is completing one of the most successful eugenics programs in history.

If you think that's hyperbole, consider that eugenics—the word itself is derived from Greek, meaning "well born"—is nothing more than an effort to control breeding to increase desirable heritable characteristics within a population. This can be done through "positive" selection, as in breeding the "right" kinds of people with each other, or in "negative" selection, which is stopping the wrong kinds of people from having children. Due to the rise of prenatal screening tests, the number of babies born with Down syndrome in the Western world has begun to significantly diminish.

Some Europeans—and journalists here in the United States—claim they are "eradicating" Down syndrome births.[23] The word "eradication" implies that an ailment is being cured or beaten by some technological advancement or medicine. Not so in this case. You are not curing the disease by selectively eradicating the people who might have it. More and more women are taking these prenatal tests, and the tests are becoming increasingly accurate.

Iceland is nearly 100 percent free of Down syndrome kids. If Iceland's policy "reflects a relatively heavy-handed genetic counseling," as well-known geneticist Kari Stefansson admits, then what will it mean when we have the science to extrapolate on these tests and pinpoint other problematic traits in people? How about children with congenital heart defects or cleft palates or sickle-cell disease or autism? Eradicate? One day a DNA test will be able to tell us virtually anything we want to know, including our tendencies. So here's the best way to frame the ugliness of these eradication policies in terms more people might care about: "Europe has made great strides in eradicating gay births" or "Europe has made great strides in eradicating low-IQ births" or "Europe has made great strides in eradicating births of those who lean toward obesity." Feel free to insert any facet of humankind that gets you most upset.

At Landspitali University Hospital, Helga Sol Olafsdottir

counsels women whose pregnancies have a chromosomal abnormality. They speak to her when deciding whether to continue or end their pregnancies. Olafsdottir tells women who are wrestling with the decision or feelings of guilt over aborting imperfect unborn babies, "This is your life—you have the right to choose how your life will look like." Well, not everyone gets to choose what his or her life looks like. Certainly not those who are "eradicated" because they suffer from disorders. "We don't look at abortion as a murder," Olafsdottir explains later. "We look at it as a thing that we ended." Once, in Europe and elsewhere, abortion was looked at as, at best, a necessary evil. A thing? Using an ambiguous noun is a cowardly way to avoid the moral questions that pop up when you have to define that "thing." And science is making it increasingly difficult to circumvent that debate.

Evidence tells us that there is pressure from state doctors to terminate the pregnancy of children with potential disabilities across Europe, not only in nations with lax ethics around human life. "In all honesty we were offered 15 terminations, even though we made it really clear that it wasn't an option for us, but they really seemed to push and really seemed to want us to terminate," Emma Mellor told the BBC a few years ago.[24] At her twenty-week scan, Emma was told her daughter had some fluid on her brain. Doctors said she was likely to be disabled. "From that moment on, they recommended we should terminate and told us to think about the effect on our son and his quality of life." As this was happening, their son, as is often the case in Britain, was on a waiting list for surgery, having been born with a hole in his heart.[25]

There is, of course, a tremendous responsibility that comes with having a Down syndrome child. In the United States around 67 percent of women who find out their child will be born with the disease opt to have an abortion. However, about 6,000 babies are born with Down syndrome every year, which is about one in every 700 babies born. From 1979 to 2003, the number of babies born with Down syndrome increased by about 30 percent. The level seems to be holding. This is probably because women are having children in later years, and those babies are disproportionately affected by Down syndrome.

Child Euthanasia

In ancient Sparta, newborn babies would first be examined by elders, and if they weren't up to snuff, without blemish, they would be left in the wilderness with the animals. Though Europe hasn't regressed quite to that point, the modern version of this practice was codified in the 2004 Groningen Protocol, named after Groningen University Medical Center, where pediatric euthanasia—already widespread in Europe at the time—was formalized.

The standards for infanticide were set forth after the *Dutch Journal of Medicine* found that twenty-two disabled newborns had been terminated by lethal injections of sedatives between 1997 and 2004. Two more recent *Lancet* studies showed that about 8 percent of all infants who die in the Netherlands are killed by doctors, or around eighty to ninety per year.[26]

Basically, if an infant's "prospects" of a future don't measure up to the doctors' expectations, that child could be euthanized under the Groningen Protocol. Considering the mind-blowing technological and medical advances we make every year—including microsurgery on fetuses—such considerations are immoral but also subjective and unscientific.

When the growing acceptance of euthanasia is secured by a growing statism, even the wishes of parents can be overridden. As Philippe Mahoux, a Socialist Party senator and sponsor of the legislation, argued, giving terminally ill children the right to "die in dignity," even before exhausting medical science, was the "ultimate gesture of humanity."[27]

Consider Alfie Evans, nearly two years old, who was hospi-
talized at Alder Hey Hospital in Liverpool in 2018 with a rare
neurodegenerative disease. He soon suffered a seizure and was
dependent on feeding and breathing machines. Before giving
up on him, the parents decided to try alternative care. A Munich clinic offered to take Alfie for treatment. As did Bambino
Gesù Pediatric Hospital in Rome, which offered to treat Alfie
with prolonged ventilator support and an experimental surgery
to keep him alive. The Italian hospital arranged for his medical
transport and for the government to grant Alfie citizenship, ensuring that legal hurdles were cleared in advance.

The NHS's British hospital would not let him leave, coming to the decision that there was no hope. The parents sued,
and a succession of British and European courts refused to allow
them to remove the boy, asserting that future medical treatment
was not in the best interest of the child. A nation with state-
run medical care and state-run hospitals decided to end the life
of the child despite the fact that other hospitals had offered to
treat him, and the parents had not consented. Justice Anthony
Hayden of the High Court claimed that living on artificial ven-
tilation undermined Alfie's "dignity," though there was no evidence that the boy was suffering.

Another officious fascist named Justice Eleanor Warwick
King, of the Court of Appeal of England and Wales, argued that
parents were too emotional to make proper decisions about their
own children. "It is clear and understandable that they *have been
unable to think through* the disadvantages for them as a family
to relocating either to Italy or Munich without the support of
their extended families and unable to speak either language,"
she noted (emphasis mine), "in order to be able to spend Alfie's
last weeks or months in what they currently regard as *a more
empathetic environment*."

When Alfie died, his father, Tom, wrote, "My gladiator
lay down his shield and gained his wings at 2:30, absolutely

heartbroken LOVE YOU MY GUY." The Associated Press noted that the hospital had withdrawn Alfie's life support, "after a series of court rulings sided with doctors." This was a lie. The court sided with *a* hospital. There were many doctors who had treated the boy.

Alfie was not the first—nor will he be the last child to be taken by the state. Charlie Gard was born in August 2016, a seemingly healthy baby. Within two months his health dramatically declined. His parents took him to London's Great Ormond Street Hospital for Children in October, where he was diagnosed with mitochondrial DNA depletion syndrome, a rare inherited condition that leads to the loss of motor skills. Doctors knew very little about the ailment, as Charlie was, according to the parents, only the sixteenth person diagnosed with the disease.

Michio Hirano, a neurologist in New York, who was working on an experimental treatment based on nucleoside supplementation, had hoped to treat the boy. Before treatment could begin Charlie had seizures that caused brain damage. Charlie's parents still wanted to try the experimental treatment and raised nearly $2 million for a transfer to a hospital in New York. The British state-run medical establishment stepped in and wouldn't let the boy be moved and announced they would remove him from his ventilators. The parents appealed the case to the Court of Appeal, the Supreme Court, and the European Court of Human Rights. All upheld the government's order. Even after receiving a letter signed by several international specialists defending the potential new treatment, in July Charlie was transferred to a hospice and mechanical ventilation was withdrawn. He died the next day at the age of eleven months and twenty-four days.

In the United States, Alfie and Charlie would have been given a better chance, free from rationing, which clearly plays a role in the decisions the state makes for parents.

A number of U.S. states have passed, or have proposed, laws

that would ban abortions sought due to fetal genetic abnormalities, such as Down syndrome, or because of the race, sex, or ethnicity of a fetus.

When pressed, Europhiles will tell you that they too are against sex-selective abortion, but there is little logic to their position. Polls from the pro-life Charlotte Lozier Institute have found that 77 percent of Americans believed abortion should be illegal if "the sole reason for seeking an abortion" was to select a boy or a girl. Once you admit that these theoretical choices equate to real-life consequences, like eugenics, you are conceding that these are lives we're talking about, not blobs.

None of these issues are simple, and we should not act as if there are easy answers. At one time, however, there were countervailing societal forces, the churches, that would create a healthy debate and offer ethical guardrails. That kind of debate barely exists today in Europe; instead a government bureaucracy decides what a life is worth and what the cost. But really, it is impossible to govern such decisions. Rather, a respect for life is predicated on a healthy societal worldview—as long as that world does not include Europe.

Can We Be Like Europe?

Europe. Their political interests are entirely distinct from ours. Their mutual jealousies, their balance of power, their complicated alliances, their forms and principles of government, are all foreign to us. They are nations of eternal war. All their energies are expended in the destruction of the labor, property and lives of their people.

—*Thomas Jefferson*

A few years ago, the Pew Research Center attempted to distill the most conspicuous differences in the way Americans and Europeans view the world. Obviously, the United States and Europe are themselves geographically, culturally, and ethnically diverse, encompassing within them an array of social outlooks and attitudes that are forged by centuries of tradition and history. Yet, it is indisputable that there are hierarchies of value that dominate Europe and the United States. Pew found important areas of divergence, which offer vital insights into our psychological and ideological differences that make European ideas—one hopes—incompatible with American life:[1]

SELF-DETERMINATION: "Americans are more likely to believe they control their own destiny."

This, of course, is simply another way of saying Americans believe they live in a meritocracy, a place where success is predicated predominately on skill, intelligence, and effort, rather than predetermined by social class, race, birth, or redistribution by the state.

Nearly 58 percent of Americans disagree with the statement "Success in life is pretty much determined by forces outside our control."[2] It is a far higher percentage than in any other European nation, though, sadly, lower than it used to be. Nearly 75 percent of Americans still say they believe hard work leads to success, as opposed to only 35 percent of Europeans. According to the World Values Survey, 70 percent of Americans believe that the poor can escape poverty if they work hard enough, but only half of Europeans agree with the sentiment. Even low-income Americans have a largely negative view of redistribution policies meant to fix inequities, compared to high levels of support from European poor.[3]

However well the meritocracy is working—or not—it says something about Americans that they view opportunity as a national ethos. It is indisputably true of every society, including our own, that to some extent external factors—luck, inherited wealth, upbringing—help determine a person's success. Indeed, "success" itself is often a subjective and multilayered idea that can mean entirely different things to different sets of people.

Americans have long touted the value of personal responsibility, often mocked by elites as hopelessly simplistic. Yet this belief continues to undercut a corrosive culture of victimhood and dependence that permeates European society. Americans should not dismiss that inherent unfairness sometimes exists in the system, but a society that values and incentivizes personal self-determination also creates a strong work ethic, a strong sense of fairness, and more opportunity. Americans are more charitable than any other people in the world, and yet the idea of living off the state or expecting someone to take care of you is still somewhat stigmatized. Europhiles find the crudity of this foundational conception of American life distasteful. Fans of European socialism like Alexandria Ocasio-Cortez lecture

Americans about how it is both "physically" and metaphorically "impossible" to pull oneself up by their bootstraps. Millions of immigrants who flood into this country every decade—including my own parents, who fled the economic "equality" of communist Europe—might be surprised to learn that success is a mythology.

Of course, Europeans do not emerge from the womb clamoring to be taken care of by the commissioners of the EU, but rather they are brought into a reality of their social situation. In France or Hungary, economic systems and cultural attitudes do not propel and celebrate individual achievement in the same way we do in the United States. Rather there is a tradition of the state treating the citizenry like a munificent parent—and that attitude is portable from the generations that lived under monarchy to those who lived under fascism and communism, and now under the bureaucratic superstate that exists in Europe today.

While Europhiles have spent years demeaning this kind of aspiration, a merit-based ideal helps diffuse class and caste systems—and helps better assimilate immigrants and creates the kind of competitiveness that Europe lacks. The fact is evident in our technological, moral, and economic success as a nation and our massive wealth, diversified lifestyles, and vocational choices. As the most America-centric politician in European history, Margaret Thatcher, once noted, "We want a society where people are free to make choices, to make mistakes, to be generous and compassionate. This is what we mean by a moral society; not a society where the state is responsible for everything, and no one is responsible for the state."[4] This is not the way in Europe. And understanding the fundamental difference in outlook goes a long way in comprehending our policy differences.

INDIVIDUALISM: "Americans tend to prioritize individual liberty, while Europeans tend to value the role of the state to ensure no one in society is in need."

Nearly 60 percent of Americans believe that allowing everyone to pursue their life's goals without interference from the state is more important than ensuring that every person live without need. Majorities in every single European nation, on the other hand, believe that it is more important for the state to guarantee *no one* suffers than to protect the rights of all individuals—an outlook that is incompatible with the idea of the American republic.

This is a false binary choice. There will always be *someone* in need. Mankind has yet to concoct any political or economic system in which society successfully guarantees that all people are taken care of. The United States has proven that allowing everyone to pursue their life's goals in an open economy is the best way to ensure that *most* citizens partake in wealth generated by a competitive capitalistic society.

Americans are no more inclined to allow enduring poverty to exist than Europeans. And though we are constantly offering opportunity to millions of new arrivals—far more overall than Europeans, despite the perceptions—we remain the wealthiest major nation in the world by nearly every measurement.

Societies that place the state's role in procuring equal outcomes over individual freedom have produced some of the most hideous outcomes ever visited upon mankind. This is not to suggest that the kind of contemporary European bureaucratism now favored by many American elites is tantamount to communism, but it is to suggest that it's destructive. Europeans are more pliable. They have a tradition of acquiescing to the state for their moral guidance and the promise of safety and equality. The European mind invites trouble. The Europhilic mind invites that trouble to the North American continent.

FREEDOM OF SPEECH: "There is greater tolerance in the U.S. than in Europe for offensive speech."

This too is misleading framing: Americans don't have any "greater tolerance" for offensive speech than Europeans; they have fostered a greater acceptance of neutral freedoms—laws and rights that apply to liberties without regard to the substance or underlying message of the expression. This is the fiber holding together American liberties.

Around 75 percent of Americans still believe citizens should be allowed to make statements that are offensive to people's religious beliefs. This is a significantly higher share of the public than in any of the European Union nations, despite the fact that organized religion—other than Islam—is dying in Europe. In Poland, Germany, and Italy, less than half of the population believe this kind of speech should be even legal. Whereas anticlericalism was a key to balancing European power, today the state—the only church with any real power on the European continent decides what is and isn't worthy of free expression.

Americans are also far more likely to say offensive statements "about minority groups" should be permitted, though this number is shrinking. This says nothing about the tolerance of the nation—the United States by every measure is more tolerant than Europe. But it does say something about Americans' affinity for liberal values.

GOD: "Religion is significantly less important to Europeans than to Americans."

Slightly over half of Americans say religion is very important in their life, nearly double the share who hold this view in Poland, which registered the highest percentage among EU nations polled. Religious life is not merely the most obvious faith-based aspect of life—moral life—but also there is civil society and the belief in the exceptionalism of its people and laws. European identity has been diluted into a mélange of vapid politically correct slogans that are increasingly encroaching on any recognizable set of useful liberal principles.

Faith, or the tenets and moral values that gird a healthy society, are portable and enduring whether Moses parted the Red Sea or not. As the historian Tom Holland noted recently, even

Western secularism is "a distinctive Christian idea and it's not remotely neutral because it obliges Muslims and Jews and Hindus and whoever to alter their understanding of themselves to fit into this template." Faith in that template engenders a belief that transcends contemporary political fads—certainly it transcends the European Union's flag, which now stands for little more than an economic arrangement and bureaucratism.

Whereas anticlericalism once balanced the power of the church with liberal ideals, there is no balance anymore. There is no anticlericalism to check the rise of vapid universalism endorsed by the European elites or the illiberal orthodoxy of political Islam. Universalism is a faith that has overtaken Europe at a rate faster than any other religious movement in its history. Universalism might be malleable and often incoherent, but it's an assault on family and life. It creates apathy and strips away identity. In this environment, Europeans are once again starting to look for meaning in hypernationalism and socialism—the two catastrophic philosophies of the twentieth century.

Europe keeps abandoning its best ideas. We have no reason to follow.

Acknowledgments

Firstly, I'm grateful to Eric Nelson for bringing me the idea of writing a book about the Europhiles who dominate American political discourse. My editor, Hannah Long, sharpened my thinking and improved the manuscript. Thanks to both, and to everyone else at Broadside, for making the book possible. I'm indebted as well to Krystina Skurk, who offered invaluable assistance in researching and synthesizing the complexities of bloated European institutions, and to Lindsay Craig at National Review Institute, who provided me with top-notch researchers Amanda Johnson, Grace Maffucci, and Anne Whelan. Thanks also to Keith Urbahn, and everyone at Javelin.

It's been a great pleasure working with Rich Lowry, Jason Steorts, Phil Klein, and Judd Berger—and all my other colleagues—at *National Review*. Thanks also to those who edit my work at other venues: Sohrab Ahmari and Adam Brodsky at the *New*

York Post, Seth Mandel at the *Washington Examiner*, and Simone Slykhous and Alessandra Caruso at Creators Syndicate.

I am lucky to have many cohorts and friends such as Charles Cooke, Mollie Hemingway, Karen and Phil Meyer, Buck Sexton, and Harris Vederman, who both support and challenge my thinking. Also, I appreciate the kind words from Victor Davis Hanson, Brian Kilmeade, Dana Loesch, Arthur Herman, and Meghan McCain.

Gratitude goes out to my brothers and their wonderful families. My amazing children continue to be a source of inspiration and happiness. Though I would be nowhere without the patience, support, and love of my wife. And, finally, thank you, Mom and Dad, for everything, but especially for defecting to ensure my life in the new world.

Notes

1. EUROPEANIZATION

1. Ryan McMaken, "3 Times as Many Europeans Move to the US, Than the Other Way Around," Mises Institute, December 6, 2018, https://mises.org/wire/3-times-many-europeans-move-us-other-way-around.
2. Rubina Pabani and Brendan Miller, "How Europeans See America," *New York Times*, October 28, 2019, https://www.nytimes.com/2019/10/28/opinion/europeans-view-americans.html.
3. Alec Gallup and Lydia Saad, "Americans Know Little About European Union," Gallup, June 16, 2004, https://news.gallup.com/poll/12043/americans-know-little-about-european-union.aspx.
4. Vijay Joshi, "America Seen from Abroad: Arrogant, Nice, Tech-Savvy, Free," Associated Press, August 5, 2016, https://www.ap.org/explore/divided-america/america-seen-from-abroad-arrogant-nice-tech-savvy-free.html.
5. Richard Pells, *Not Like Us: How Europeans Have Loved, Hated, and Transformed American Culture Since World War II* (New York: Basic Books, 1998), 4.

2. THE NORDIC "UTOPIAS"

1. P. J. O'Rourke, *Eat the Rich: A Treatise on Economics* (Boston: Atlantic Monthly Press, 1999), 185.
2. Jeffrey D. Sachs, "The Social Welfare State, beyond Ideology," *Scientific American*, November 2006, https://www.scientificamerican.com/article/the-social-welfare-state/.
3. Paul Krugman, "Socialist Hellhole Blogging," *New York Times*,

August 11, 2011, https://krugman.blogs.nytimes.com/2011/08/19/socialist-hellhole-blogging/.

4. *Washington Post* staff, "The CNN Democratic Debate Transcript, Annotated," CNN, October 13, 2015, https://www.washingtonpost.com/news/the-fix/wp/2015/10/13/the-oct-13-democratic-debate-who-said-what-and-what-it-means/.

5. Staff, "Full Transcript: Ninth Democratic Debate in Las Vegas," February 20, 2020, https://www.nbcnews.com/politics/2020-election/full-transcript-ninth-democratic-debate-las-vegas-n1139546.

6. Heritage Foundation, 2020 Index of Economic Freedom, 2020, https://www.heritage.org/index/.

7. World Bank, "Ease of Doing Business Rankings," 2019, https://www.doingbusiness.org/en/rankings.

8. "The Next Supermodel," *Economist*, February 2, 2013, https://www.economist.com/leaders/2013/02/02/the-next-supermodel.

9. Kerry Jackson, "Denmark Tells Bernie Sanders It's Had Enough of His 'Socialist' Slurs," *Investor's Business Daily*, November 9, 2015, https://www.investors.com/politics/commentary/denmark-tells-bernie-sanders-to-stop-calling-it-socialist/.

10. Andreas Bergh, "The Rise, Fall and Revival of the Swedish Welfare State: What Are the Policy Lessons from Sweden?," Research Institute of Industrial Economics, 2011, https://www.ifn.se/wfiles/wp/wp873.pdf.

11. Rainer Zitelmann, "The Myth of Nordic Socialism," *Barrons*, April 3, 2019, https://www.barrons.com/articles/the-myth-of-nordic-socialism-51554296401.

12. Ibid.

13. Richard H. Pletcher, "Sweden: Gross Domestic Product (GDP) Per Capita in Current Prices from 1985 to 2025," Statista, January 20, 2021, https://www.statista.com/statistics/375643/gross-domestic-product-gdp-per-capita-in-sweden/.

14. Nima Sanandaji, *Scandinavian Unexceptionalism: Culture, Markets and the Failure of Third-Way Socialism* (London: Institute of Economic Affairs, 2015), 62.

15. Sweden Sverige, "Sweden and Migration," https://sweden.se/migration/.

16. Ran Abramitzky, Leah Platt Boustan, and Katherine Eriksson, "Europe's Tired, Poor, Huddled Masses: Self-Selection and Economic Outcomes in the Age of Mass Migration," *American Economic Review*, August 2012, https://www.ncbi.nlm.nih.gov/pmc/articles/PMC4651453/.

17. Ran Abramitzky, Leah Platt Boustan, and Katherine Eriksson, "To the New World and Back Again: Return Migrants in the Age of

Mass Migration," *ILR Review*, Cornell University, August 28, 2017, https://journals.sagepub.com/doi/10.1177/0019793917726981.

18. Aamna Mohdin, "The Most Refugee-Friendly Country in Europe Is Growing Weary," Quartz, September 7, 2016, https://qz.com/774427/the-most-refugee-friendly-country-in-europe-is-growing-weary/.

19. Adam Taylor, "Denmark Puts Ad in Lebanese Newspapers: Dear Refugees, Don't Come Here," *Washington Post*, September 7, 2015, https://www.washingtonpost.com/news/worldviews/wp/2015/09/07/denmark-places-an-advertisement-in-lebanese-newspapers-dear-refugees-dont-come-here/.

20. "Baden-Württemberg stoppt vorerst Aufnahme von Flüchtlingen," *Frankfurter Allgemeine Zeitung*, September 9, 2015, http://www.faz.net/aktuell/politik/fluechtlingskrise/daenische-bahn-stoppt-zugverkehr-aus-deutschland-13793739.html.

21. Sweden Sverige, "Sweden and Migration," https://sweden.se/migration/.

22. David Crouch, "Sweden Slams Shut Its Open-Door Policy Towards Refugees," *Guardian*, November 24, 2015, https://www.theguardian.com/world/2015/nov/24/sweden-asylum-seekers-refugees-policy-reversal.

23. "Facts About Migration, Integration and Crime in Sweden," Ministry for Foreign Affairs, Government Offices of Sweden, February 23, 2017, https://www.government.se/articles/2017/02/facts-about-migration-and-crime-in-sweden/.

24. Paulina Neuding, "Sweden's Violent Reality Is Undoing a Peaceful Self-Image," *Politico*, April 16, 2018, https://www.politico.eu/article/sweden-bombings-grenade-attacks-violent-reality-undoing-peaceful-self-image-law-and-order/.

25. Nima Sanandaji, "So Long, Swedish Welfare State?," *Foreign Policy*, September 5, 2018, https://foreignpolicy.com/2018/09/05/so-long-swedish-welfare-state/.

26. Christopher Caldwell, *Reflections on the Revolution in Europe: Immigration, Islam, and the West* (New York: Doubleday, 2019), 111.

27. Tino Sanandaji, "What Is the Truth About Crime and Immigration in Sweden?," *National Review*, February 25, 2017, https://www.nationalreview.com/2017/02/sweden-crime-rates-statistics-immigration-trump-fox-news/.

28. Lee Roden, "Why Sweden Doesn't Keep Stats on Ethnicity and Crime," *Local*, May 8, 2018, https://www.thelocal.se/20180508/why-sweden-doesnt-keep-stats-on-ethnic-background-and-crime.

29. Sanandaji, "What Is the Truth about Crime and Immigration in Sweden?"

30. Stephen Brown, "Sweden Freaks Out," *Politico*, July 11, 2018,

https://www.politico.eu/article/sweden-joins-the-club-far-right
-democrats-jimmie-akesson-stefan-lofven-general-election/.

31. Rafaela Lindeberg, "Unemployment Is Haunting Sweden Years After the Immigration Boom," Bloomberg, November 2, 2018, https://
www.bloomberg.com/news/articles/2018-11-02/unemployment-is
-haunting-sweden-years-after-the-immigration-boom/.

32. "Ancestry in Minnesota," Statistical Atlas, September 4, 2018,
https://statisticalatlas.com/state/Minnesota/Ancestry.

33. Benny Carlson and Stefanie Chambers, "A Tale of Twin Cities and
Somalis Being Trumped," *MinnPost*, May 23, 2017, https://www
.minnpost.com/community-voices/2017/05/tale-twin-cities-and
-somalis-being-trumped/.

34. Johan Norberg, "Swedish Models," *National Interest*, June 1, 2006,
https://nationalinterest.org/article/swedish-models-869.

35. Jan-Emmanuel De Neve, John Helliwell, Richard Layard, and
Jeffrey D. Sachs, "World Happiness Report 2020," Sustainable
Development Solutions Network, March 20, 2020, https://world
happiness.report/ed/2020/#read.

36. James J. Heckman and Rasmus Landersø, "The Scandinavian Fantasy: The Sources of Intergenerational Mobility in Denmark and the
U.S.," National Bureau of Economic Research, July 2016, https://
www.nber.org/papers/w22465.

37. Saska Saarikoski, "Maailman suosituin presidentti," *Helsingin Sa-
nomat*, November 4, 2019, https://www.hs.fi/kuukausiliite/art-20
00006290539.html.

38. Maria Cramer, "Smile? The Results from the 2020 World Happiness Report Are In," *New York Times*, March 20, 2020, https://www
.nytimes.com/2020/03/20/world/europe/world-happiness-report
.html.

39. Matt Reynolds, "Scandinavia's Reign as the Happiest Place on Earth
Is Ending," *Wired*, July 31, 2019, https://www.wired.co.uk/article
/worlds-happiest-country-scandinavia.

40. Michael Booth, "The Danish Don't Have the Secret to Happiness,"
Atlantic, January 30, 2015, https://www.theatlantic.com/health
/archive/2015/01/the-danish-dont-have-the-secret-to-happiness
/384930/.

41. Ibid.

42. Sarah Boseley, "Nordic Countries' 'Happy' Reputation Masks Sadness of Young, Says Report," *Guardian*, August 27, 2018, https://
www.theguardian.com/world/2018/aug/25/nordic-countries
-happy-reputation-masks-sadness-of-young-says-report.

43. "Crisis Point: Well-Being of Young People Still Defined by the Economic Crisis," European Foundation for the Improvement of Living and Working Conditions, July 4, 2019.

44. O'Rourke, *Eat the Rich*, 158.

45. Nima Sanandaji, "The Swedish Lesson: Welfare States Create Moral Hazard," *National Review*, May 17, 2019, https://www.national review.com/2019/05/nordic-countries-scale-back-welfare-states/.

46. Seth Motel, "5 Facts on How Americans View Taxes," Pew Research Center, April 10, 2015, https://www.pewresearch.org/fact -tank/2015/04/10/5-facts-on-how-americans-view-taxes/.

47. Elke Asen, "Insights into the Tax Systems of Scandinavian Countries," Tax Foundation, February 24, 2020, https://taxfoundation .org/bernie-sanders-scandinavian-countries-taxes/.

48. Ibid.

49. "Global Revenue Statistics Database," Organisation for Economic Co-operation and Development, 2018, https://stats.oecd.org/Index .aspx?DataSetCode=RS_GBL.

50. Asen, "Insights into the Tax Systems of Scandinavian Countries."

51. Terry Moran, "Obama: No 'Easy Out' for Wall Street," ABC News, February 10, 2009, https://abcnews.go.com/Politics/Business/story ?id=6844330&page=1/.

3. EUROPE'S HEALTH CARE DISASTERS

1. Roger Cohen, "The Public Imperative," *New York Times*, October 4, 2009, https://www.nytimes.com/2009/10/05/opinion/05iht-edcohen .html.

2. Aaron Carroll and Austin Frakt, "The Best Health Care System in the World: Which One Would You Pick?," *New York Times*, September 18, 2017, https://www.nytimes.com/interactive/2017/09/18 /upshot/best-health-care-system-country-bracket.html.

3. Erika Edwards and Lauren Dunn, "Is Germany's Health Care System a Model for the U.S.?," NBC News, June 30, 2019, https://www .nbcnews.com/health/health-news/edscap-s-health-care-system -model-u-s-n1024491.

4. "The Fix for American Health Care Can Be Found in Europe," *Economist*, August 10, 2017, https://www.economist.com/united -states/2017/08/10/the-fix-for-american-health-care-can-be-found -in-europe.

5. Charlotte Morabito, "France's Health-Care System Was Ranked as the World's Best—Here's How It Compares with the US," CNBC,

May 17, 2019, https://www.cnbc.com/2019/05/17/france-versus-the
-united-states-how-the-two-nations-health-care-systems-compare
.html.

6. Lisa Rapaport, "U.S. Health Spending Twice Other Countries' with
    Worse Results," Reuters, March 13, 2018, https://www.reuters.com
    /article/us-health-spending/u-s-health-spending-twice-other
    -countries-with-worse-results-idUSKCN1GP2YN.

7. Press release, "Jayapal, Dingell and More Than 100 Co-Sponsors
    Introduce Medicare for All Act of 2019," Pramila Jayapal, Febru-
    ary 28, 2019, https://jayapal.house.gov/2019/02/28/jayapal-dingell
    -and-more-than-100-co-sponsors-introduce-medicare-for-all-act-of
    -2019/.

8. "Life Expectancy and Healthy Life Expectancy," World Health
    Organization, https://www.who.int/data/gho/data/themes/topics
    /indicator-groups/indicator-group-details/GHO/life-expectancy
    -and-healthy-life-expectancy.

9. Ashish K. Jha, Irene Papanicolas, and Liana R. Woskie, "Health
    Care Spending in the United States and Other High-Income
    Countries," *Journal of the American Medical Association*, March
    13, 2018, https://jamanetwork.com/journals/jama/article-abstract
    /2674671.

10. Gorav Ailawadi, Castigliano M. Bhamidipati, David R. Jones, Ir-
    ving L. Kron, Damien J. LaPar, Carlos M. Mery, Bruce D. Schirmer,
    and George J. Stukenborg, "Primary Payer Status Affects Mortality
    for Major Surgical Operations," *Annals of Surgery*, April 6, 2010,
    https://www.ncbi.nlm.nih.gov/pmc/articles/PMC3071622/.

11. Avik Roy, "The Myth of Americans' Poor Life Expectancy," *Forbes*,
    November 23, 2011, https://www.forbes.com/sites/theapothecary
    /2011/11/23/the-myth-of-americans-poor-life-expectancy/.

12. Scott Gottlieb, "Medicaid Is Worse Than No Coverage at All," *Wall
    Street Journal*, March 10, 2011, https://www.wsj.com/articles/SB10
    001424052748704758904576188280858303612.

13. Avik Roy, "Why Medicaid Is a Humanitarian Catastrophe,"
    Forbes, May 2, 2011, https://www.forbes.com/sites/theapothecary
    /2011/03/02/why-medicaid-is-a-humanitarian-catastrophe/.

14. Roy, "The Myth of Americans' Poor Life Expectancy."

15. Amelia Bertozzi-Villa, Laura Dwyer-Lindgren, Rebecca W. Stubbs
    et al., "Inequalities in Life Expectancy Among US Counties, 1980
    to 2014," *Journal of the American Medical Association*, July 2017,
    https://jamanetwork.com/journals/jamainternalmedicine/fullarticle
    /2626194.

16. "Average Annual Miles per Driver by Age Group," U.S. Department

of Transportation, Federal Highway Administration, March 29, 2018, https://www.fhwa.dot.gov/ohim/onh00/bar8.htm.

17. UK Department for Transport, "National Travel Survey," https://www.gov.uk/government/collections/national-travel-survey-statistics.

18. Robert L. Ohsfeldt and John E. Schneider, "The Business of Health: The Role of Competition, Markets, and Regulation," American Enterprise Institute, October 3, 2006, http://www.aei.org/press/the-business-of-health/.

19. Nicholas Kristof (@nickkristof), "Hm. The US ranks 41 in child mortality. An American child is 55 percent more likely to die by age 19 than kids in other OECD countries. An American woman is three times as likely to die in pregnancy or childbirth. Three US counties have shorter life expectancy than Cambodia," Twitter, April 9, 2020, 9:52 a.m., https://twitter.com/nickkristof/status/1248247527696035842.

20. Sarah Kliff, "American Kids Are 70 Percent More Likely to Die Before Adulthood Than Kids in Other Rich Countries," Vox, June 8, 2018, https://www.vox.com/health-care/2018/1/8/16863656/childhood-mortality-united-states/.

21. Gary Price and Tim Norbeck, "Infant Mortality Isn't a True Measure of a Successful Healthcare System," *Forbes*, April 12, 2016, https://www.forbes.com/sites/physiciansfoundation/2016/04/12/infant-mortality-not-a-true-measure-of-a-successful-health-care-system/.

22. Sally Pipes, "U.S. Has the Worst Health Care? Not by a Long Shot," *Forbes*, July 14, 2014, https://www.forbes.com/sites/sallypipes/2014/07/14/u-s-has-the-worst-health-care-not-by-a-long-shot/.

23. Scott W. Atlas, "Infant Mortality: A Deceptive Statistic," *National Review*, September 14, 2014, https://www.nationalreview.com/2011/09/infant-mortality-deceptive-statistic-scott-w-atlas/.

24. Robert Woods, "Long-Term Trends in Fetal Mortality: Implications for Developing Countries," World Health Organization Bulletin, April 1, 2008, https://www.who.int/bulletin/volumes/86/6/07-043471/en/.

25. Heather Jordan, "Baby Who Weighed Less Than 1 Pound at Birth Gets to Go Home, Dad Says It's 'Nothing Short of a Miracle,'" *Saginaw News*, November 4, 2020, https://www.mlive.com/news/saginaw-bay-city/2020/11/baby-who-weighed-less-than-1-pound-at-birth-gets-to-go-home-dad-says-its-nothing-short-of-a-miracle.html.

26. Jha, Papanicolas, and Woskie, "Health Care Spending in the United States and Other High-Income Countries."

27. Marilyn Geewax, "Why Americans Spend Too Much," National Public Radio, December 6, 2011, https://www.npr.org/2011/12/05/143149947/why-americans-spend-too-much.

28. "Clinical Trials Map," United States National Library of Medicine, https://clinicaltrials.gov/ct2/search/map.

29. "All Nobel Prizes in Physiology or Medicine," Nobel Prize, https://www.nobelprize.org/prizes/lists/all-nobel-laureates-in-physiology-or-medicine/.

30. Michael Drummond, Beena Bhuiyan Khan, and Corinna Sorenson, "Medical Technology as a Key Driver of Rising Health Expenditure: Disentangling the Relationship," *ClinicoEconomics and Outcomes Research*, May 30, 2013, https://www.ncbi.nlm.nih.gov/pmc/articles/PMC3686328/.

31. Aaron E. Carroll, "Why Survival Rate Is Not the Best Way to Judge Cancer Spending," *New York Times*, April 13, 2015, https://www.nytimes.com/2015/04/14/upshot/why-survival-rate-is-not-the-best-way-to-judge-cancer-spending.html.

32. Stacy Simon, "Facts & Figures 2020 Reports Largest One-Year Drop in Cancer Mortality," American Cancer Society, January 8, 2020, https://www.cancer.org/latest-news/facts-and-figures-2020.html.

33. "Health at a Glance 2019," Organisation for Economic Co-operation and Development, November 7, 2019, https://www.oecd.org/health/health-systems/health-at-a-glance-19991312.htm.

34. Laura Joszt, "The US Has Higher Incidence, Survival of Rare Cancers Compared with Europe," *American Journal of Managed Care*, June 6, 2020, https://www.ajmc.com/view/the-us-has-higher-incidence-survival-of-rare-cancers-compared-with-europe.

35. Hector Florimon, "Why the US Spends More on Health Care Than Other Countries, but Doesn't Fare Better: Study," ABC News, September 12, 2019, https://abcnews.go.com/Health/us-spends-health-care-countries-fare-study/story?id=53710650.

36. Thomas Sullivan, "A Tough Road: Cost to Develop One New Drug Is $2.6 Billion; Approval Rate for Drugs Entering Clinical Development Is Less Than 12%," *Policy & Medicine*, March 21, 2019, https://www.policymed.com/2014/12/a-tough-road-cost-to-develop-one-new-drug-is-26-billion-approval-rate-for-drugs-entering-clinical-de.html.

37. Editorial Board, "Why Are Drugs Cheaper in Europe?," *Wall Street Journal*, October 28, 2018, https://www.wsj.com/articles/why-are-drugs-cheaper-in-europe-1540760855.

38. Robert Moffit, *No Choice, No Exit* (Washington, DC: Heritage Foundation, 2020), 246, https://www.heritage.org/article/the-truth-about-government-controlled-health-care.
39. Ziba Kashef, "FDA Approves Drugs More Quickly Than Peer Agency in Europe," *Yale News*, April 5, 2017, https://news.yale.edu/2017/04/05/fda-approves-drugs-more-quickly-peer-agency-europe.
40. Alexandra Nightingale, "Brief: More Rigorous Patent Examination in US Than Europe and Australia?," *Intellectual Property Watch*, November 2, 2016, https://www.ip-watch.org/2016/11/02/rigorous-patent-examination-us-europe-australia/.
41. Nicholas S. Downing, Joseph S. Ross, and Audrey D. Zhang, "Regulatory Review of New Therapeutic Agents—FDA versus EMA, 2011–2015," *New England Journal of Medicine*, April 6, 2017, https://www.nejm.org/doi/full/10.1056/NEJMc1700103#t=article.
42. "International Physician Compensation Report 2019. Do US Physicians Have It Best?," *Medscape*, September 16, 2019, https://www.medscape.com/slideshow/2019-international-compensation-report-6011814.
43. Lisa Rapaport, "U.S. Relies Heavily on Foreign-Born Healthcare Workers," Reuters, December 4, 2018, https://www.reuters.com/article/us-health-professions-us-noncitizens/u-s-relies-heavily-on-foreign-born-healthcare-workers-idUSKBN1O32FR.
44. Anthony Pearson and Nicola Triglione, "Italian Lessons for U.S. Healthcare—the Skeptical Cardiologist Hosts an Italian Cardiologist," *MedPage Today*, February 15, 2020, https://www.medpagetoday.com/blogs/skeptical-cardiologist/84888?.
45. Sally Pipes, "U.K.'s Healthcare Horror Stories Ought to Curb Dems' Enthusiasm for Single-Payer," *Forbes*, October 1, 2018, https://www.forbes.com/sites/sallypipes/2018/10/01/u-k-s-healthcare-horror-stories-ought-to-curb-dems-enthusiasm-for-single-payer/?sh=4a99c3a23099.
46. Ibid.
47. Denis Campbell, "NHS Suffering Worst Ever Staff and Cash Crisis, Figures Show," *Guardian*, September 11, 2018, https://www.theguardian.com/society/2018/sep/11/nhs-suffering-worst-ever-staff-cash-crisis-figures-show.
48. Anonymous, "My Job as a Doctor in Today's NHS Is Draining Me of Humanity," *Guardian*, February 7, 2019, https://www.theguardian.com/society/2019/feb/07/job-doctor-todays-nhs-draining-humanity.
49. Sally Pipes, "God Save the Queen's Health Care System," *Investor's*

Business Daily, February 2, 2018, https://www.investors.com/politics /columnists/sally-c-pipes-god-save-the-queens-health-care-system/.

50. Sarah Smith, "Nurses Quit NHS to Work in Lidl Because Pay, Hours and Benefits Better," *London Economic*, July 2, 2018, https:// www.thelondoneconomic.com/news/nurses-quit-nhs-to-work-in -lidl-because-pay-hours-and-benefits-better/02/07/.

51. Silvia Amaro, "Lacking Beds, Masks and Doctors, Europe's Health Services Struggle to Cope with the Coronavirus," CNBC, April 3, 2020, https://www.cnbc.com/2020/04/03/coronavirus-italy-spain -uk-health-services-struggle-to-cope.html.

52. David Jiménez, "Spain's Lethal Secret: We Didn't Have 'the Best Health Care in the World,'" *New York Times*, April 13, 2020, https://www.nytimes.com/2020/04/13/opinion/spain-coronavirus -hospitals.html.

53. Paul Krugman, "The Swiss Menace," *New York Times*, April 16, 2009, https://www.nytimes.com/2009/08/17/opinion/17krugman .html.

54. Chris Pope, "Medicare for All? Lessons from Abroad for Comprehensive Health-Care Reform," Manhattan Institute, November 19, 2019, https://www.manhattan-institute.org/using-lessons-from-inter national-health-care-medicare-for-all.

55. Ezra Klein, "In the UK's Health System, Rationing Isn't a Dirty Word," Vox, January 28, 2020, https://www.vox.com/2020/1 /28/21074386/health-care-rationing-britain-nhs-nice-medicare -for-all.

56. Avik Roy, "Socialized Medicine Is Bad for Your Health," *National Review*, May 16, 2019, https://www.nationalreview.com/magazine /2019/06/03/socialized-medicine-is-bad-for-your-health/.

57. Joy Ogden, "QALYs and Their Role in the NICE Decision-Making Process," *Prescriber*, April 2017, https://wchh.onlinelibrary.wiley .com/doi/pdf/10.1002/psb.1562.

58. "Procedures of Limited Clinical Value," Ration Watch, http://www .rationwatch.co.uk/ccgs/ (accessed November 14, 2020).

59. "Patients Are Being Denied Vital Cataract Surgery," RNIB, March 20, 2019, https://www.rnib.org.uk/patients-are-being-denied-vital -cataract-surgery.

60. "Thousands in Britain Left to Go Blind Due to Eye Surgery Rationing: Report," *Straits Times*, April 6, 2019, https://www.straits times.com/world/europe/thousands-in-britain-left-to-go-blind -due-to-eye-surgery-rationing-report.

61. Nick Triggle, "Lucentis: An NHS Dilemma," BBC News, August 27, 2008, http://news.bbc.co.uk/2/hi/health/7582740.stm.

62. Arthur Chambers, "Trends in U.S. Health Travel Service Trade," Office of Industries: USITC Executive Briefing on Trade, August 2015, https://www.usitc.gov/publications/332/executive_briefings/chambers_health-related_travel_final.pdf, 1.

63. Denis Campbell, "NHS Opens Clinic to Help Child Addicts of Computer Games," *Guardian*, October 7, 2019, https://www.theguardian.com/society/2019/oct/08/nhs-opens-clinic-to-help-child-addicts-of-computer-games.

64. Ibid.; Sally Pipes, *False Premise, False Promise: The Disastrous Reality of Medicare for All* (Pacific Research Center, 2020), 120.

65. Ross Clark, "Sex Addicts May Get Free Treatment on NHS so Why Are Taxpaying Britons Being Denied Hernia Operations?," *Daily Mail*, July 11, 2018, https://www.dailymail.co.uk/debate/article-5944631/Sex-addicts-free-treatment-NHS-taxpaying-Britons-denied-hernia-operations.html.

66. Ibid.

67. "NHS Hospitals Need Plan to Tackle Backlog of Patients, Warns RCS," Royal College of Surgeons of England, March 14, 2019, https://www.rcseng.ac.uk/news-and-events/media-centre/press-releases/nhs-stats-march-2019/.

68. Denis Campbell, "NHS Hospital Waiting Lists Could Hit 10 Million in England This Year," *Guardian*, June 9, 2020, https://www.theguardian.com/society/2020/jun/10/nhs-hospital-waiting-lists-could-hit-10-million-in-england-this-year.

69. "NHS Combined Performance Summary December–January 2020," National Healthcare System, February 13, 2020, https://www.england.nhs.uk/statistics/wp content/uploads/sites/2/2020/02/Combined-Performance-Summary-February-December-January-data-2020-oi2U9.pdf.

70. Susannah Thraves, "My Wait for NHS Surgery Has Caused Me Further Pain," *Guardian*, August 7, 2019, https://www.theguardian.com/commentisfree/2019/aug/07/wait-nhs-surgery-pain-patients-england-distress.

71. James C. Capretta, "Market-Driven Health Care Is Worth the Effort," American Enterprise Institute, February 26, 2020, https://www.aei.org/articles/market-driven-health-care-is-worth-the-effort/.

72. Sally Pipes, "Britain's Version of 'Medicare for All' Is Struggling with Long Waits for Care," *Forbes*, April 1, 2019, https://www.forbes.com/sites/sallypipes/2019/04/01/britains-version-of-medicare-for-all-is-collapsing/?sh=41afe50136b8.

73. Denis Campbell, "Thousands of Patients Die Waiting for Beds in Hospitals—Study," *Guardian*, December 10, 2019, https://www

.theguardian.com/society/2019/dec/10/thousands-of-patients-die
-waiting-for-beds-in-hospitals-study.

74. Richard Vernalls and Jane Kirby, "Two Patients Die on Trolleys in Same A&E in One Week as NHS Struggles to Cope," *Independent*, January 6, 2017, https://www.independent.co.uk/life-style/health -and-families/health-news/worcestershire-hospital-patients-die -trolleys-and-e-nhs-crisis-a7513546.html.

75. Pipes, "U.K.'s Healthcare Horror Stories Ought to Curb Dems' Enthusiasm for Single-Payer."

76. Sarah Johnson, "Patient Safety Hit by Lack of Staff, Warn 80% of NHS Workers," *Guardian*, March 17, 2018, https://www.theguardian .com/society/2018/mar/18/hospitals-staff-shortage-nursing-nhs -rcn-patient-care-sarah-johnson-survey.

4. "THE UNITED STATES OF EUROPE"

1. Steven G. Calabresi, "Scalia on Writing Well, Originalism, and a Turkey Hunting Mishap," *Washington Post*, November 3, 2017, https://www.washingtonpost.com/outlook/scalia-on-writing-well -originalism-and-a-turkey-hunting-mishap/2017/11/03/778f8202 -b364-11e7-a908-a3470754bbb9_story.html.

2. Speech by M. Paul-Henri Spaak, president of the Ad Hoc Assembly, March 9, 1953, during a formal sitting at the Maison de l'Europe in Strasbourg, http://www.epgencms.europarl.europa.eu/cmsdata /upload/475124d2-aac4-4f48-bcf2-6e93774953ee/10068947 _speech_spaak_EN.PDF.

3. Ted R. Bromund, "The Top Ten US Myths About the European Union," Heritage Foundation, January 25, 2016, https://www.heritage .org/europe/commentary/the-top-ten-us-myths-about-the-european -union.

4. Timothy S. Boylan, "The Framing of the EU Constitution: An American Constitutional Perspective," *Journal of Political Science*, November 2005, https://digitalcommons.coastal.edu/cgi/viewcontent .cgi?article=1297&context=jops.

5. "Treaty for Establishing a Constitution for Europe," European Communities, 2005, https://europa.eu/european-union/sites/europaeu /files/docs/body/treaty_establishing_a_constitution_for_europe _en.pdf/.

6. Ruth Bader Ginsburg, "'A Decent Respect to the Opinions of [Human]kind': The Value of a Comparative Perspective in Constitutional Adjudication," *FIU Law Review*, Spring 2016, https://

ecollections.law.fiu.edu/cgi/viewcontent.cgi?referer=https://www
.google.com/&httpsredir=1&article=1006&context=lawreview.

7. Adam Liptak, "'We the People' Loses Appeal with People Around
the World," *New York Times*, February 6, 2012, https://www.nytimes
.com/2012/02/07/us/we-the-people-loses-appeal-with-people
-around-the-world.html.

8. Luigi Barzini, *The Europeans* (New York: Penguin Books, 1984), 37.

9. John Pinder and Simon Usherwood, *The European Union: A Very Short
Introduction*, 3rd ed. (Oxford: Oxford University Press, 2013), 49.

10. Michael Ashcroft, "How the United Kingdom Voted on
Thursday . . . and Why," Lord Ashcroft Polls, June 24, 2016, https://
lordashcroftpolls.com/2016/06/how-the-united-kingdom-voted
-and-why/.

11. Huw Jones and Marine Strauss, "Britain and EU Split over Financial
Market Access," Reuters, February 11, 2020, https://www.reuters
.com/article/britain-eu-equivalence/update-2-britain-eu-split-over
-financial-market-access-idUSL8N2AB373.

12. Benjamin Wallace-Wells, "Brexit Makes the U.S. the Last, Best Hope
for Liberalism," *New Yorker*, June 24, 2016, https://www.newyorker
.com/news/benjamin-wallace-wells/brexit-creates-a-lonely-new
-american-exceptionalism.

13. "The European Single Market," European Commission, https://ec
.europa.eu/growth/single-market_en.

14. Bromund, "The Top Ten US Myths About the European Union."

15. Jakub Grygiel, "The Status of the EU: A Frustrated Empire Built
on the Wrong Assumption," Hoover Institution, August 12, 2020,
https://www.hoover.org/research/status-eu-frustrated-empire
-built-wrong-assumption.

16. Kalina Oroschakoff, "The Politics of the Green Deal," *Politico*, October 27, 2020, https://www.politico.eu/article/chapter-two-the
-politics-of-the-green-deal/.

17. "How Much Legislation Comes from Europe?," House of Commons
Library, October 13, 2010, http://researchbriefings.files.parliament
.uk/documents/RP10-62/RP10-62.pdf, 1.

18. Carol Harlow, "European Administrative Law and the Global Challenge," RSC Working Paper No. 98/23, 1998.

19. "How Much Legislation Comes from Europe?," 8.

20. Ibid., 1.

21. Ibid.

22. Ibid., 9.

23. Elizabeth Warren, "A Plan for Economic Patriotism," Team

Warren, June 4, 2019, https://medium.com/@teamwarren/a-plan
-for-economic-patriotism-13b879f4cfc7.

24. Edward Malnick, "EU Lays Down the Law on Coffee Making," *Telegraph*, April 19, 2014, https://www.telegraph.co.uk/news/world
news/europe/10776587/EU-lays-down-the-law-on-coffee-making
.html.

25. Richard Williams, "The Brexit Vote Is a Referendum on the European
Union's Thousands of Stifling Regulations," *Reason*, June 22, 2016,
https://reason.com/2016/06/22/the-brexit-vote-is-a-referendum
-on-the-e/.

26. "Americans' Budget Share for Total Food Was at a Historical Low
of 9.5 Percent in 2019," USDA, June 15, 2020, https://www
.ers.usda.gov/data-products/chart-gallery/gallery/chart-detail
/?chartId=76967; Katy Askew, "Food Prices in Europe Rising at
'Rapid Rate': Where Are the Most Expensive Countries to Eat?,"
Foodnavigator.com, August 12, 2019, https://www.foodnavigator
.com/Article/2019/08/12/Food-prices-in-Europe-rising-at-rapid
-rate-Where-are-the-most-expensive-countries-to-eat.

27. Philip Booth, "Europe's Single Market Isn't a Free Market," *Wall
Street Journal*, December 23, 2011, https://www.wsj.com/articles
/SB10001424052970204552304577112072693595352.

28. Walter W. Eubanks, "The European Union's Response to the 2007–
2009 Financial Crisis," Congressional Research Service, August 13,
2010, https://fas.org/sgp/crs/row/R41367.pdf, 4.

29. Ibid.

30. "Harmonised Standards," European Commission, https://ec.europa.eu
/growth/single-market/european-standards/harmonised-standards
_en.

31. "Conformity Assessment," European Commission, https://ec.europa
.eu/growth/single-market/goods/building-blocks/conformity
-assessment_en.

32. "Industry Groups and Self-Regulatory Organizations," North American Securities Administrators Association, https://www.nasaa.org
/2618/industry-groups-and-self-regulatory-organizations/.

33. Press release, "European Commission Swears Oath to Respect the
EU Treaties," European Commission, May 3, 2010, https://ec.europa
.eu/commission/presscorner/detail/en/IP_10_487.

34. Max Bergmann, "Embrace the Union," Center for American Progress, October 31, 2019, https://www.americanprogress.org/issues
/security/reports/2019/10/31/476483/embrace-the-union/.

35. Victor Morton, "French Ambassador Uses Pearl Harbor Day to Blast
U.S. for Betraying France in 1930s," *Washington Times*, December 7,

2017, https://www.washingtontimes.com/news/2017/dec/7/gerard
-araud-pearl-harbor-day-us-betrayed-france-1/.
36. "Fiscal Year Ending June 30, 1948," FRASER, Federal Reserve,
https://fraser.stlouisfed.org/title/budget-united-states-government
-54/fiscal-year-ending-june-30-1948-19001.
37. "Foreign Assistance Act of 1948 (April 3, 1948)," George C. Marshall Foundation.
38. William S. Smith, "The Republican War over Germany," *Hill*,
June 18, 2020, https://thehill.com/opinion/international/503384-the
-republican-war-over-germany.
39. "Defence Expenditure of NATO Countries (2013–2019)," North
Atlantic Treaty Organization, November 2019, https://www.nato
.int/nato_static_fl2014/assets/pdf/pdf_2019_11/20191129_pr
-2019-123-en.pdf.
40. Robin Emmott, "Germany Commits to NATO Spending Goal
by 2031 for First Time," Reuters, November 7, 2019, https://www
.reuters.com/article/us-germany-nato/germany-commits-to-nato
-spending-goal-by-2031-for-first-time-idUSKBN1XH1IK.
41. Ted R. Bromund, "Not All U.S. Allies Are Created Equal," Heritage Foundation, May 2, 2018, https://www.heritage.org/europe
/commentary/not-all-us-allies-are-created-equal.
42. Philip Oltermann, "'Regrettable': Germany Reacts to Trump Plan
to Withdraw US Troops," *Guardian*, June 6, 2020, https://www
.theguardian.com/world/2020/jun/06/regrettable-germany-reacts
-to-trump-plan-to-withdraw-us-troops.
43. "Germany Is Doomed to Lead Europe," *Economist*, June 25, 2020,
https://www.economist.com/europe/2020/06/25/germany-is
-doomed-to-lead-europe.
44. Jon Stone, "Germany Now 'Biggest Breaker of EU Rules,' According to Official Figures," *Independent*, February 7, 2018, https://www
.independent.co.uk/news/uk/politics/angela-merkel-germany
-breaks-more-eu-rules-worst-bottom-class-a8198271.html.

5. AMERICA IS FAR MORE TOLERANT THAN EUROPE

1. Bukola Adebayo, "Nigeria Overtakes India in Extreme Poverty
Ranking," CNN, June 26, 2018, http://www.cnn.com/2018/06/26
/africa/nigeria-overtakes-india-extreme-poverty-intl/index.
2. Molly Fosco, "The Most Successful Ethnic Group in the U.S. May
Surprise You," Ozy, June 6, 2018, http://www.ozy.com/around-the
-world/the-most-successful-ethnic-group-in-the-u-s-may-surprise
-you/86885/.

3. "Drain or Gain?," *Economist*, May 28, 2011, http://www.economist
   .com/finance-and-economics/2011/05/26/drain-or-gain.

4. News release, "Report Finds Immigrants Come to Resemble
   Native-Born Americans over Time, but Integration Not Always
   Linked to Greater Well-Being for Immigrants," National Academies of Sciences, Engineering, and Medicine, September 21, 2015,
   https://www.nationalacademies.org/news/2015/09/report-finds
   -immigrants-come-to-resemble-native-born-americans-over-time
   -but-integration-not-always-linked-to-greater-well-being-for
   -immigrants.

5. Cameron Easley, "Support for Black Lives Matter Stretches Over
   to the Other Side of the Atlantic," *Morning Consult*, June 25, 2020,
   http://www.morningconsult.com/2020/06/25/black-lives-matter
   -protests-europe-support/.

6. Robin Wright, "To the World, We're Now America the Racist and
   Pitiful," *New Yorker*, July 3, 2020, https://www.newyorker.com
   /news/our-columnists/to-the-world-were-now-america-the-racist
   -and-pitiful.

7. Kim Hjelmgaard, "'I'm Leaving, and I'm Just Not Coming Back':
   Fed Up with Racism, Black Americans Head Overseas," *USA Today*, June 26, 2020, http://www.usatoday.com/story/news/world
   /2020/06/26/blaxit-black-americans-leave-us-escape-racism-build
   -lives-abroad/3234129001/.

8. Barrett Holmes Pitner, "Viewpoint: Why Racism in US Is Worse
   Than in Europe," BBC News, May 17, 2018, http://www.bbc.com
   /news/world-us-canada-44158098.

9. Nicole Phillip, "My Very Personal Taste of Racism Abroad," *New York
   Times*, October 23, 2018, https://www.nytimes.com/2018/10/23
   /travel/racism-travel-italy-study-abroad.html.

10. Maya Lyght, "Being Black Abroad: Europe Edition," Center for
    Global and Intercultural Study, University of Michigan, Octo-
    ber 12, 2018, https://lsa.umich.edu/cgis/news-events/all-news/being
    -black-abroad--europe-edition.html.

11. Lorraine Brown and Ian Jones, "Encounters with Racism and the
    International Student Experience," ResearchGate, September 2011,
    https://www.researchgate.net/publication/233027322_Encounters
    _with_racism_and_the_international_student_experience.

12. "Second European Union Minorities and Discrimination Survey:
    Being Black in the EU," European Union Agency for Fundamen-
    tal Rights, November 23, 2018, https://fra.europa.eu/sites/default
    /files/fra_uploads/fra-2018-being-black-in-the-eu_en.pdf.

13. Max Fisher, "A Fascinating Map of the World's Most and Least

Racially Tolerant Countries," *Washington Post*, May 15, 2013, https://www.washingtonpost.com/news/worldviews/wp/2013/05/15/a-fascinating-map-of-the-worlds-most-and-least-racially-tolerant-countries/.

14. Jacob Poushter and Janell Fetterolf, "How People Around the World View Diversity in Their Countries," Pew Research Center, April 22, 2019, https://www.pewresearch.org/global/2019/04/22/how-people-around-the-world-view-diversity-in-their-countries/.

15. Bruce Drake and Jacob Poushter, "In Views of Diversity, Many Europeans Are Less Positive Than Americans," Pew Research Center, July 12, 2016.

16. Juliana Menasce Horowitz, "Americans See Advantages and Challenges in Country's Growing Racial and Ethnic Diversity," Pew Research Center, May 9, 2019.

17. Wright, "To the World, We're Now America the Racist and Pitiful."

18. "Second European Union Minorities and Discrimination Survey: Being Black in the EU."

19. "2021: Snapshot of Race and Home Buying in America," National Association of Realtors, https://cdn.nar.realtor/sites/default/files/documents/2021-snapshot-of-race-and-home-buyers-in-america-report-02-19-2021.pdf.

20. "A Higher Share of Black-Owned Businesses Are Women-Owned Than Non-Black Businesses," USA Facts, February 11, 2021, https://usafacts.org/articles/black-women-business-month.

21. Randeep Ramesh, "Black People More Likely to Be Jobless in Britain Than US, Research Reveals," *Guardian*, April 12, 2012, https://www.theguardian.com/world/2012/apr/13/black-people-unemployed-britain-us.

22. Jeanna Smialek, "Minority Women Are Winning the Jobs Race in a Record Economic Expansion," *New York Times*, July 1, 2019, https://www.nytimes.com/2019/07/01/business/economy/minority-women-hispanics-jobs.html.

23. Lucy Williamson, "Colonial Abuses Haunt France's Racism Debate," BBC News, June 18, 2020, https://www.bbc.com/news/world-europe-53095738.

24. Illa Kane, "France, Major Actor in Enslavement of Africans," Anadolu Agency, November 13, 2019, https://www.aa.com.tr/en/africa/france-major-actor-in-enslavement-of-africans/1644213.

25. Paul Johnson, *Modern Times: The World from the Twenties to the Nineties* (New York: Harper Perennial Classics, 2001), 150.

26. Emma-Kate Symons, "Don't Believe Anyone in France Who Says They Don't See Race," Quartz, October 21, 2014, https://qz.com

/283120/dont-believe-anyone-in-france-who-says-they-dont-see
-race/.

27. Jacopo Barigazzi, "'No Doubt' Europe Better Than US on Race Issues, EU Commissioner Says," *Politico*, June 10, 2020, https://www
.politico.eu/article/margaritis-schinas-eu-better-than-us-on-race
-issues/.

28. Luke Hurst, "All-White European Commission Debate on Racism
'Would Be Ridiculous,' Says Ex-MEP Magid Magid," *Euronews*,
June 19, 2020, https://www.euronews.com/2020/06/19/all-white
-european-commission-debate-on-racism-would-be-ridiculous-says
-ex-mep-magid-magid.

29. Ryan Heath, "Brussels Is Blind to Diversity," *Politico*, December 11,
2017, https://www.politico.eu/article/brussels-blind-to-diversity
-whiteout-european-parliament/.

30. Galaxy Henry, "Racism Persists in the Heart of the EU," *Politico*,
June 18, 2019, https://www.politico.eu/article/europe-struggles
-combatting-racial-discrimination-brussels-bubble/.

31. "Annual Diversity and Inclusion Report 2018," North Atlantic
Treaty Organization, https://www.nato.int/nato_static_fl2014/assets
/pdf/2020/7/pdf/2018-annual-diversity_inclusion_report.pdf.

32. Loveday Morris, "Germany's Only Black Member of Parliament
Says the Country Needs to Face Its Racism," *Washington Post*, June
19, 2020, https://www.washingtonpost.com/world/europe/black
-lives-matter-germany-karamba-diaby/2020/06/18/a9ad114e-acba
-11ea-a43b-be9f6494a87d_story.html.

33. Patrick Smith, "Soccer in the Spotlight as Europe Grapples with
Racism On and Off the Field," NBC News, April 14, 2019, https://
www.nbcnews.com/news/world/soccer-spotlight-europe-grapples
-racism-field-n992911.

34. Holly Yan, Lauren Russell, and Boriana Milanova, "Bananas Thrown
at Italy's First Black Minister Cecile Kyenge," CNN, July 29, 2013,
https://www.cnn.com/2013/07/28/world/europe/italy-politics
-racism.

35. "Experiences and Perceptions of Antisemitism: Second Survey
on Discrimination and Hate Crime Against Jews in the EU," European Union Agency for Fundamental Rights, 2018, https://fra
.europa.eu/sites/default/files/fra_uploads/fra-2018-experiences
-and-perceptions-of-antisemitism-survey_en.pdf.

36. William A. Galston, "Anti-Semitism Soars in Eastern Europe," *Wall
Street Journal*, November 26, 2019, https://www.wsj.com/articles
/anti-semitism-soars-in-eastern-europe-11574812176.

37. Raphael Ahren, "In Landmark Ruling, EU's Top Court Says Settlement

Product Labeling Mandatory," *Times of Israel*, November 12, 2019, https://www.timesofisrael.com/in-landmark-ruling-eus-top -court-says-settlement-product-labeling-mandatory/.

38. Benjamin Weinthal, "German Court Calls Synagogue Torching an Act to 'Criticize Israel,'" *Jerusalem Post*, January 13, 2017, https://www.jpost.com/Diaspora/German-court-calls-synagogue-torching -an-act-to-criticize-Israel-478330.

39. Toby Axelrod, "Synagogue Arson Not Anti-Semitic—or So Rules German Court," *Forward*, January 15, 2017, https://www.forward .com/news/breaking-news/360019/german-court-affirms-ruling -that-said-synagogue-arson-isn-t-anti-semitic/.

40. "Les 'gilets jaunes': Une forte porosité à la rhétorique complot- iste," Département Opinion et Stratégies d'Entreprises, February 2019, https://www.ifop.com/wp-content/uploads/2019/02/Focus n188-Les-gilets-jaunes-une-forte-porosit%C3%A9-%C3%A0-la-r h%C3%A9torique-complotiste.pdf.

41. JTA, "In French Poll, Majority Say Zionism Is a Jewish Conspiracy," *Times of Israel*, May 26, 2018, https://www.timesofisrael.com/in -french-poll-majority-say-zionism-is-a-jewish-conspiracy/.

42. Adam Nossiter, "'They Spit When I Walked in the Street': The 'New Anti-Semitism' in France," *New York Times*, July 27, 2018.

43. "France Anti-Semitism: Jewish Graves Defaced with Nazi Swasti- kas," BBC News, December 4, 2019.

44. Edward Cody, "Rabbi, Three Children Shot Dead Outside Jewish School in France," *Washington Post*, March 19, 2012, https://www .washingtonpost.com/world/europe/father-two-children-shot -dead-outside-jewish-school-in-france/2012/03/19/gIQAclfUMS _story.

45. "Brussels Jewish Museum Killings: Mehdi Nemmouche Trial Be- gins," BBC News, January 10, 2019, https://www.bbc.com/news /world-europe-46822469.

46. Aurelien Breeden, "At Trial, Jewish Victims of 2015 Paris Attack Ask: Why the Hatred?," *New York Times*, September 27, 2020, https://www.nytimes.com/2020/09/27/world/europe/france -attacks-supermarket-charlie-hebdo-trial.html.

47. James McAuley, "How the Murders of Two Elderly Jewish Women Shook France," *Guardian*, November 27, 2018, https://www.theguardian.com/world/2018/nov/27/how-the-murders -of-two-elderly-jewish-women-shook-france-antisemitism-mireille -knoll-sarah-halimi.

48. Agence France-Presse, "Two Men to Stand Trial in France for Kill- ing of Jewish Woman, 85," *Guardian*, July 13, 2020, https://www

.theguardian.com/world/2020/jul/13/two-men-to-stand-trial-in
-france-for-killing-of-jewish-woman-85.

49. Griff Witte and Anthony Faiola, "France Sends 10,000 Troops
Across Country, Protecting Hundreds of Jewish Sites," *Washington
Post*, January 12, 2015, https://www.washingtonpost.com/world
/hollande-calls-crisis-meeting-10000-extra-forces-sent-to
-protect-people-of-france/2015/01/12/63610982-9a34-11e4-a7ee-
526210d665b4_story.html.

50. Toby Axelrod, "American Tourist Attacked in Berlin After Saying
He Was Jewish," *Jerusalem Post*, June 20, 2019, https://www.jpost
.com/Diaspora/American-tourist-attacked-in-Berlin-after-saying
-he-was-Jewish-593090.

51. Geir Moulson, "Merkel Slams Anti-Semitism 'Disgrace' on Jewish Group's 70th," Associated Press, September 15, 2020, https://
apnews.com/article/race-and-ethnicity-angela-merkel-berlin-anti
-semitism-germany-f1824f9dd8c49805034eed40f5a4b5ac.

52. Rick Noack and Luisa Beck, "Video Shows Belt-Wielding Assail-
ant Screaming 'Jew' as He Attacks Two People on a Berlin Street,"
Washington Post, April 19, 2018, https://www.washingtonpost.com
/news/worldviews/wp/2018/04/19/belt-wielding-assailant-screams
-jew-as-he-attacks-two-on-a-berlin-street/.

53. "Anti-Semitic Acts in Tampere and Turku, as Finland's Leaders
Mark Holocaust," *News Now Finland*, January 27, 2020, https://
www.newsnowfinland.fi/domestic/anti-semitic-acts-in-tampere
-and-turku-as-finlands-leaders-mark-holocaust.

54. JTA, "Norwegian Rapper Curses 'the F***ing Jews' at Diversity Concert," *Times of Israel*, June 19, 2018, https://www.timesofisrael.com
/norwegian-rapper-curses-the-fing-jews-at-diversity-concert/.

55. "Religious Communities and Life Stance Communities," Central
Bureau of Statistics, Norway, December 8, 2020, https://www.ssb
.no/en/kultur-og-fritid/statistikker/trosamf/aar.

56. Norwegian Civil Penal Code § 135, https://lovdata.no/dokument
/NLO/lov/1902-05-22-10/KAPITTEL_2-6#KAPITTEL_2-6.

57. Cnaan Liphshiz, "Norwegian Rapper Who Cursed Jews During Performance Not Charged with Hate Speech," *Haaretz*, March 13, 2019,
https://www.haaretz.com/world-news/europe/norwegian-rapper
-who-cursed-jews-during-performance-not-charged-with-hate-spe
ech-1.7018462.

58. Jeremy Rifkin, *The European Dream: How Europe's Vision of the
Future Is Quietly Eclipsing the American Dream* (Oxford: Jeremy P.
Tarcher, 2004), 247.

6. IMAGINE, NO COUNTRIES

1. Kate Ferguson and David Hughes, "National Borders Are 'the Worst Invention Ever,' Says EC Chief Jean-Claude Juncker," *Independent*, August 22, 2016, https://www.independent.co.uk/news/world /europe/national-borders-are-worst-invention-ever-says-ec-chief -jean-claude-juncker-a7204006.html.
2. "Migrant Crisis: Migration to Europe Explained in Seven Charts," BBC News, March 4, 2016, https://www.bbc.com/news/world-europe -34131911.
3. "Europe's Growing Muslim Population," Pew Research Center, November 29, 2017, https://www.pewforum.org/2017/11/29/europes -growing-muslim-population/.
4. Ibid.
5. "Number of Refugees to Europe Surges to Record 1.3 Million in 2015," Pew Research Center, August 2, 2016, https://www.pew research.org/global/2016/08/02/number-of-refugees-to-europe -surges-to-record-1-3-million-in-2015/.
6. "Europe's Growing Muslim Population."
7. Ibid.
8. Nicholas Watt and Patrick Wintour, "How Immigration Came to Haunt Labour: The Inside Story," *Guardian*, March 24, 2015, https:// www.theguardian.com/news/2015/mar/24/how-immigration -came-to-haunt-labour-inside-story.
9. "Integration Policy Flopping in Germany," *American Interest*, June 22, 2017, https://www.the-american-interest.com/2017/06/22/integration -policy-flopping-germany/.
10. Anushka Asthana, "Islamophobia Holding Back UK Muslims in Workplace, Study Finds," *Guardian*, September 7, 2017, https://www .theguardian.com/society/2017/sep/07/islamophobia-holding-back -uk-muslims-in-workplace-study-finds.
11. Alex Nowrasteh, "Muslim Immigration and Integration in the United States and Western Europe," Cato Institute, October 31, 2016, https://www.cato.org/blog/muslim-immigration-integration -united-states-western-europe.
12. "The Somali Diaspora in Kensington and Chelsea," Kensington and Chelsea Council, March 2011, https://www.councilofsomaliorgs .com/sites/default/files/resources/Somali_Diaspora_in_Kensington _Chelsea.pdf, 6.
13. Deborah Potter, "Muslims in Germany," PBS, Religion & Ethics Newsweekly, October 30, 2009, https://www.pbs.org/wnet/religion

andethics/2009/10/30/october-30–2009-muslims-in-germany
/4787/.

14. Mark Joseph Stern, "The Supreme Court Lets Trump Punish Immigrants Who May Be a 'Public Charge,'" *Slate*, January 27, 2020, https://slate.com/news-and-politics/2020/01/supreme-court
-public-charge-immigrant-ban.html.

15. Christopher Richardson, "We Must Abolish the 'Public Charge' Rule," *Washington Post*, August 15, 2019, https://www.washington
post.com/opinions/2019/08/15/we-must-abolish-public-charge
-rule/.

16. Masha Gessen, "Trump's Immigration Rule Is Cruel and Racist—but It's Nothing New," *New Yorker*, January 29, 2020, https://www
.newyorker.com/news/our-columnists/trumps-immigration-rule
-is-cruel-and-racistbut-its-nothing-new.

17. Besheer Mohamed, "New Estimates Show U.S. Muslim Population Continues to Grow," Pew Research Center, January 3, 2018, https://
www.pewresearch.org/fact-tank/2018/01/03/new-estimates-show
-u-s-muslim-population-continues-to-grow/.

18. "Demographic Portrait of Muslim Americans," Pew Research Center, July 26, 2017, https://www.pewforum.org/2017/07/26/demographic
-portrait-of-muslim-americans/.

19. Jason Deparle, "Why the U.S. Is So Good at Turning Immigrants into Americans," *Atlantic*, November 2013, https://www.theatlantic
.com/magazine/archive/2013/11/assimilation-nation/309518/.

20. "U.S. Muslims Concerned About Their Place in Society, but Continue to Believe in the American Dream," Pew Research Center, July 26, 2017, https://pewresearch.tumblr.com/post/163445720855/overall
-muslims-in-the-united-states-perceive-a.

21. Andrew Hussey, "La Haine 20 Years On: What Has Changed?," *Guardian*, May 3, 2015, https://www.theguardian.com/film/2015
/may/03/la-haine-film-sequel-20-years-on-france.

22. Caldwell, *Reflections on the Revolution in Europe*, 113.

23. Fabien Jobard, "An Overview of French Riots: 1981–2004," in Dave Waddington, Fabien Jobard, and Mike King, *Rioting in the UK and France: A Comparative Analysis* (London: Willan, 2009), 27–38.

24. Ibid., 3.

25. Ibid., 4.

26. Ibid., 5.

27. Caldwell, *Reflections on the Revolution in Europe*, 102.

28. Hussey, "La Haine 20 Years On."

29. Caldwell, *Reflections on the Revolution in Europe*, 112.

30. Ibid., 103.

31. John Leicester, "Anti-Police Violence Surges in the Tough Suburbs of Paris," *U.S. News & World Report*, November 5, 2019, https://www.usnews.com/news/world/articles/2019-11-05/anti-police -violence-surges-in-the-tough-suburbs-of-paris.
32. Caldwell, *Reflections on the Revolution in Europe*, 100.
33. Ibid., 101.
34. Paulina Neuding, "Living in Fear," *Spectator*, February 10, 2018, https://www.spectator.co.uk/article/living-in-fear.
35. Ibid.
36. Joel Kotkin, "Europe's Fading Cosmopolitan Dream," *City Journal*, August 12, 2019.
37. Caldwell, *Reflections on the Revolution in Europe*, 111.
38. Justin Penrose, "The 200 Foreign Suspects Arrested Every Day in London," *Daily Mirror*, October 7, 2012, https://www.mirror.co.uk /news/uk-news/the-200-foreign-suspects-arrested-every-1364331.
39. Ibid.
40. Jack Heffernan, "Travel Warning: Amsterdam Destroyed by Immigrants," *Live Trading News*, July 29, 2018, https://www.livetrading news.com/travel-warning-amsterdam-destroyed-by-immigrants -99292.html.
41. Melinda Wenner Moyer, "Undocumented Immigrants Are Half as Likely to Be Arrested for Violent Crimes as U.S.-Born Citizens," *Scientific American*, December 7, 2020, https://www.scientificamerican .com/article/undocumented-immigrants-are-half-as-likely-to-be -arrested-for-violent-crimes-as-u-s-born-citizens/
42. Rich Morin, "Crime Rises Among Second-Generation Immigrants as They Assimilate," Pew Research Center, October 15, 2013, https:// www.pewresearch.org/fact-tank/2013/10/15/crime-rises among -second-generation-immigrants-as-they-assimilate/.
43. Caldwell, *Reflections on the Revolution in Europe*, 110.
44. Ibid.
45. George Martin, "Most Germans Now Fear 'No-Go Zones' Where They Believe Police Are Too Afraid to Patrol, New Poll Shows," *Daily Mail*, April 16, 2018, https://www.dailymail.co.uk/news/article -5620795/Most-Germans-fear-no-zones-believe-police-afraid -patrol.html.
46. Adam Shaw, "Angela Merkel Admits That 'No-Go Zones' Exist in Germany," Fox News, March 1, 2018, https://www.foxnews.com /world/angela-merkel-admits-that-no-go-zones-exist-in-germany.
47. Rebecca Camber, "'No Porn or Prostitution': Islamic Extremists Set Up Sharia Law Controlled Zones in British Cities," *Daily Mail*, July 28, 2011, https://www.dailymail.co.uk/news/article-2019547

/Anjem-Choudary-Islamic-extremists-set-Sharia-law-zones-UK
-cities.html.

48. Sam Jones, "Muslim Vigilantes Jailed for 'Sharia Law' Attacks in London," *Guardian*, December 6, 2013, https://www.theguardian .com/uk-news/2013/dec/06/muslim-vigilantes-jailed-sharia-law -attacks-london.

49. Carol Kuruvilla, "Extremist 'Muslim Patrol' Attempting to Enforce Sharia Law in East London Is Condemned by England's Imams," *Daily News*, February 2, 2013, https://www.nydailynews.com/news /world/muslim-patrol-enforcing-sharia-e-london-article-1.12538 93.

50. Camber, "'No Porn or Prostitution.'"

51. Shaw, "Angela Merkel Admits That 'No-Go Zones' Exist in Germany."

52. "Sharia Law in UK Is 'Unavoidable,'" BBC News, February 7, 2008, http://news.bbc.co.uk/2/hi/uk_news/7232661.stm.

53. Caldwell, *Reflections on the Revolution in Europe*, 108.

54. Emil Pain, "The Decline of Multiculturalism," Russia in Global Affairs, March 27, 2011, https://eng.globalaffairs.ru/articles/the -decline-of-multiculturalism/.

55. Bruce Bawer, "Young Afghans in Sweden," Gatestone Institute, January 20, 2018, https://www.gatestoneinstitute.org/11768/sweden -afghans-immigration.

56. Robin Simcox, "European Islamist Plots and Attacks Since 2014— and How the U.S. Can Help Prevent Them," Heritage Foundation, August 1, 2017, https://www.heritage.org/europe/report/european -islamist-plots-and-attacks-2014-and-how-the-us-can-help-prevent -them?_ga=2.97201943.94278987.1607905764-658918599.1 607905764.

57. Ibid.

58. "Terrorism in Europe—Statistics & Facts," Statista, October 12, 2020, https://www.statista.com/topics/3788/terrorism-in-europe/.

59. Robin Simcox, "Scandinavian Approach to Counterterrorism, Islamist Ideology Is Flawed," *Daily Signal*, May 11, 2018, https:// www.dailysignal.com/2018/05/11/scandinavian-approach-to -counterterrorism-islamist-ideology-is-fatally-flawed/.

60. Saphora Smith, Nancy Ing, and Tim Stelloh, "French Authorities Say Suspect in Nice Church Attacks Is a Tunisian National," NBC News, October 29, 2020, https://www.nbcnews.com/news/world /two-dead-others-injured-suspected-terrorist-attack-french-church -n1245222.

61. "France Teacher Attack: Seven Charged over Samuel Paty's Killing,"

BBC News, October 22, 2020, https://www.bbc.com/news/world-europe-54632353.

62. "Vienna Shooting: Austria Hunts Suspects After 'Islamist Terror' Attack," BBC News, November 3, 2020, https://www.bbc.com/news/world-europe-54788613.

63. Frances Perraudin, "Half of All British Muslims Think Homosexuality Should Be Illegal, Poll Finds," *Guardian*, April 11, 2016, https://www.theguardian.com/uk-news/2016/apr/11/british-muslims-strong-sense-of-belonging-poll-homosexuality-sharia-law.

64. Bruce Bawer, "A Problem with Muslim Enclaves," *Christian Science Monitor*, June 30, 2003, https://www.csmonitor.com/2003/0630/p09s01-coop.html.

65. "Migrant Child Brides Put Europe in a Spin," BBC News, September 30, 2016, https://www.bbc.com/news/world-europe-37518289

66. Rhea Wessel, "European Immigrants Continue to Be Forced into Marriages," *World Politics Review*, January 31, 2007, https://www.worldpoliticsreview.com/articles/509/european-immigrants-continue-to-be-forced-into-marriage.

67. Rick Noack, "Leaked Document Says 2,000 Men Allegedly Assaulted 1,200 German Women on New Year's Eve," *Washington Post*, July 11, 2016, https://www.washingtonpost.com/news/world views/wp/2016/07/10/leaked-document-says-2000-men-allegedly-assaulted-1200-german-women-on-new-years-eve/?noredirect=on.

68. Alison Smale, "As Germany Welcomes Migrants, Sexual Attacks in Cologne Point to a New Reality," *New York Times*, January 14, 2016, https://www.nytimes.com/2016/01/15/world/europe/as-germany-welcomes-migrantssexual-attacks-in-cologne-point-to-a-new-reality.html.

69. "'Cologne Is Every Day': Europe's Rape Epidemic," News.com.au, March 12, 2016, https://www.news.com.au/finance/economy/world-economy/cologne-is-every-day-europes-rape-epidemic/news-story/e2e618e17ad4400b5ed65045e65e141d.

70. "Sweden Rape: Most Convicted Attackers Foreign-Born, Says TV," BBC News, August 22, 2018, https://www.bbc.com/news/world-europe-45269764.

71. Ibid.

72. Ibid.

73. Luke Harding, "Angela Merkel Defends Germany's Handling of Refugee Influx," *Guardian*, September 15, 2015, https://www.theguardian.com/world/2015/sep/15/angela-merkel-defends-germanys-handling-of-refugee-influx.

74. Melissa Eddy, "German Far Right and Counterprotesters Clash in

Chemnitz," *New York Times*, August 28, 2018, https://www.nytimes
.com/2018/08/28/world/europe/chemnitz-protest-germany.html.

75. "Factbox: German Far-Right Attacks in Recent Years," Reuters,
February 20, 2020, https://www.reuters.com/article/us-germany
-shooting-farright-factbox/factbox-german-far-right-attacks-in
-recent-years-idUSKBN20E1SS.

76. Crispian Balmer, "Despite Falling Numbers, Immigration Remains
Divisive EU Issue," Reuters, May 14, 2019, https://www.reuters.com
/article/us-eu-election-migrants/despite-falling-numbers-immigration
-remains-divisive-eu-issue-idUSKCN1SK1GD.

77. Ana Gonzalez-Barrera and Phillip Connor, "Around the World,
More Say Immigrants Are a Strength Than a Burden," Pew Research
Center, March 14, 2019, https://www.pewresearch.org/global/2019
/03/14/around-the-world-more-say-immigrants-are-a-strength
-than-a-burden/.

78. Alexander Stille, "How Matteo Salvini Pulled Italy to the Far
Right," *Guardian*, August 9, 2018, https://www.theguardian.com
/news/2018/aug/09/how-matteo-salvini-pulled-italy-to-the-far-right.

79. Sylvia Poggioli, "Long a Bastion of the Left, Tuscany Is Turning Hard
Right," National Public Radio, August 14, 2019, https://www.npr
.org/2019/08/14/749898871/long-a-bastion-of-the-left-tuscany-is
-turning-hard-right.

80. Julian Coman, "'Italians First': How the Populist Right Became
Italy's Dominant Force," *Guardian*, December 1, 2018, https://www
.theguardian.com/world/2018/dec/01/italians-first-matteo-salvini
-the-league-rise-rightwing-populism.

81. Marton Dunai, "'The Wave Has Reached Us': EU Gropes for Answers to Migrant Surge," Reuters, August 25, 2015, https://www
.reuters.com/article/us-europe-migrants/the-wave-has-reached
-us-eu-gropes-for-answers-to-migrant-surge-idUSKCN0QU1BC20
150825.

82. "Slovak PM Says Will Never Support Mandatory Quotas for Migrants," Reuters, September 25, 2015, https://www.reuters.com/article
/us-europe-migrants-slovakia/slovak-pm-says-will-never-support
-mandatory-quotas-for-migrants-idUSKCN0RF1LL20150915.

83. "Advocate General Sharpston: The Court Should Rule That, by Refusing to Comply with the Provisional and Time-Limited Mechanism for the Mandatory Relocation of Applicants for International
Protection, Poland, Hungary and the Czech Republic Have Failed
to Fulfil Their Obligations Under EU Law," Court of Justice of the
European Union, October 31, 2019, https://curia.europa.eu/jcms
/upload/docs/application/pdf/2019-10/cp190133en.pdf.

84. Samuel Osborne, "World's Most and Least Welcoming Countries for Migrants," *Independent*, August 23, 2017, https://www.independent.co.uk/news/world/politics/world-welcoming-migrant-countries-least-most-uk-refugee-crisis-us-australia-eastern-europe-a7908766.html.

85. "U.S. Humanitarian Assistance in Response to the Syrian Crisis," White House, Office of the Press Secretary, September 24, 2013, https://obamawhitehouse.archives.gov/the-press-office/2013/09/24/fact-sheet-us-humanitarian-assistance-response-syrian-crisis.

86. "UNHCR Global Resettlement Statistical Report 2014," United Nations Refugee Agency, https://www.unhcr.org/52693bd09.html.

87. Annett Meiritz and Dara Lind, "Why Germany Just Closed Its Borders to Refugees," *Vox*, September 14, 2015, https://www.vox.com/2015/9/13/9319741/germany-borders-merkel.

88. Kenan Malik, "The Failure of Multiculturalism," *Foreign Affairs*, March/April 2015, https://www.foreignaffairs.com/articles/western-europe/2015-02-18/failure-multiculturalism.

7. RICHER THAN YOU

1. Nick Romeo, "What Can America Learn from Europe About Regulating Big Tech?," *New Yorker*, August 18, 2020, https://www.newyorker.com/tech/annals-of-technology/what-can-america-learn-from-europe-about-regulating-big-tech.

2. Marley Coyne, Andrea Murphy, Hank Tucker, and Halah Touryalai, "Global 2000: The World's Largest Public Companies," *Forbes*, May 13, 2020, https://www.forbes.com/global2000/#5780fe83335d.

3. Ibid.

4. Jon Porter, "Apple and Samsung Dominate Top Selling Phone Lists for 2019," Verge, February 28, 2020, https://www.theverge.com/2020/2/28/21157386/iphone-best-selling-phone-worldwide-xr-11-samsung-a-series-counterpoint-research.

5. "Fostering Peer-to-Peer Learning in Entrepreneurship Education," EU Innovation Trends, May 3, 2019, https://www.innovationtrends.eu/news/fostering-peer-peer-learning-entrepreneurship-education.

6. "The Complete List of Unicorn Companies," CB Insights, https://www.cbinsights.com/research-unicorn-companies (accessed November 13, 2020).

7. Scott Austin, Chris Canipe, and Sarah Slobin, "The Billion Dollar Startup Club," *Wall Street Journal*, February 18, 2015, https://www.wsj.com/graphics/billion-dollar-club/.

8. Ilan Rozenkopf, Pål Erik Sjåtil, and Sebastian Stern, "How Purpose-Led

Missions Can Help Europe Innovate at Scale," McKinsey & Company, December 10, 2019, https://www.mckinsey.com/featured -insights/europe/how-purpose-led-missions-can-help-europe -innovate-at-scale.

9. "National Innovation Policies: What Countries Do Best and How They Can Improve," Information Technology & Innovation Foundation, June 13, 2019, https://itif.org/publications/2019/06/13 /national-innovation-policies-what-countries-do-best-and-how-they -can-improve.

10. "Your Startup Has a 1.28% Chance of Becoming a Unicorn," CB Insights, May 25, 2015, https://www.cbinsights.com/research/unicorn -conversion-rate/.

11. Ryan Singel, "Silicon Valley Conference About Failing Is Big Success," *Wired*, October 28, 2009, https://www.wired.com/2009/10 /failcon-succeeds/.

12. "Les misérables," *Economist*, July 28, 2012, https://www.economist .com/briefing/2012/07/28/les-miserables.

13. Ibid.

14. Edward Robinson, "Why It's So Hard for Entrepreneurs to Get Really Rich in Europe," *Financial Review*, October 4, 2019, https:// www.afr.com/technology/why-it-s-so-hard-for-entrepreneurs-to -get-really-rich-in-europe-20191003-p52xau.

15. "Why Are European Banks Merging?," *Economist*, September 20, 2020, https://www.economist.com/finance-and-economics/2020/09 /10/why-are-european-banks-merging.

16. "Youth Self-Employment and Entrepreneurship Activities," *The Missing Entrepreneurs 2019: Policies for Inclusive Entrepreneurship*, Organisation for Economic Co-operation and Development, https://www .oecd-ilibrary.org/sites/3ec10f3b-en/index.html?itemId=/content /component/3ec10f3b-en.

17. "37% of Europeans Would Like to Be Their Own Boss," Europa-Wire, January 9, 2013, https://news.europawire.eu/37-of-europeans -would-like-to-be-their-own-boss-19537648532/eu-press-release /2013/01/09/23/22/35/5669/.

18. James B. Stewart, "A Fearless Culture Fuels U.S. Tech Giants," *New York Times*, June 18, 2015, https://www.nytimes.com/2015/06/19 /business/the-american-way-of-tech-and-europes.html.

19. South West News Service, "Most Americans Dream of Being Their Own Boss," *New York Post*, January 17, 2018, https://nypost.com /2018/01/17/most-americans-dream-of-being-their-own-boss/.

20. Simon Duke, "Europe's Labour Laws and Welfare Systems Make Workers Lazy, Says Chinese Finance Chief," *Daily Mail*, Novem-

ber 12, 2011, https://www.dailymail.co.uk/news/article-2058441
/Europes-labour-laws-make-workers-lazy-says-Chinese-finance
-chief.html.

21. Jessica Dickler, "Many US Workers Are Going to Lose Half Their
Vacation Time This Year," CNBC, November 20, 2018, https://www
.cnbc.com/2018/11/20/us-workers-to-forfeit-half-their-vacation
-time-this-year.html.

22. "Hours Worked," Organisation for Economic Co-operation and Development, https://data.oecd.org/emp/hours-worked.htm (accessed
December 15, 2020).

23. Derek Thompson, "Workism Is Making Americans Miserable,"
Atlantic, February 24, 2019, https://www.theatlantic.com/ideas
/archive/2019/02/religion-workism-making-americans-miserable
/583441/.

24. "Work and Workplace," Gallup, https://news.gallup.com/poll/1720
/work-work-place.aspx.

25. Karlyn Bowman, "AEI Public Opinion Study: The State of the American Worker, 2018," American Enterprise Institute, August 31, 2018,
https://www.aei.org/research-products/report/aei-public-opinion
-study-the-state-of-the-american-worker-2018/.

26. David Spiegel, "85% of American Workers Are Happy with Their
Jobs, National Survey Shows," CNBC, April 2, 2019, https://www
.cnbc.com/2019/04/01/85percent-of-us-workers-are-happy-with
-their-jobs-national-survey-shows.html.

27. Shawn M. Carter, "More Than Half of Americans Are Satisfied with
Their Jobs—Here's Why," Fox Business News, August 19, 2019,
https://www.foxbusiness.com/features/more-than-half-of-americans
-are-satisfied-with-their-jobs-the-highest-amount-in-two-decades.

28. Gary White, "Compare U.S. Labor Laws and European Labor
Laws," Chron, https://smallbusiness.chron.com/compare-us-labor-laws
-european-labor-laws-62420.html.

29. Dylan Matthews, "Europe Could Have the Secret to Saving America's Unions," Vox, April 17, 2017, https://www.vox.com/policy
-and-politics/2017/4/17/15290674/union-labor-movement-europe
-bargaining-fight-15-ghent.

30. Nowrasteh, "Muslim Immigration and Integration in the United
States and Western Europe."

31. Shiv Malik and Caelainn Barr, "European Job Market Is Rigged
Against Younger Workers, Says Draghi," *Guardian*, March 11, 2016,
https://www.theguardian.com/world/2016/mar/11/european-job
-market-is-rigged-against-younger-workers-says-draghi.

32. Guntram Wolff, "Europe Can't Afford to Lose Another Generation

to Youth Unemployment," *Guardian*, November 11, 2020, https://www.theguardian.com/world/commentisfree/2020/nov/11/europe-cant-afford-to-lose-another-generation-to-youth-unemployment.

33. Katie Sanders, "The United States Is 'Behind Many Countries in Europe in Terms of the Ability of Every Kid in America to Get Ahead,'" PolitiFact, December 19, 2013, https://www.politifact.com/factchecks/2013/dec/19/steven-rattner/it-easier-obtain-american-dream-europe/.

34. Alissa J. Rubin, "France Lets Workers Turn Off, Tune Out and Live Life," *New York Times*, January 2, 2017, https://www.nytimes.com/2017/01/02/world/europe/france-work-email.html.

35. Kerry Close, "The Real Reason the French Work Less Than Americans Do," *Time*, January 3, 2017, https://time.com/4620759/european-american-work-life-balance/.

36. Hugh Schofield, "The Plan to Ban Work Emails Out of Hours," BBC News, May 11, 2016, https://www.bbc.com/news/magazine-36249647.

37. Kim Willsher, "Health Workers Say 'Non' as 35-Hour Week Takes Blame for France's Problems," *Guardian*, May 30, 2015, https://www.theguardian.com/world/2015/may/30/35-hour-week-french-say-no-to-changes-reform.

38. John Gage, "AOC Invokes MLK to Defend Comments Calling 'Bootstrap' Meritocracy 'a Joke,'" *Washington Examiner*, February 6, 2020, https://www.washingtonexaminer.com/news/aoc-invokes-mlk-to-defend-comments-calling-bootstrap-meritocracy-a-joke.

39. Facundo Alvaredo, Bertrand Garbinti, and Thomas Piketty, "On the Share of Inheritance in Aggregate Wealth: Europe and the United States, 1900–2010," Paris School of Economics, October 29, 2015, http://piketty.pse.ens.fr/files/AlvaredoGarbintiPiketty2015.pdf.

40. Catherine Clifford, "Nearly 68% of the World's Richest People Are 'Self-Made,' Says New Report," CNBC, September 26, 2019, https://www.cnbc.com/2019/09/26/majority-of-the-worlds-richest-people-are-self-made-says-new-report.html.

41. Steven N. Kaplan and Joshua D. Rauh, "Family, Education, and Sources of Wealth among the Richest Americans, 1982–2012," *American Economic Review*, May 2013, https://www.jstor.org/stable/23469721?seq=1.

42. Robert Arnott, William Bernstein, and Lillian Wu, "The Myth of Dynastic Wealth: The Rich Get Poorer," *Cato Journal*, fall 2015, https://www.cato.org/sites/cato.org/files/serials/files/cato-journal/2015/9/cj-v35n3-1_0.pdf.

43. Caroline Freund and Sarah Oliver, "The Origins of the Superrich:

The Billionaire Characteristics Database," Peterson Institute for International Economics, February 2016, https://www.piie.com /publications/wp/wp16-1.pdf.

44. Marketwired, "BMO Private Bank Changing Face of Wealth Study: Two-Thirds of Nation's Wealthy Are Self Made Millionaires," Yahoo! Finance, June 13, 2013, https://finance.yahoo.com/news/bmo -private-bank-changing-face-110000839.html.

45. Jon Bakija, Adam Cole, and Bradley T. Heim, "Jobs and Income Growth of Top Earners and the Causes of Changing Income In- equality: Evidence from U.S. Tax Return Data," U.S. Department of the Treasury, April 2012, https://web.williams.edu/Economics /wp/BakijaColeHeimJobsIncomeGrowthTopEarners.pdf.

46. "U.S. Trust Insights on Wealth and Worth Survey," Bank of Amer- ica Private Wealth Management, U.S. Trust, 2015, https://www .privatebank.bankofamerica.com/publish/content/application/pdf /GWMOL/USTp_ARTNTGDB_2016-05.pdf.

47. "All Nobel Prizes," Nobel Prize, https://www.nobelprize.org/prizes /lists/all-nobel-prizes/.

48. Stuart Anderson, "Immigrant Nobel Prize Winners Keep Lead- ing the Way for America," Forbes, October 14, 2019, https://www .forbes.com/sites/stuartanderson/2019/10/14/immigrant-nobel -prize-winners-keep-leading-the-way-for-america/#740b9e744d4b.

49. Kevin D. Williamson, "How America Became the World's Brain," National Review, October 13, 2020, https://www.nationalreview .com/the-tuesday/how-america-became-the-worlds-brain/

50. "Trends in U.S. Study Abroad," NAFSA: Association of Interna- tional Educators, https://www.nafsa.org/policy-and-advocacy/policy -resources/trends-us-study-abroad.

51. Hans Wiesendanger, "A History of OTL," Stanford University, Of- fice of Technology Licensing, https://otl.stanford.edu/history-otl.

52. Tom Fairless, "Europe Is Struggling to Foster a Startup Culture," Wall Street Journal, May 18, 2015, https://www.wsj.com/articles /europe-is-struggling-to-foster-a-startup-culture-1431992065.

53. Ibid.

54. Joseph E. Stiglitz, "The American Economy Is Rigged," Scientific American, November 1, 2018, https://www.scientificamerican.com /article/the-american-economy-is-rigged/.

55. Stephen Rose, "The Growing Size and Incomes of the Upper Middle Class," Urban Institute, June 21, 2016, https://www.urban.org/research /publication/growing-size-and-incomes-upper-middle-class.

56. Mark J. Perry, "US Middle Class Has Disappeared into Higher- Income Groups; Recent Stagnation Explained by Changing Household

Demographics?," American Enterprise Institute, February 4, 2015, https://www.aei.org/publication/middle-class-disappeared-higher-income-groups-recent-stagnation-explained-changing-household-demographics/.

57. Rakesh Kochhar, "Middle Class Fortunes in Western Europe," Pew Research Center, April 24, 2017, https://www.pewresearch.org/global/2017/04/24/middle-class-fortunes-in-western-europe/.

58. Liz Alderman, "Europe's Middle Class Is Shrinking. Spain Bears Much of the Pain," *New York Times*, February 14, 2019, https://www.nytimes.com/2019/02/14/business/spain-europe-middle-class.html.

59. Scott Horsley, "Why America's 1-Percenters Are Richer Than Europe's," National Public Radio, December 5, 2019, https://www.npr.org/2019/12/05/783001561/why-americas-1-percenters-are-richer-than-europe-s.

60. Taige Jensen and Nayeema Raza, "Please Stop Telling Me America Is Great," *New York Times*, July 1, 2019, https://www.nytimes.com/2019/07/01/opinion/america-great.html.

61. Jack Ewing, "United States Is the Richest Country in the World, and It Has the Biggest Wealth Gap," *New York Times*, September 23, 2020, https://www.nytimes.com/2020/09/23/business/united-states-is-the-richest-country-in-the-world-and-it-has-the-biggest-wealth-gap.html.

62. Glenn Phelps and Steve Crabtree, "Worldwide, Median Household Income About $10,000," Gallup, December 16, 2013, https://news.gallup.com/poll/166211/worldwide-median-household-income-000.aspx.

63. "U.S. GDP as % of World GDP" (source: World Bank), YCharts, https://ycharts.com/indicators/us_gdp_as_a_percentage_of_world_gdp.

64. Joseph W. Sullivan, "American Economic Growth: First in Its Class," *National Review*, July 28, 2020, https://www.nationalreview.com/2020/07/coronavirus-economy-american-economic-growth-outpaces-other-countries/.

65. Ryan McMaken, "The Poor in the US Are Richer Than the Middle Class in Much of Europe," Mises Institute, October 16, 2015, https://mises.org/wire/poor-us-are-richer-middle-class-much-europe.

66. "General Government Spending," Organisation for Economic Co-operation and Development, https://data.oecd.org/gga/general-government-spending.htm.

67. "The Middle Class Always Pays," *Wall Street Journal*, November 28,

2019, https://www.wsj.com/articles/the-middle-class-always-pays
-11574967052.

68. Adam Michel and Travis Nix, "Europeans Work 2 Months Longer Than Americans Do to Pay Their Tax Bill," Heritage Foundation, June 24, 2019, https://www.heritage.org/taxes/commentary/europeans-work-2-months-longer-americans-do-pay-their-tax-bill.

69. Cristina Enache, "Sources of Government Revenue in the OECD," Tax Foundation, February 11, 2021, https://taxfoundation.org/publications/sources-of-government-revenue-in-the-oecd/.

70. Shawn Langlois, "Americans Are Bad at Saving Money, but Europeans Are Much Worse," MarketWatch, January 26, 2017, https://www.marketwatch.com/story/americans-are-bad-at-saving-money-but-europeans-are-much-worse-2017-01-26.

71. Arthur Neslen, "The Rise and Fall of Fracking in Europe," *Guardian*, September 29, 2016, https://www.theguardian.com/sustainable-business/2016/sep/29/fracking-shale-gas-europe-opposition-ban.

72. "Global Electricity Prices for Households in September 2020, by Select Country (in U.S. Dollars per Kilowatt Hour)," Statista, https://www.statista.com/statistics/263492/electricity-prices-in-selected-countries/ (accessed January 6, 2021).

73. "German Consumers Paying Record Prices for Power: Portal," Reuters, January 15, 2019, https://www.reuters.com/article/us-germany-energy-retail/german-consumers-paying-record-prices-for-power-portal-idUSKCN1P9233.

74. Roger Andrews, "The Causes of the Differences between European and US Residential Electricity Rates," Energy Matters, April 30, 2018, http://euanmearns.com/the-causes-of-the-differences-between-european-and-us-residential-electricity-rates/.

75. "How Much Tax Do We Pay on a Gallon of Gasoline and on a Gallon of Diesel Fuel?," EIA, https://www.eia.gov/tools/faqs/faq.php?id=10&t=10 (accessed December 28, 2020).

76. Elke Asen, "Gas Taxes in Europe," Tax Foundation, August 15, 2019, https://taxfoundation.org/gas-taxes-europe-2019/.

77. Oroschakoff, "The Politics of the Green Deal."

8. THE END OF FAITH

1. Michiel Van de Kamp, "Large Number of Dutch Churches to Close in Near Future," Crux, August 5, 2019, https://cruxnow.com/church-in-europe/2019/08/large-number-of-dutch-churches-to-close-in-near-future/.

2. Naftali Bendavid, "Europe's Empty Churches Go on Sale," *Wall Street*

Journal, January 2, 2015, https://www.wsj.com/articles/europes-empty -churches-go-on-sale-1420245359.

3. Harriet Sherwood, "Muslim Population in Some EU Countries Could Triple, Says Report," *Guardian*, November 29, 2017, https:// www.theguardian.com/world/2017/nov/29/muslim-population-in -europe-could-more-than-double.

4. Stephen Bullivant, "Europe's Young Adults and Religion: Findings from the European Social Survey (2014–16) to Inform the 2018 Synod of Bishops," Benedict XVI Centre for Religion and Society, 2018, https://www.stmarys.ac.uk/research/centres/benedict-xvi/docs /2018-mar-europe-young-people-report-eng.pdf.

5. Michael Lipka, "10 Facts About Atheists," Pew Research Center, December 6, 2019, https://www.pewresearch.org/fact-tank/2019 /12/06/10-facts-about-atheists/.

6. Harriet Sherwood, "Nearly 50% Are of No Religion—but Has UK Hit 'Peak Secular'?," *Guardian*, May 13, 2017, https://www.the guardian.com/world/2017/may/13/uk-losing-faith-religion-young -reject-parents-beliefs.

7. Neha Sahgal, "10 Key Findings about Religion in Western Europe," Pew Research Center, May 29, 2018, https://www.pewresearch.org /fact-tank/2018/05/29/10-key-findings-about-religion-in-western -europe/.

8. Sigal Samuel, "Atheists Are Sometimes More Religious Than Chris- tians," *Atlantic*, May 31, 2018, https://www.theatlantic.com/inter national/archive/2018/05/american-atheists-religious-european -christians/560936/.

9. Jessica Martinez, "Study: 2.6 Billion of World Population Expected to Be Christian by 2020," *Christian Post*, July 19, 2013, https://www .christianpost.com/news/study-2-6-billion-of-world-population -expected-to-be-christian-by-2020.html.

10. Harriet Sherwood, "Religion: Why Faith Is Becoming More and More Popular," *Guardian*, August 27, 2018, https://www.theguardian .com/news/2018/aug/27/religion-why-is-faith-growing-and-what -happens-next.

11. Caldwell, *Reflections on the Revolution in Europe*, 182.

12. Linley Sanders, "Who Is Proud to Be an American?," YouGov, June 23, 2020, https://today.yougov.com/topics/politics/articles-reports /2020/06/23/proud-american-poll.

13. Associated Press, "White Evangelicals the Most Patriotic, Poll Finds," *USA Today*, June 28, 2013, https://www.usatoday.com/story /news/nation/2013/06/28/rns-evangelical-patriotic/2473971/.

14. "From John Adams to Massachusetts Militia, 11 October 1798,"

Founders Online, https://founders.archives.gov/documents/Adams /99-02-02-3102.

15. Michelle Boorstein, "The 'Star-Spangled Banner' in Church? Some Christians Are Questioning the Mix of Patriotism and God," *Washington Post*, July 1, 2018, https://www.washingtonpost.com/news /acts-of-faith/wp/2018/07/01/star-spangled-banner-in-church -sunday-christians-debating-god-and-country-anew/.

16. "Religion's Relationship to Happiness, Civic Engagement and Health Around the World," Pew Research Center, January 31, 2019, https:// www.pewforum.org/2019/01/31/religions-relationship-to-happ iness-civic-engagement-and-health-around-the-world/.

17. Stephanie Pappas, "Why Religion Makes People Happier (Hint: Not God)," Live Science, December 7, 2010, https://www.livescience .com/9090-religion-people-happier-hint-god.html.

18. Janell Ross, "Americans Are Patriotic, Honest, Lazy and Selfish, According to Americans," *Washington Post*, December 12, 2015, https://www.washingtonpost.com/news/the-fix/wp/2015/12/12 /americans-arent-terribly-impressed-with-americans/.

19. Gordon C. Nagayama Hall, "Is Narcissism the Cost of Being an American?," *Psychology Today*, April 24, 2018, https://www.psychology today.com/us/blog/life-in-the-intersection/201804/is-narcissism -the-cost-being-american.

20. Paul Krugman, "The Cult of Selfishness Is Killing America," *New York Times*, July 27, 2020, https://www.nytimes.com/2020/07/27 /opinion/us-republicans-coronavirus.html.

21. Alexis de Tocqueville, *Democracy in America* (New York: Bantam Classic, 2000), 71.

22. Ricky Gervais, "The Difference Between American and British Humour," *Time*, November 9, 2011, https://time.com/3720218 /difference-between-american-british-humour/.

23. "Who Gives Most to Charity?," Philanthropy Roundtable, https:// www.philanthropyroundtable.org/almanac/statistics/who-gives.

24. Jon Clifton, "The Most Generous Countries in the World," Gallup, December 12, 2018, https://news.gallup.com/opinion/gallup/2451 92/generous-countries-world.aspx.

25. "Who Gives Most to Charity?"

26. Ben Steverman, "Rich Americans Are Donating More from Huge Charity Stockpiles," Bloomberg, July 16, 2020, https://www.bloom berg.com/news/articles/2020-07-16/rich-americans-are-drawing -down-their-massive-charity-stockpiles.

27. Paul Sullivan, "Philanthropy Rises in Pandemic as Donors Heed the Call for Help," *New York Times*, July 26, 2020, https://www.nytimes

.com/2020/06/26/your-money/philanthropy-pandemic-coronavirus
.html.

28. Alex Daniels, "Religious Americans Give More, New Study
Finds," *Chronicle of Philanthropy*, November 25, 2013, https://
www.philanthropy.com/article/Religious-Americans-Give-More
/153973#:~:text=The%20more%20important%20religion%20is,
65%20percent%20give%20to%20charity.

29. "Americans Donated More Than $3 Billion to Tsunami Relief Efforts,
Study Finds," Center on Philanthropy at Indiana University, December 19, 2006, https://philanthropynewsdigest.org/news/americans
-donated-more-than-3-billion-to-tsunami-relief-efforts-study-finds.

30. Laura Hollis, "The Generosity of Americans," Creators Syndicate, Real-
ClearPolitics, December 18, 2018, https://www.realclearpolitics.com
/articles/2018/12/28/the_generosity_of_americans_139032.html.

31. "Charities Aid Foundation World Giving Index: 10th Edition," October 2019, https://www.cafonline.org/docs/default-source/about-us
-publications/caf_wgi_10th_edition_report_2712a_web_101019
.pdf.

32. Daniels, "Religious Americans Give More, New Study Finds."

33. Lucas Manfredi, "Rioters Destroy Bar Bought with Minnesota Firefighter's Life Savings," Fox Business News, May 31, 2020, https://
www.foxbusiness.com/money/rioters-minnesota-bar-firefighter
-life-savings.

34. Albert J. Menendez and Edd Doerr, eds., *Great Quotations on Religious Freedom* (New York: Prometheus, 2002), 73.

35. Chad Day, "Americans Have Shifted Dramatically on What Values
Matter Most," *Wall Street Journal*, August 25, 2019, https://www
.wsj.com/articles/americans-have-shifted-dramatically-on-what
-values-matter-most-11566738001.

9. THOUGHT POLICE

1. Emily Bazelon, "The First Amendment in the Age of Disinforma-
tion," *New York Times*, October 13, 2020, https://www.nytimes
.com/2020/10/13/magazine/free-speech.html.

2. Eddie Scarry, "CNN's Chris Cuomo: Hate Speech 'Excluded from
Protection' in Constitution," *Washington Examiner*, May 6, 2015,
https://www.washingtonexaminer.com/cnns-chris-cuomo-hate
-speech-excluded-from-protection-in-constitution.

3. Laura Beth Nielsen, "The Case for Restricting Hate Speech," *Los Angeles Times*, June 21, 2017, https://www.latimes.com/opinion/op-ed
/la-oe-nielsen-free-speech-hate-20170621-story.html.

4. Dylan Lyons, "Why Do So Many People Smoke Cigarettes in Europe?," *Babbel Magazine*, February 23, 2019, https://www.babbel.com/en/magazine/smoking-in-europe.
5. Sintia Radu, "Countries with the Highest Rates of Suicide," *U.S. News & World Report*, June 20, 2018, https://www.usnews.com/news/best-countries/slideshows/countries-with-the-highest-suicide-rates.
6. Richard Stengel, "Why America Needs a Hate Speech Law," *Washington Post*, October 29, 2019, https://www.washingtonpost.com/opinions/2019/10/29/why-america-needs-hate-speech-law/.
7. Shannon Van Sant, "Russia Criminalizes the Spread of Online News Which 'Disrespects' the Government," National Public Radio, May 18, 2019, https://www.npr.org/2019/03/18/704600310/russia-criminalizes-the-spread-of-online-news-which-disrespects-the-government.
8. Eugene Volokh, "Supreme Court Unanimously Reaffirms: There Is No 'Hate Speech' Exception to the First Amendment," *Washington Post*, Volokh Conspiracy blog, June 19, 2017, https://www.washingtonpost.com/news/volokh-conspiracy/wp/2017/06/19/supreme-court-unanimously-reaffirms-there-is-no-hate-speech-exception-to-the-first-amendment/.
9. Robert Khan, "Why Do Europeans Ban Hate Speech? A Debate Between Karl Loewenstein and Robert Post," *Hofstra Law Review* 31, no. 3, article 2 (2013), https://scholarlycommons.law.hofstra.edu/cgi/viewcontent.cgi?article=2701&context=hlr.
10. "Copenhagen, Speech, and Violence," *New Yorker*, February 14, 2015, https://www.newyorker.com/news/news-desk/copenhagen-speech-violence.
11. David Shimer, "Germany Raids Homes of 36 People Accused of Hateful Postings over Social Media," *New York Times*, June 20, 2017, https://www.nytimes.com/2017/06/20/world/europe/germany-36-accused-of-hateful-postings-over-social-media.html.
12. "German Hate Speech Law Tested as Twitter Blocks Satire Account," Reuters, January 3, 2018, https://www.reuters.com/article/us-germany-hatecrime/german-hate-speech-law-tested-as-twitter-blocks-satire-account-idUSKBN1ES1AT.
13. "Umgang der Justiz mit Antisemitismus wirft Fragen auf," *Jüdische Allgemeine*, February 2, 2021, https://www.juedische-allgemeine.de/politik/umgang-der-justiz-mit-antisemitismus-wirft-fragen-auf/.
14. Erik Kirschbaum, "In Germany, It Can Be a Crime to Insult Someone in Public," *Los Angeles Times*, September 6, 2016, https://www.latimes.com/world/europe/la-fg-germany-insult-law-snap-story.html.
15. Christopher F. Schuetze, "Germany Criminalizes Burning of E.U.

and Other Foreign Flags," *New York Times*, July 16, 2020, https://www
.nytimes.com/2020/05/16/world/europe/germany-flag-burning
-law.html.

16. Merrit Kennedy, "Germany Is Scrapping Law That Bans Insulting
Foreign Leaders," National Public Radio, January 25, 2017, https://
www.npr.org/sections/thetwo-way/2017/01/25/511611581/germany
-is-scrapping-law-that-bans-insulting-foreign-leaders.

17. "Jailed and Wanted Journalists in Turkey (as of January 8, 2021),"
Stockholm Center for Freedom, https://stockholmcf.org/updated
-list/.

18. Ece Toksabay, "Turkish Journalist Denies Sending Subliminal Message on Eve of Coup," Reuters, June 21, 2017, https://www.reuters
.com/article/us-turkey-security-journalists/turkish-journalist-denies
-sending-subliminal-message-on-eve-of-coup-idUSKBN19C2HL.

19. Jon Fingas, "Germany Backs Fines for Social Networks That Ignore Hate Speech," Engadget, April 5, 2017, https://www.engadget
.com/2017-04-05-germany-backs-fines-for-online-hate-speech.html.

20. "French MPs Back Giving Online Platforms 24 Hours to Remove
Hate Speech," France 24, April 7, 2019, https://www.france24.com
/en/20190704-french-mps-back-giving-online-platforms-24-hours
-remove-hate-speech.

21. Emmanuel Macron, "Speech by the President of the Republic, Emmanuel Macron, at the Congress of the United States of America,"
Élysée, April 25, 2018, https://www.elysee.fr/emmanuel-macron
/2018/04/25/speech-by-the-president-of-the-republic-emmanuel
-macron-at-the-congress-of-the-united-states-of-america.en.

22. "French Opposition, Twitter Users Slam Macron's Anti-Fake-News
Plans," Reuters, January 5, 2018, https://www.reuters.com/article
/us-france-macron-fakenews/french-opposition-twitter-users-slam
-macrons-anti-fake-news-plans-idUSKBN1EU161.

23. Victoria Song, "Twitter Uses France's Own Fake News Law to Block
French Voter Registration Campaign," Gizmodo, April 3, 2019,
https://gizmodo.com/twitter-uses-frances-own-fake-news-law-to
-block-french-1833781703.

24. "Requests to Delist Content Under European Privacy Law," Google
Transparency Report, https://transparencyreport.google.com/eu
-privacy/overview?hl=en.

25. Kirk Arner and Harold Furchtgott-Roth, "Europe's 'Right to Be Forgotten' Threatens Free Speech," RealClearMarkets, February 18, 2020,
https://www.realclearmarkets.com/articles/2020/02/18/europes
_right_to_be_forgotten_threatens_free_speech_104081.html.

26. Stuart Lauchlan, "Pedophiles and Politicos Rewrite History through

Europe's 'Right to Be Forgotten,'" Diginomica, May 18, 2014, https://diginomica.com/pedophiles-politicos-rewrite-history-europes-right-forgotten.

27. Suzanne Daley, "On Its Own, Europe Backs Web Privacy Fights," *New York Times*, August 9, 2011, https://www.nytimes.com/2011/08/10/world/europe/10spain.html.

28. Agence France- Presse, "German Court Backs Murderer's 'Right to Be Forgotten,'" Courthouse News Service, November 27, 2019, https://www.courthousenews.com/german-court-backs-murderers-right-to-be-forgotten/.

29. Arner and Furchtgott-Roth, "Europe's 'Right to Be Forgotten' Threatens Free Speech."

30. Ibid.

31. Paul Chadwick, "Should We Forget about the 'Right to Be Forgotten'?," *Guardian*, March 5, 2018, https://www.theguardian.com/commentisfree/2018/mar/05/right-to-be-forgotten-google-europe-ecj-data-spain.

32. Arner and Furchtgott-Roth, "Europe's 'Right to Be Forgotten' Threatens Free Speech."

33. Rebecca Heilweil, "How Close Is an American Right-to-Be-Forgotten?," *Forbes*, March 4, 2018, https://www.forbes.com/sites/rebeccaheilweil1/2018/03/04/how-close-is-an-american-right-to-be-forgotten/#61d56125626e.

34. Brooke Auxier, "Most Americans Support Right to Have Some Personal Info Removed from Online Searches," Pew Research Center, January 27, 2020, https://www.pewresearch.org/fact-tank/2020/01/27/most-americans-support-right-to-have-some-personal-info-removed-from-online-searches/.

35. Leo Kelion, "Google Wins Landmark Right to Be Forgotten Case," BBC News, September 24, 2019, https://www.bbc.com/news/technology-49808208.

36. Stephanie Bodoni, "Facebook May Be Told to Censor Users' Hateful Posts Globally," Bloomberg, June 4, 2019, https://www.bloomberg.com/news/articles/2019-06-04/facebook-risks-global-hunt-for-offensive-posts-under-eu-law.

37. "'Gay' Police Horse Case Dropped," BBC News, January 12, 2006, http://news.bbc.co.uk/2/hi/uk_news/england/oxfordshire/4606022.stm.

38. "CPS Backs 'Insulting' Law Change," BBC News, December 10, 2012, https://www.bbc.com/news/uk-20666099.

39. Associated Press, "UK Judge: Police Probe of 'Transphobic' Tweets Was Unlawful," ABC News, February 14, 2020, https://abcnews

.go.com/International/wireStory/uk-judge-police-probe-transphobic
-tweets-unlawful-68984071.

40. South Yorkshire Police (@syptweet), "Hate can be any incident or
crime, motivated by prejudice or hostility (or perceived to be so)
against a person's race, religion, sexual orientation, transgender identity or disability. Hate hurts and nobody should have to tolerate it. Report it and put a stop to it #HateHurts," Twitter, September 9, 2018,
2:15 p.m., https://twitter.com/syptweet/status/1038853324970315
779.

41. Izzy Lyons, Jack Hardy, and Martin Evans, "Police Record 120,000
'Non-Crime' Hate Incidents That May Stop Accused Getting Jobs,"
Telegraph, February 14, 2020, https://www.telegraph.co.uk/news
/2020/02/14/police-record-120000-non-crime-incidents-may-stop
-accused-getting/.

42. Lucy Campbell, "Police Investigate David Starkey over Slavery Remarks to Darren Grimes," *Guardian*, October 13, 2020, https://
www.theguardian.com/culture/2020/oct/13/police-investigate
-david-starkey-over-slavery-remarks-to-daren-grimes.

43. "Free to Disagree," Savanta: ComRes, August 18, 2020, https://
2sjjwunnql41ia7ki31qqub1-wpengine.netdna-ssl.com/wp-content
/uploads/2020/08/Final-Free-to-Disagree-Scotland-Poll-Tables
-20200814_Private.pdf.

44. Chris Musson, "New Scottish Laws on Hate Crimes against Groups
Will Carry up to Seven-Year Jail Sentence," *Scottish Sun*, April
24, 2020, https://www.thescottishsun.co.uk/news/scottish-news
/5527475/scottish-laws-hate-crime-jail-sentence/.

45. Jacob Poushter, "40% of Millennials OK with Limiting Speech Offensive to Minorities," Pew Research Center, November 20, 2015, https://
www.pewresearch.org/fact-tank/2015/11/20/40-of-millennials
-ok-with-limiting-speech-offensive-to-minorities/.

46. Peter Moore, "Half of Democrats Support a Ban on Hate Speech,"
YouGov, May 20, 2015, https://today.yougov.com/topics/politics
/articles-reports/2015/05/20/hate-speech.

47. "The 2019 State of the First Amendment Survey," First Amendment Center of the Freedom Forum Institute, https://www.freedom
foruminstitute.org/wp-content/uploads/2019/06/SOFAreport
2019.pdf.

48. Howard Kurtz, "Many Republicans Say Trump Should Have Power
to Shut Down Media Outlets," Fox News, August 9, 2018, https://
www.foxnews.com/politics/many-republicans-say-trump-should
-have-power-to-shut-down-media-outlets.

10. THE FUTURE MUST NOT BELONG TO THOSE WHO SLANDER THE PROPHET

1. Dina Vakil, "'Don't Allow Religious Hooligans to Dictate Terms,'" *Times of India*, January 26, 2008, http://archive.is/ecOpa#selection -4157.0-4157.50.
2. Brian Winston, *The Rushdie Fatwa and After: A Lesson to the Circumspect* (London: Palgrave Macmillan, 2014).
3. Andrew Anthony, "How One Book Ignited a Culture War," *Guardian*, January 10, 2009, https://www.theguardian.com/books/2009 /jan/11/salman-rushdie-satanic-verses.
4. Steven Weisman, "Japanese Translator of Rushdie Book Found Slain," *New York Times*, July 12, 1991, https://archive.nytimes.com /www.nytimes.com/books/99/04/18/specials/rushdie-translator .html?mcubz=0.
5. Henrik Pryser Libell and Richard Martyn Hemphill, "25 Years Later, Norway Files Charges in Shooting of 'Satanic Verses' Publisher," *New York Times*, October 10, 2018, https://www.nytimes .com/2018/10/10/world/europe/norway-satanic-verses.html.
6. Tara John, "Iranian Hardliners Raise Bounty on Salman Rushdie to Almost $4 Million," *Time*, February 23, 2016, https://time.com /4233580/fatwa-salman-rushdie-iran/.
7. Kenan Malik, "Shadow of the Fatwa," *Eurozine*, December 16, 2008, https://www.eurozine.com/shadow-of-the-fatwa/.
8. Asra Q. Nomani, "You Still Can't Write About Muhammad," *Wall Street Journal*, August 6, 2008, https://www.wsj.com/articles/SB12 1797979078815073.
9. Winston, *The Rushdie Fatwa and After*, 99.
10. Daniel Kalder, "In Search of the Jewel of Medina Controversy," *Guardian*, March 5, 2009, https://www.theguardian.com/books /booksblog/2009/mar/05/sherry-jones-jewel-medina.
11. Alison Flood, "Muhammad Novel Publisher Undeterred by Firebomb Attack," *Guardian*, September 29, 2008, https://www.the guardian.com/books/2008/sep/29/jewel.of.medina.firebomb.
12. Julian Petley, *Censorship: A Beginner's Guide* (Oxford: Oneworld Publications, 2009), 157.
13. Owen Bowcott, "Arrest Extremist Marchers, Police Told," *Guardian*, February 6, 2006, https://www.theguardian.com/uk/2006/feb /06/raceandreligion.muhammadcartoons.
14. "Germany's Thilo Sarrazin in Court over Controversial Book on Islam," *Deutsche Welle*, July 9, 2018, https://www.dw.com/en/germanys

-thilo-sarrazin-in-court-over-controversial-book-on-islam/a-44583
174.

15. "Mozart Opera Dropped Due to Terror Threat," *Deutsche Welle*, September 26, 2006, https://www.dw.com/en/mozart-opera-dropped
-due-to-terror-threat/a-2186167.

16. Mark Brown, "Gallery Removes Naked Nymphs Painting to 'Prompt
Conversation,'" *Guardian*, January 31, 2018, https://www.theguardian
.com/artanddesign/2018/jan/31/manchester-art-gallery-removes
-waterhouse-naked-nymphs-painting-prompt-conversation.

17. Lorena Muñoz-Alonso, "Security Threats Force London's V&A to Remove Prophet Muhammad Artwork," Artnet News, January 26, 2015,
https://news.artnet.com/exhibitions/security-threats-force-londons
-va-to-remove-prophet-muhammad-artwork-232724.

18. Lucy Williamson, "Samuel Paty: Beheading of Teacher Deepens
Divisions over France's Secular Identity," BBC News, October 20,
2020, https://www.bbc.com/news/world-europe-54602171.

19. Ibid.

20. "BBC Radio 4 Today Muslim Poll," Savanta: ComRes, February 25,
2015, https://comresglobal.com/polls/bbc-radio-4-today-muslim
-poll/.

21. Shadi Hamid, "The Major Roadblock to Muslim Assimilation in Europe," Brookings Institution, August 18, 2011, https://www.brook
ings.edu/opinions/the-major-roadblock-to-muslim-assimilation
-in-europe/.

22. "Ytringsfrihed i Danmark," Justitsministeriet, 2019, https://www
.justitsministeriet.dk/sites/default/files/media/Pressemeddelelser
/pdf/2020/ytringsfrihedsundersoegelse.pdf.

23. Ben Ellery, "Police Arrest Preacher, 64, and Grab His Bible . . . for
Promoting Christianity: Pastor Accused of Hate Speech for 'Racist'
Comments about Islam Wins £2,500 Payout from Scotland Yard,"
Daily Mail, July 27, 2019, https://www.dailymail.co.uk/news/article
-7293257/Police-arrest-preacher-64-grab-Bible-promoting-Christ
ianity.html.

24. "There Are 'Limitations' to Free Speech, Says London Mayor after
Street Preacher's Arrest," *Christianity Today*, March 22, 2019, https://
christiantoday.com/article/there-are-limitations-to-free-speech
-says-london-mayor-after-street-preachers-arrest/132049.htm.

25. "Mehrheit der Deutschen äußert sich in der Öffentlichkeit nur vorsichtig," *Welt*, May 22, 2019, https://www.welt.de/politik/article
193977845/Deutsche-sehen-Meinungsfreiheit-in-der-Oeffent
lichkeit-eingeschraenkt.html.

26. "Compilation of Venice Commission Opinions and Reports Concerning Freedom of Expression and Media," European Commission for Democracy Through Law, September 19, 2016, https://www.venice.coe.int/webforms/documents/?pdf=CDL-PI(2016)011-e.

27. "Austrian Politician Calls Prophet Muhammad a 'Child Molester,'" *Spiegel International*, January 14, 2008, https://www.spiegel.de/international/europe/campaigns-of-intolerance-austrian-politician-calls -prophet-muhammad-a-child-molester-a-528549.html.

28. Jamie Dettmer, "In Europe, Calls Grow Louder for United Front Against 'Political Islam,'" Voice of America, November 5, 2020, https://www.voanews.com/europe/europe-calls-grow-louder-united-front -against-political-islam.

II. EUROPE AS RETIREMENT HOME

1. George Weigel, "Catholic Lite and Europe's Demographic Suicide," First Things, May 24, 2017, https://www.firstthings.com/web -exclusives/2017/05/catholic-lite-and-europes-demographic-suicide.

2. Jacob Ausubel, "Populations Skew Older in Some of the Countries Hit Hard by COVID-19," Pew Research Center, April 22, 2020, https://www.pewresearch.org/fact-tank/2020/04/22/populations -skew-older-in-some-of-the-countries-hit-hard-by-covid-19/.

3. Ibid.

4. "In Charts: Europe's Demographic Time-Bomb," *Financial Times*, January 13, 2020, https://www.ft.com/content/49e1e106-0231-11ea -b7bc-f3fa4e77dd47.

5. Simona Varrella, "Number of Births in Italy from 2010 to 2019," Statista, January 4, 2021, https://www.statista.com/statistics/781315 /number-of-births-in-italy/.

6. Lizzy Davies, Anne Penketh, Stephen Burgen, Helena Smith, and Remi Adekoya, "Marriage Falls out of Favour for Young Europeans as Austerity and Apathy Bite," *Guardian*, July 25, 2014, https:// www.theguardian.com/lifeandstyle/2014/jul/25/marriage-young -europeans-austerity.

7. Andy Kiersz and Madison Hoff, "The 20 Fastest-Shrinking Countries in the World," *Business Insider*, July 16, 2020, https://www .businessinsider.com/the-fastest-shrinking-countries-in-the-world -declining-populations.

8. Bryce J. Christensen, "Motherhood in Peril—in Europe and Elsewhere," Mercatornet, June 18, 2018, https://mercatornet.com/mother hood-in-perilin-europe-and-elsewhere/22777/.

9. "In Europe, Muslims Projected to Have More Children Than Non-Muslims," Pew Research Center, November 22, 2017, https://www.pewforum.org/2017/11/29/europes-growing-muslim-population/pf_11-29-17_muslims-update-16/.

10. Caldwell, *Reflections on the Revolution in Europe*, 57.

11. "Half a Million Poles Applied for Settled Status in UK," *Poland In*, January 17, 2020, https://polandin.com/46238042/half-a-million-poles-applied-for-settled-status-in-uk.

12. "World Population Data Sheet with Focus on Changing Age Structures," Population Reference Bureau, https://www.prb.org/2018-world-population-data-sheet-with-focus-on-changing-age-structures/.

13. Ivana Draženović, Marina Kunovac, and Dominik Pripužić, "Dynamics and Determinants of Migration—the Case of Croatia and Experience of New EU Member States," Croatian National Bank, June 3–5, 2018, https://www.hnb.hr/documents/20182/2101832/24-dec-drazenovic-kunovac-pripuzic.pdf.

14. Gordon Sander, "Latvia, a Disappearing Nation," *Politico*, January 5, 2018, https://www.politico.eu/article/latvia-a-disappearing-nation-migration-population-decline/.

15. Suzanne Daley and Nicholas Kulish, "Germany Fights Population Drop," *New York Times*, August 13, 2013, https://www.nytimes.com/2013/08/14/world/europe/germany-fights-population-drop.html.

16. "World Population Ageing 2015," United Nations Department of Economic and Social Affairs Population Division, https://www.un.org/en/development/desa/population/publications/pdf/ageing/WPA2015_Report.pdf, 69.

17. "Poverty Increasingly Threatens Elderly Germans, Says Study," *Deutsche Welle*, September 12, 2019, https://www.dw.com/en/poverty-increasingly-threatens-elderly-germans-says-study/a-50393805.

18. "World Population Ageing 2015," 34.

19. Nicholas Gailey, "Europe Is Destined to Age—but Not to Suffer the Consequences," *Foreign Policy*, January 24, 2020, https://foreignpolicy.com/2020/01/24/europe-eu-aging-migration-fertility-population-strategy-disaster/.

20. Katinka Barysch, "Why Europeans Don't Have Babies," Center for European Reform, June 29, 2007, https://www.cer.eu/insights/why-europeans-don%E2%80%99t-have-babies.

21. "Ban Tells European Parliament to Work Together to Address Challenge of Migration," *UN News*, May 27, 2015, https://news.un.org/en/story/2015/05/499952-ban-tells-european-parliament-work-together-address-challenge-migration.

22. Christopher Ingraham, "Charted: The Religions That Make the Most Babies," *Washington Post*, May 12, 2015, https://www.washington post.com/news/wonk/wp/2015/05/12/charted-the-religions-that -make-the-most-babies/.

23. Joseph A. Bulbulia, Eleanor A. Power, Benjamin G. Purzycki, John H. Shaver, Rebecca Sear, Mary K. Shenk, Richard Sosis, and Joseph Watts, "Church Attendance and Alloparenting: An Analysis of Fertility, Social Support and Child Development among English Mothers," Royal Society, June 29, 2020, https://royalsocietypublishing .org/doi/10.1098/rstb.2019.0428#d403693e1.

24. "How Do Countries Fight Falling Birth Rates?," BBC News, January 15, 2020, https://www.bbc.com/news/world-europe-51118616.

25. "Hungary Population 1950–2021," Macrotrends, https://www.macro trends.net/countries/HUN/hungary/population

26. Esteban Ortiz-Ospina and Max Roser, "Marriages and Divorces," Our World in Data, https://ourworldindata.org/marriages-and-divorces.

27. Statista Research Department, "Marriage Rates in the United States in 2019, by State," Statista, February 16, 2021, https:// www.statista.com/statistics/227305/highest-marriage-rates-by-us -state/.

28. Michael Lipka and Benjamin Wormald, "How Religious Is Your State?," Pew Research Center, February 29, 2016, https://www.pew research.org/fact-tank/2016/02/29/how-religious-is-your-state/.

29. Julia Belluz, "The Historically Low Birthrate, Explained in 3 Charts," Vox, January 13, 2020, https://www.vox.com/science-and -health/2018/5/22/17376536/fertility-rate-united-states-births -women.

30. Jeremy Carl, "Here's Why It Matters That Americans Are Having Fewer Children Than Ever Before," Fox News, May 20, 2018, https://www.foxnews.com/opinion/heres-why-it-matters-that -americans-are-having-fewer-children-than-ever-before.

31. Gayle L. Reznik, Dave Shoffner, and David A. Weaver, "Coping with the Demographic Challenge: Fewer Children and Living Longer," Social Security, Office of Policy, Bulletin 66, no. 4 (2005/2006), https://www.ssa.gov/policy/docs/ssb/v66n4/v66n4p37.html.

32. Tara Law, "Women Are Now the Majority of the U.S. Workforce— but Working Women Still Face Serious Challenges," *Time*, January 16, 2020, https://time.com/5766787/women-workforce/.

33. Gretchen Livingston, "Birth Rates Lag in Europe and the U.S., but the Desire for Kids Does Not," Pew Research Center, April 11, 2014, https://www.pewresearch.org/fact-tank/2014/04/11/birth-rates -lag-in-europe-and-the-u-s-but-the-desire-for-kids-does-not/.

34. Shiv Malik, "The Dependent Generation: Half Young European Adults Live with Their Parents," *Guardian*, March 24, 2014, https://www.theguardian.com/society/2014/mar/24/dependent-generation-half-young-european-adults-live-parents.

35. Greg Hurst, "Climate Change Fears Put Young Couples Off Having Children, YouGov Poll Shows," *Sunday Times*, January 3, 2020, https://www.thetimes.co.uk/article/climate-change-fears-put-young-couples-off-having-children-yougov-poll-shows-7shvzvhll.

36. Corey J. A. Bradshaw and Barry W. Brook, "Human Population Reduction Is Not a Quick Fix for Environmental Problems," *Proceedings of the National Academy of Sciences of the United States of America*, October 27, 2014, https://www.ncbi.nlm.nih.gov/pmc/articles/PMC4246304/.

37. "World Bank Forecasts Global Poverty to Fall Below 10% for First Time; Major Hurdles Remain in Goal to End Poverty by 2030," World Bank, October 4, 2015, https://www.worldbank.org/en/news/press-release/2015/10/04/world-bank-forecasts-global-poverty-to-fall-below-10-for-first-time-major-hurdles-remain-in-goal-to-end-poverty-by-2030.

38. Sid Perkins, "The Best Way to Reduce Your Carbon Footprint Is One the Government Isn't Telling You About," *Science*, July 11, 2017, https://www.sciencemag.org/news/2017/07/best-way-reduce-your-carbon-footprint-one-government-isn-t-telling-you-about.

39. Sophie Lewis, "More Than 11,000 Scientists Officially Declare a 'Climate Emergency,'" CBS News, November 3, 2019, https://www.cbsnews.com/news/scientists-officially-declare-climate-emergency-untold-suffering-study-today-2019-11-05/.

40. Leila Ettachfini, "A Third of Young Adults Agree with AOC: Climate Change Affects Family Planning," Vice, March 5, 2019, https://www.vice.com/en/article/nexkvz/alexandria-ocasio-cortez-climate-change-birth.

41. Maggie Astor, "No Children Because of Climate Change? Some People Are Considering It," *New York Times*, February 5, 2018, https://www.nytimes.com/2018/02/05/climate/climate-change-children.html.

42. Virginia Pelley, "This Extreme Sect of Vegans Thinks Your Baby Will Destroy the Planet," *Marie Claire*, January 29, 2019, https://www.marieclaire.com/culture/a14751412/antinatalism/.

43. Eliza Relman and Walt Hickey, "More Than a Third of Millennials Share Rep. Alexandria Ocasio-Cortez's Worry about Having Kids While the Threat of Climate Change Looms," *Business Insider*, March 4, 2019, https://www.businessinsider.com/millennials

-americans-worry-about-kids-children-climate-change-poll-2019
-3.

44. Frank Newport and Joy Wilke, "Desire for Children Still Norm in U.S.," Gallup, September 25, 2013, https://news.gallup.com/poll /164618/desire-children-norm.aspx.

45. Claire Cain Miller, "The U.S. Fertility Rate Is Down, Yet More Women Are Mothers," *New York Times*, January 18, 2018, https:// www.nytimes.com/2018/01/18/upshot/the-us-fertility-rate-is -down-yet-more-women-are-mothers.html.

12. THE SANCTITY OF LIFE

1. Peter Singer, "The Sanctity of Life," *Foreign Policy*, October 20, 2009, https://foreignpolicy.com/2009/10/20/the-sanctity-of-life/.

2. Ezekiel Emanuel, "Why I Hope to Die at 75," *Atlantic*, October 2014, https://www.theatlantic.com/magazine/archive/2014/10/why-i -hope-to-die-at-75/379329/.

3. Megan Brenan, "Americans' Strong Support for Euthanasia Persists," Gallup, May 31, 2018, https://news.gallup.com/poll/235145 /americans-strong-support-euthanasia-persists.aspx.

4. Madeline Kennedy, "Euthanasia Rising in Belgium, Including More Who Are Not Terminally Ill," Reuters, September 15, 2016, https:// www.reuters.com/article/us-health-euthanasia-belgium/euthanasia -rising-in-belgium-including-more-who-are-not-terminally-ill-idU SKCN11M03D.

5. Kenneth Chambaere, Joachim Cohen, Luc Deliens, and Sigrid Dierickx, "Euthanasia in Belgium: Trends in Reported Cases between 2003 and 2013," *Canadian Medical Association Journal*, November 1, 2016, https://www.cmaj.ca/content/188/16/E407.

6. Samuel Petrequin, "Report: Belgian Nursing Homes Failed Patients amid Pandemic," Associated Press, November 16, 2020, https://ca.finance.yahoo.com/news/report-belgium-nursing-homes -failed-081102784.html.

7. Graeme Hamilton, "Death by Doctor: Controversial Physician Has Made His Name Delivering Euthanasia When No One Else Will," *National Post*, January 25, 2015, https://nationalpost.com/news /canada/death-by-doctor-controversial-physician-has-made-his -name-delivering-euthanasia-when-no-one-else-will.

8. Andrew Keh, "The Champion Who Picked a Date to Die," *New York Times*, December 5, 2019, https://www.nytimes.com/interactive /2019/12/05/sports/euthanasia-athlete.html.

9. Charles Lane, "Europe's Sinister Expansion of Euthanasia," *Wash-*

ington Post, August 19, 2015, https://www.washingtonpost.com
/opinions/euthanasias-slippery-slope/2015/08/19/4c13b12a-45cf
-11e5-8ab4-c73967a143d3_story.html.

10. Cecilia Rodriguez, "Euthanasia Tourism: Is the E.U. Encouraging Its Growth?," *Forbes*, May 17, 2019, https://www.forbes.com
/sites/ceciliarodriguez/2019/03/17/euthanasia-tourism-is-the-e-u
-encouraging-its-growth/#523d371b229b.

11. "Belgian Rapist Van Den Bleeken Refused 'Right to Die,'" BBC
News, January 6, 2015, https://www.bbc.com/news/world-europe
-30699780.

12. Nicola Davis, "Euthanasia and Assisted Dying Rates Are Soaring.
But Where Are They Legal?," *Guardian*, July 15, 2019, https://www
.theguardian.com/news/2019/jul/15/euthanasia-and-assisted-dying
-rates-are-soaring-but-where-are-they-legal.

13. Ritwik Roy, "Euthanasia Tourists, Especially from France, Flock-
ing to Belgium for a Lethal Dose," *International Business Times*,
August 19, 2016, https://www.ibtimes.com.au/euthanasia-tourists
-especially-france-flocking-belgium-lethal-dose-1525927.

14. "'Induced' Deaths Rise in Netherlands, Sparking Concerns from
Doctors, Ethicists," Catholic News Agency, January 22, 2019,
https://www.catholicnewsagency.com/news/induced-deaths-rise
-in-netherlands-sparking-concerns-from-doctors-ethicists-11567.

15. "More Euthanasia in the Netherlands, Nearly All Cases in Line with
the Rules," *Dutch News*, March 7, 2018, https://www.dutchnews
.nl/news/2018/03/more-euthanasia-in-the-netherlands-nearly-all
-cases-in-line-with-the-rules/.

16. "Dutch Euthanasia Case: Doctor Acted in Interest of Patient, Court
Rules," BBC News, September 11, 2019, https://www.bbc.com/news
/world-europe-49660525.

17. Christopher de Bellaigue, "Death on Demand: Has Euthanasia Gone
Too Far?," *Guardian*, January 18, 2019, https://www.theguardian
.com/news/2019/jan/18/death-on-demand-has-euthanasia-gone
-too-far-netherlands-assisted-dying.

18. Wesley J. Smith, "Dutch Doctors Killed 431 Without Request in
2015," *National Review*, July 3, 2017, https://www.nationalreview
.com/corner/dutch-doctors-killed-431-without-request-2015/.

19. Wesley J. Smith, "Doctors Induce Twenty-Five Percent of Dutch
Deaths," *National Review*, January 21, 2019, https://www.national
review.com/corner/doctors-induce-twenty-five-percent-of-dutch
-deaths/.

20. Robert Booth, "'Do Not Resuscitate' Orders Caused Potentially
Avoidable Deaths, Regulator Finds," *Guardian*, December 2, 2020,

https://www.theguardian.com/society/2020/dec/03/do-not-resus
citate-orders-caused-potentially-avoidable-deaths-regulator-finds.

21. Mark Hodges, "Dutch Research Institute Chillingly Tells Man with Down Syndrome How Much He Costs Society," LifeSiteNews, December 18, 2017, https://www.lifesitenews.com/news/watch-dutch -research-institute-chillingly-tells-man-with-down-syndrome-how.

22. David Forte, "From Termination to Extermination: The International Down Syndrome Genocide," Public Discourse, July 23, 2018, https://www.thepublicdiscourse.com/2018/07/21996/.

23. Julian Quiñones and Arijeta Lajka, "'What Kind of Society Do You Want to Live In?': Inside the Country Where Down Syndrome Is Disappearing," CBS News, August 14, 2017, https://www.cbsnews .com/news/down-syndrome-iceland/.

24. Charlie Jones, "Down's Syndrome: 'In All Honesty We Were Offered 15 Terminations,'" BBC News, October 25, 2020, https:// www.bbc.com/news/uk-england-beds-bucks-herts-51658631.

25. Ibid.

26. Wesley J. Smith, "Is the Dutch Gronningen Infanticide Protocol Akin to the Nazi Doctors?," First Things, September 8, 2010, https:// www.firstthings.com/blogs/firstthoughts/2010/09/is-the-dutch -gronningen-infanticide-protocol-akin-to-the-nazi-doctors.

27. Andrew Higgins, "Belgian Senate Votes to Allow Euthanasia for Terminally Ill Children," New York Times, December 12, 2013, https://www.nytimes.com/2013/12/13/world/europe/belgian -senate-votes-to-allow-euthanasia-for-terminally-ill-children.html.

CAN WE BE LIKE EUROPE?

1. Richard Wike, "5 Ways Americans and Europeans Are Different," Pew Research Center, April 19, 2016, https://www.pewresearch .org/fact-tank/2016/04/19/5-ways-americans-and-europeans-are -different/.

2. "Emerging and Developing Economies Much More Optimistic Than Rich Countries about the Future," Pew Research Center, October 9, 2014, https://www.pewresearch.org/global/2014/10/09/emerging -and-developing-economies-much-more-optimistic-than-rich-coun tries-about-the-future/.

3. Alberto Alesina and Stefanie Stantcheva, "Mobility: Real and Perceived," City Journal, Autumn 2019, https://www.city-journal.org /economic-mobility.

4. Margaret Thatcher, "Speech to Zurich Economic Society," March 14, 1977, https://www.margaretthatcher.org/document/103336.

Bibliography

Ali, Ayaan Hirsi. 2007. *Infidel*. Atria Books.

———. 2021. *Prey: Immigration, Islam, and the Erosion of Women's Rights.* Harper.

Barzini, Luigi. 1984. *The Europeans.* Penguin Books.

Bergin, Joseph. 2015. *A History of France.* Macmillan Essential Histories.

Berman, Russell. 2008. *Anti-Americanism in Europe: A Cultural Problem.* Hoover Institution Press.

Blanning, T. C. W. 1996. *The Oxford History of Modern Europe.* Oxford University Press.

Blanning, Tim, and David Cannadine. 2008. *The Pursuit of Glory: The Five Revolutions That Made Modern Europe: 1648–1815.* Penguin Books.

Booker, Christopher, and Richard North. 2016. *Great Deception: The True Story of Britain and the European Union.* Bloomsbury Continuum.

Booth, Michael. 2016. *The Almost Nearly Perfect People.* Picador.

Bradford, Anu. 2020. *The Brussels Effect: How the European Union Rules the World.* Oxford University Press.

Caldwell, Christopher. 2009. *Reflections on the Revolution in Europe: Immigration, Islam, and the West.* Doubleday.

Campbell, Kenneth L. 2007. *A History of the British Isles: Prehistory to the Present.* Bloomsbury.

Chin, Rita. 2017. *The Crisis of Multiculturalism in Europe: A History.* Princeton University Press.

Connelly, John. 2020. *From Peoples into Nations: A History of Eastern Europe.* Princeton University Press.

Davies, Norman. 1999. *Europe: A History.* Harper Perennial.

Drozdiak, William. 2017. *Fractured Continent: Europe's Crises and the Fate of the West*. W. W. Norton.

Fenby, Jonathan. 2016. *The History of Modern France*. Simon & Schuster.

Ferguson, Niall. 2011. *Civilization: The West and the Rest*. Penguin.

———. 2004. *Empire: How Britain Made the Modern World*. Penguin.

Fulbrook, Mary. 2014. *A History of Germany 1918–2014: The Divided Nation*. Wiley-Blackwell.

Guizot, François. 2013. *The History of Civilization in Europe*. Liberty Fund.

Hazard, Paul. 2013. *The Crisis of the European Mind: 1680–1715*. New York Review of Books Classics.

Hill, Steven. 2010. *Europe's Promise: Why the European Way Is the Best Hope in an Insecure Age*. University of California Press.

Hitchcock, William I. 2004. *The Struggle for Europe: The Turbulent History of a Divided Continent, 1945 to the Present*. Anchor.

Inglehart, Ronald, and Pippa Norris. 2019. *Cultural Backlash: Trump, Brexit, and Authoritarian Populism*. Cambridge University Press.

Johnson, Paul. 2001. *Modern Times: The World from the Twenties to the Nineties*. Harper Perennial Classics.

Judt, Tony. 2006. *Postwar: A History of Europe Since 1945*. Penguin Books.

Kershaw, Ian. 2020. *The Global Age: Europe 1950–2017*. Penguin Books.

Kirchick, James. 2017. *The End of Europe: Dictators, Demagogues, and the Coming Dark Age*. Yale University Press.

Krastev, Ivan. 2017. *After Europe*. University of Pennsylvania Press.

Lindemann, Albert S. 2013. *A History of Modern Europe: From 1815 to the Present*. Wiley-Blackwell.

Lowe, Keith. 2012. *Savage Continent: Europe in the Aftermath of World War II*. St. Martin's Press.

Markovits, Andrei S. 2009. *Uncouth Nation: Why Europe Dislikes America*. Princeton University Press.

Marr, Andrew. 2017. *A History of Modern Britain*. Pan Books.

Mason, David S. 2011. *A Concise History of Modern Europe: Liberty, Equality, Solidarity*. Rowman & Littlefield.

Mazower, Mark. 2009. *Dark Continent: Europe's Twentieth Century*. Vintage.

McCormick, John, and Jonathan Olsen. 2013. *The European Union: Politics and Policies*. Westview Press.

Mearsheimer, John J. 2003. *The Tragedy of Great Power Politics*. W. W. Norton.

Murray, Douglas. 2018. *The Strange Death of Europe: Immigration, Identity, Islam*. Bloomsbury Continuum.

Norwich, John Julius. 2018. *A History of France*. Atlantic Monthly Press.

Orlow, Dietrich. 2018. *A History of Modern Germany: 1871 to Present*. Routledge.

O'Rourke, P. J. 1999. *Eat the Rich: A Treatise on Economics*. Atlantic Monthly Press.

Pells, Richard. 1998. *Not Like Us: How Europeans Have Loved, Hated, and Transformed American Culture Since World War II*. Basic Books.

Pinder, John. 2013. *European Union: A Very Short Introduction*. Oxford University Press.

Revel, Jean François. 2003. *Anti-Americanism*. Encounter Books.

Rifkin, Jeremy. 2005. *The European Dream: How Europe's Vision of the Future Is Quietly Eclipsing the American Dream*. Jeremy P. Tarcher/ Penguin.

Roberts, Andrew. 2007. *A History of the English-Speaking Peoples Since 1900*. Harper.

Royle, Edward. 2016. *Modern Britain: A Social History*. 3rd ed. Bloomsbury.

Sanandaji, Nima. 2015. *Scandinavian Unexceptionalism: Culture, Markets and the Failure of Third-Way Socialism*. Institute of Economic Affairs.

Sayle, Timothy Andrews. 2019. *Enduring Alliance: A History of NATO and the Postwar Global Order*. Cornell University Press.

Simms, Brendan. 2013. *Europe: The Struggle for Supremacy, from 1453 to the Present*. Basic Books.

Smith, Helmut Walser. 2020. *Germany: A Nation in Its Time: Before, During, and After Nationalism, 1500–2000*. Liveright.

Snyder, Timothy. 2018. *The Road to Unfreedom: Russia, Europe, America*. Duggan Books.

Sowerwine, Charles. 2018. *France Since 1870: Culture, Politics and Society*. Springer.

Strong, Roy. 2019. *The Story of Britain: A History of the Great Ages: From the Romans to the Present*. Pegasus Books.

Verhofstadt, Guy. 2017. *Europe's Last Chance: Why the European States Must Form a More Perfect Union*. Hachette.

Wakeman, Rosemary. 2020. *A Modern History of European Cities: 1815 to the Present*. Bloomsbury Academic.

Index

About the Author

David Harsanyi is a senior writer at the *National Review*, a nationally syndicated columnist, and the author of five books. He is a frequent contributor to the *New York Post*, and his work has also been featured in the *Wall Street Journal*, the *Washington Post*, Reason, and *USA Today*, among numerous other publications. He has appeared on Fox News, CNN, MSNBC, NPR, *ABC World News Tonight*, *NBC Nightly News*, and dozens of radio talk shows across the country.